DID MOSES
REALLY HAVE HORNS?

DID MOSES REALLY HAVE HORNS?

*And Other Myths
about Jews and Judaism*

RIFAT SONSINO

URJ PRESS

New York, New York

Library of Congress Cataloging-in-Publication Data

Sonsino, Rifat, 1938–
Did Moses really have horns? and other myths about Jews and Judaism / Rifat Sonsino.
    p. cm.
  Includes bibliographical references.
  ISBN 978-0-8074-1060-8
  1. Judaism—Doctrines. I. Title.
  BM602.S66 2008
  296—dc22

                                                                    2008040234

Photo Credits: URJ Press is grateful to the following individuals and institutions for granting
permission to print their photographs in this publication. **Allinari/Art Resource:** p.1. **Erich
Lessing/Art Resource:** p. 12. **Erich Lessing/Art Resource:** p. 25. **Erich Lessing/Art Resource:** p. 38.
The Metropolitan Museum of Art/Art Resource: p. 47. **Scala/Art Resource:** p. 60.
Bildarchiv Preussischer Kulturbesitz/Art Resource: p. 65. **Réunion des Musées Nationax/Art
Resource:** p. 70. **Erich Lessing/Art Resource:** p. 82. **Réunion des Musées Nationax/Art Resource:**
p.97. **Scala/Art Resource:** p. 112. **Scala/Ministero per i Beni e le Attività culturali/Art Resource:**
p. 121. **Malcah Zeldis/Art Resource:** p. 134. **Scala/Art Resource:** p. 144. **Erich Lessing/Art Resource:**
p. 155. **The Jewish Museum/Art Resource:** p. 165. **Israel Government Press Office:** p. 177.

To my parents
Albert and Victoria Sonsino, z"l
and
to my beloved grandchildren
Ariella and Dalia Sonsino
Avi and Talya Seri

Contents

Preface

In the Western world, we are the beneficiaries of an edifying tradition that has its roots in the context of the ancient Near East. This tradition, reflected in the Hebrew Bible, includes foundational myths, such as Creation, the Flood, the Exodus, the Revelation of Torah, the conquest of Canaan, and others. Over the centuries, these narratives were collected, revised, updated, and changed in response to the current conditions of the authors, compilers, or editors. The end result is a rich tapestry of stories that have shaped our identities today. This study proposes to examine these myths in greater detail by subjecting them to historical and textual criticism.

A few points on nomenclature: Some of these myths come from very ancient times in Jewish history. In order to place the narratives in an historical timeline, it is necessary to know something about the periodization of Jewish history, a topic that is highly controversial among scholars. In this book, using broad categories, the biblical period is taken to refer to the period from Creation to the destruction of the Second Temple in 70 C.E., even though the last three hundred years or so are also known as the Hellenistic period. The early Rabbinic period formally begins about the year 70 C.E. and goes through the sixth century C.E., with the completion of the Jerusalem and then the Babylonian Talmud. The medieval period in Jewish history is much longer than its Western division of historical times, and goes from the seventh to the nineteenth century. Finally, the modern period refers to the nineteenth century to the present time.

In biblical times, the First Temple period is from the construction of the Temple by King Solomon in the tenth century B.C.E. until its destruction by the Babylonians in 586 B.C.E. The exilic period, the time the Israelites spent in Babylonia, was relatively short, about fifty years; it started with the destruction of the First Temple and ended in 538 B.C.E., when Cyrus, the new Persian king, issued his famous decree allowing the Israelites to go back to their homeland. Some remained, but others took advantage of this offer and returned. They rebuilt the Second Temple (ca. 520 B.C.E.), thus initiating what is now called the postexilic period or the Second Commonwealth. The Second Temple was dedicated in 515 B.C.E., considerably enlarged by the Judean king Herod the Great (37–4 B.C.E.), and ultimately destroyed by the Romans in 70 C.E.

A number of ancient Near Eastern nations will be mentioned in this book. Among them the following are the most important: The Sumerians lived from the fourth millennium to about 1950 B.C.E. in lower Mesopotamia, north of the Persian Gulf, where the rivers Tigris and Euphrates meet. The Assyrian Empire was a powerhouse in upper Mesopotamia, from the sixteenth century to 612 B.C.E., when Nineveh, its capital, was captured by Nabopolassar, king of Babylonia. The Babylonians, both during the Old Babylonian and the Neo-Babylonian periods, lived in the middle of Mesopotamia and ruled a large empire from about 1800 to 539 B.C.E., when Cyrus, the Persian king, ended their dominion. The ancient Egyptians had a very long history, from 3000 to the fourth century B.C.E. The first reference to the Israelites outside of the Bible comes from the Egyptian Mernepta Stele in the thirteenth century B.C.E.

The origin of the word "Hebrew" is obscure. The connection between "Hebrew" and the marauders that swept through ancient Canaan called "Hap/biru" is highly contested. In the Bible, the term "Hebrew" is often used by the Israelites whenever they identified themselves to non-Jews. Thus, for instance, Abram/Abraham, the first patriarch, is called ha-ivri, "the Hebrew" (Gen. 14:13). Similarly, Jonah identified himself as a Hebrew to the sailors

---

MAJOR HISTORICAL PERIODS IN JEWISH HISTORY

Biblical Period:
  Mosaic: 1400–1200 B.C.E.?
  Joshua: 1200 B.C.E.?
  "Judges": 1200–1000 B.C.E.?
  The Monarchy (Kings Saul, David, and Solomon): 1000–930 B.C.E.?
  Destruction of the Northern Kingdom of Israel: 722 B.C.E.
  Destruction of the First Temple: 586 B.C.E.
  The Return from Babylonia: 538 B.C.E.
  Dedication of the Second Temple: 515 B.C.E.
  Hellenistic Period: 333–63 B.C.E.
  Roman Period: 63 B.C.E.–330 C.E.
  Destruction of the Second Temple: 70 C.E.
Rabbinic Period: 70 C.E. to the end of the sixth century
Medieval Period: seventh to nineteenth century
Modern Period: nineteenth century to present day

---

who wanted to heave him overboard (Jon. 1:9). The English word "Israelite" (to be distinguished from "Israeli," which means a citizen of Israel today) applies to Jews who lived during most of the biblical period, until the destruction of the First Temple in 586 B.C.E., when the kingdom of Judah was then named Yehud (Judea) by the Persians. It is from this word that the term "Jew" eventually appeared.

A few years ago, when I shared my ideas on the development of these myths with Rabbi Hara Person, the former editor in chief of URJ Press, she encouraged me to turn them into a full-size book. I express my gratitude to her for her enthusiasm and support throughout the project. I also wish to thank Michael H. Goldberg, the new editor in chief, for completing the job most efficiently.

My wife, Ines, read most of the chapters with an eye toward comprehension and clarity. I am deeply thankful to her. Similarly, I am indebted to my colleague and friend Rabbi Donald Splansky of Framingham, MA, for making valuable suggestions on a few essays included in this book. Obviously, if there are mistakes or omissions, they belong to me.

To all the staff of the URJ Press, including Elizabeth Gutterman, Rebecca Rosenfeld, Judith Bacharach, Ron Ghatan, Michael Silber, Victor Ney, Chris Aguero, and Debra Hirsch Corman, I extend my deepest thanks for their diligent work.

All translations of texts from the Pentateuch, unless otherwise indicated, are based on *The Torah: A Modern Commentary*, Revised Edition, edited by W. Gunther Plaut (New York: URJ Press, 2005). The rest of the biblical quotes are based, unless otherwise specified, on the translation from *Tanakh: The Holy Scriptures* (Philadelphia: Jewish Publication Society, 1999).

Editor's Note

This book uses the following guidelines for transliterating Hebrew into English:

"ch" for ח and כ
"f" for פ
"k" for כ and ק
"tz" for צ
"i" for א
"e" for אֶ
"ei" for א
"a" for א and אַ
"o" for א, אוֹ, and *kamatz katan*
"u" for א and אוּ
"ai" for אַי

Myths and Legends

This book, aimed at an educated laity, will discuss many of the biblical and postbiblical myths and legends, and follow their development into the Rabbinic period and modern times. We will explore how these ancient stories entered the Israelite culture, how they were reframed, and how they evolved.

In some cases, we will discover that some of these foundational myths, like the Creation story, were deeply entrenched in the ancient Near Eastern milieu but were radically transformed by the biblical authors/editors. In other cases, such as the story of the Flood, a particular myth was taken over in its broad outline but was provided with a new rationale. Some of the myths (e.g., the Exodus from Egypt) were part of the biblical tradition going back to antiquity, whereas others (e.g., Moses's "horns" or Jonah's "whale") emerged long after the Hebrew Scriptures were canonized.

Some myths and legends were preserved in a variety of versions; the older ones were subjected to constant editing and therefore changes. For example, the festival of Chanukah, which commemorates the rededication of the Second Temple by the Maccabees in the second century B.C.E., in time assumed mythic proportions. Similarly, great leaders like King David became the source of elaborate legends, multiplying in time. In some cases, myths and legends like Jonah and the "whale" or Moses's "horns" evolved because of faulty translations. Reflecting the thinking and hopes of later times, some explanations, such as the conquest of Canaan or the use of the sukkah, were projected back to the past. We also have myths that are based on multiple or even conflicting memories of ancient times, like the crossing of the wilderness after the Exodus. Some even derive from long-standing traditions colored by pure imagination, such as what happened at the top of Mount Sinai. In the Rabbinic period and beyond, a number of gaps in the ancient narratives were filled with new information. For example, Noah's wife, whose name is not recorded in the Bible, received a name in the Rabbinic literature. Similarly, the Rabbis speculated as to what happened at Mount Sinai when Moses received the Decalogue.

We do not know exactly who wrote down these ancient stories. Some ancient authors or editors collected, copied, and recopied the material over a long period of time. It is also likely that a number of individuals added glosses here and there, rewrote whole passages, or provided new rationales. What is remarkable is that at the end, all of these foundational myths and imaginative legends, which are considered to be the building blocks of the Israelite religious history, were edited in stages, slowly becoming the sacred patrimony of Judaism; for many people, these myths and legends were so special that they were deemed worthy of ascription to God. (See Chapter 1 about the editing process of the Five Books of Moses.)

As we read these ancient stories, we must pay attention to their literary background, the cultural environment out of which they grew, and the new forms they assumed in time. Only then can we fully appreciate their message and hopefully integrate their teachings in our daily life.

What Is a Myth?

In our everyday language, a myth refers to something that is untrue, clearly unreliable, and even fanciful. In religious discourse, however, a myth is a story that reflects an aspect of the cosmic order. As such, as one scholar notes, "the myth captures the integrating pattern that pulls together various dimensions of our experience."[1] Another argues, "If a narrative is concerned with the world of the gods, or if gods are to a considerable extent involved in it, we may speak of a myth."[2] For the purpose of this book, the definition found in W. Gunther Plaut's *The Torah: A Modern Commentary* will be used as a guideline: a myth is "a tale involving human beings and divine powers, a tale that was understood as having happened and that by its existence expressed, explained, or validated important aspects of existence."[3] In this definition, the term "myth" is not restricted to the actions of divine beings, but deals with narratives that involve human beings as well as divine powers. Plaut provides what he calls "the Eden myth" as an example, which tries to explain the origin of death in Judaism. The term "mythology" will be used to refer to activities involving only gods, which figure in ancient documents, whether Greek, Mesopotamian, or Egyptian.

It is important to remember that myths are not fictions created out of nowhere. Some of them may even have a kernel of historicity behind them. On the other hand, they are not, nor do they pretend to be, objectively, factually true. Their purpose is to explain and elucidate some of the fundamental beliefs by referring to some ancient event or person that brought order or new insight into our emerging world.

Another term that will be used throughout this book is "legend." The dictionary definition of "legend" is "a story coming down from the past, especially one popularly regarded as historical although not verifiable."[4] European literature contains many examples, such as Alexander the Great cutting the Gordian knot; Robin Hood robbing the rich to feed the poor; William Tell, the marksman with the crossbow; and the exploits of King Arthur of England. In American folklore, one can think of Davy Crockett or the pirate Blackbeard. One scholar, narrowing the definition, states, "If the men or place or occasions which are central to the narrative are of religious significance—priests or prophets, sanctuaries or festivals—then we call such a narrative a legend."[5] Following Plaut's commentary, the word "legend" will be defined here as "a saga of the past, amplified by folk memory, which usually neither validates nor explains."[6] An example of this in the Bible would be Jacob's prowess in lifting the stone off the mouth of the well to impress Rachel (Gen. 29:10).

It must be acknowledged, however, that in the ancient Near East it is not always easy to differentiate "myth," which deals with gods interacting with humans, from "legend," which refers to the exaggerated acts of heroes. The main reason is because in the ancient world, there is no such thing as the modern divide between "religious" and "secular." Everything is infused by

God. Everything is religious. God is active or behind every human act. Even when the text deals with legendary material describing the deeds of leading personalities, God is always present in the background. A good example of this is the Book of Esther. God is not mentioned here, but there are clear allusions to the Divine (e.g., "if you keep silent in this crisis, relief and deliverance will come to the Jews from another quarter" [Est. 4:14]) or religious acts (e.g., fasting, which is not done for health purposes, but to appeal to God's mercy [Est. 4:16]).

Mythologies in the Ancient Near East

Ancient Near Eastern literature, whether Sumerian, Akkadian, or Ugaritic, contains much mythological material. Egyptian and Greek mythologies are also extensive. In these narratives, humans, gods, and other divine beings interact frequently. In the Akkadian *Epic of Gilgamesh*, for example, the hero is half-human and half-divine.

Many of these stories appear to be etiological in nature; that is, they try to explain why things are as they are. Thus, the Mesopotamian *Enuma Elish* ("When on High") deals with the creation of the universe; the *Epic of Gilgamesh* covers the questions of immortality and the Flood; in the Ugaritic *Baal and Anat* stories, we learn about the interaction between gods and humanity; in the Egyptian *Hymn to Aton*, we are told how Aton was elevated to become the sole patron of Egypt. In other cases, however, as an ancient Near Eastern specialist observed, "texts that we regard as myths were originally only pretexts for incantations to ward off the evils they described, like toothache (*The Worm and Toothache*), broken shoulder-blades (*Adapa*) or pestilence (*Irra*)."[7]

These epics and mythologies freely circulated in the entire ancient Near East, and undoubtedly affected the Israelites, for they too were part of the cultural continuum that covered the entire region. What is noteworthy is how the biblical authors/editors transformed them.

Myths and Mythology in the Bible

One of the remarkable features about the Bible is that, in its present form, it contains many myths but hardly any mythology. The final authors/editors did an effective job of eliminating nearly all references to ancient god-stories. They did this in order to preserve a monotheistic outlook and ideology in Israel. Thus, for example, in dealing with ancient myths such as Creation or the Flood, the authors/editors centered the stories on the one invisible God. Even when they made allusions to natural forces, which in ancient mythologies clearly referred to various deities, they subordinated them to a single deity, namely *YHVH*, the ineffable personal name of the Israelites' God. During the creation of the universe, for instance, the Israelite God acts alone, even when consulting with the heavenly hosts (Gen. 1:26). Angels are not viewed as independent deities but are subservient to the Eternal; even Satan in the Book of Job does God's bidding. In the Book of Psalms it is God alone, and not Baal of the Canaanite divine council, who is behind all the natural phenomena: "The voice of the Eternal kindles flames of fire; the voice of the Eternal convulses the wilderness; the Eternal convulses the wilderness of Kadesh" (Ps. 29:7). Similarly, even though in Ugaritic texts Baal is known as the one who "rides upon the clouds" (*ANET*, 130), in the Bible that honor is attributed to God: "Sing to God, chant hymns to God's name; extol God who rides the clouds; the Eternal is God's name" (Ps. 68:5; see also Isa. 19:1).

The only exception to a mythological text in the Bible is a cryptic passage found in Genesis 6:1–4 where heavenly beings marry humans. As many scholars have already recognized, this is most likely a tiny fragment, or a combination of at least two parallel stories, belonging to a much longer mythological story that somehow crept into the Scriptures. In it we are told that after Creation, as people started to multiply upon the earth, certain "divine beings" (*b'nei ha-elohim* in Hebrew) saw that women were very pretty. Therefore, from among them "they took wives for themselves, as they chose" (Gen. 6:2). Sexual intercourse between divinities and humans is well-known in ancient Near Eastern texts as well as in Greek mythologies, but does not appear in the Bible with the exception of this passage. This biblical text also mentions the existence of Nephilim (Gen. 6:4), who perhaps were the children of this divine-human encounter. We do not know who these people were. In Num. 13:33 there is a reference to Nephilim, who are described as "giants." In some postbiblical texts, these creatures are considered "fallen angels" (see Enoch 6–8; 2 Pet. 2:4; Jude 6). Some of the Rabbis, however, say that they were the noble descendants of Seth, the son of Adam and presumably of Eve (Gen. 5:3), who had intermarried with the children of Cain (see Ibn Ezra, for example).

The fragment in Genesis 6:1–4 also contains a note stating that God put a limit to human life: "Then the Eternal One said, "My spirit will not forever

endure [*yadon*, meaning unclear] the humans, as they are but fallible flesh—
their lifespan shall be [only] 120 years" (Gen. 6:3). The number 120 represents the ideal human life in the Bible (e.g., Moses lived to be 120 [Deut.
31:2, 34:7]). Why this limitation? Maybe God realized that humanity is, in
the words of a biblical scholar, "in danger of overreaching itself."[8] According
to another scholar, "the story of the primeval titans emerges as a moral in-
dictment, and therefore as a compelling motive for the coming disaster."[9]
For soon afterward, the Flood arrives!

Oral Transmission

Ancient Israelites, like people all over the world, enjoyed telling stories. Parents used stories to regale their children with the exploits of their ancestors,
religious teachers told stories to teach their students about the marvelous
workings of God or other divine beings, and scribes recopied epics of long
standing.

Writing is known to have existed in the ancient Near East going as far
back as the Sumerians in the fourth millennium B.C.E. and most likely existed
among the Israelites not too long after they emerged onto the historical scene
in the thirteenth century B.C.E. Yet the textual evidence we have so far
strongly points to the fact that at least until the seventh century B.C.E., ancient Israel was largely nonliterate. This does not mean that they were illit-
erate but that they generally transmitted their stories in an oral fashion.[10]

The Bible makes many references to "listening," which assumes orality.
Thus, for example, Deuteronomy, which dates from about the seventh century B.C.E., urges the Israelites to "keep these words . . . in your heart" (Deut.
6:6) and repeats the words that "Moses addressed to all Israel" (Deut. 1:1).
Turning to the people, it also proclaims, "Hear, O Israel! The Eternal is our
God, the Eternal alone" (Deut. 6:4). Similarly, the prophets address the Israelites, saying, "Hear this, O priests, / Attend, O House of Israel, / And give ear,
O royal house" (Hosea 5:1), or, "Hear the word which the Eternal has spoken
to you, O House of Israel" (Jer. 10:1), and the Book of Proverbs teaches, "Listen, my child, to your father's instructions" (e.g., 1:8; 4:1, 4:10, 4:20). In time,
all these oral stories, along with a number of written texts, were progressively
combined and edited to form what is now known as the Hebrew Bible.

The German biblical scholar Herman Gunkel (1862–1932), the main
proponent of form criticism, suggested that a long oral folk literature preceded our written texts. Many stories, parables, myths, and even laws were

preserved in human memory for centuries and transmitted from one generation to another by word of mouth. Eventually, these were committed to writing, and even after that, they were revised, reedited, or simply changed. By analyzing the forms of these literary genres, Gunkel argued, we may be able to discover their *sitz im leben*, literally their "situation in life," which is the sociological background that gave rise to these forms, and follow their development into what eventually became our sacred Scriptures.

However, it is impossible to state categorically and in every case that orality preceded literacy. Very often the two forms existed concurrently. Thus, for example, *Sefer ha-Yashar*, the Book of Yashar, a collection of heroic war songs, seems to have existed in the early biblical period (Josh. 10:13; II Sam. 1:18); whereas most people preferred to transmit their messages orally, some prophets or government officials used the written method to communicate or record. Jeremiah had a secretary, Baruch, to whom he dictated a message (Jer. 36:4). When King Hezekiah recovered from his illness, he wrote a poem (*michtav l'Hizkiyahu*, "a writing of Hezekiah" [Isa. 38:9]). Deuteronomy instructs a husband who wishes to divorce his wife to give her a "bill of divorcement" (*sefer k'ritut* [Deut. 24:1]), and Queen Esther's ordinance "was recorded in a scroll" (*nichtav basefer* [Est. 9:32]).

In the ancient Near East, early writing was usually in the hands of priests or scribes. Many of these individuals wrote business contracts, sent out official documents, or copied ancient stories. Archeologists have discovered thousands of clay tablets as well as stone monuments that contain such written material in Mesopotamia and even a few cuneiform texts in Canaan.

In ancient Israel, one of the earliest written documents to have been discovered is the Gezer Calendar. It reads like a poetic text of agricultural activities. Found by the British archaeologist R. A. S. Macalister in 1908, it is written in Old Hebrew script, and is dated to around the tenth century B.C.E. It identifies the seasons going from autumn to summer as follows:

His two months are (olive) harvest,
His two months are planting (grain),
His two months are late planting;
His month is hoeing up of flax,
His month is harvest of barley,
His month is harvest and feasting;
His two months are vine-tending,
His month is summer fruit. (*ANET*, 320).

We do not know who wrote this text or its purpose. Some scholars argue that it was a student's memory exercise. Others maintain that it was a popular folk song.

Scribes

In the ancient Near East, scribes were highly skilled individuals. The earliest reference to a "scribe" (*sofer*) in the Bible is in the Song of Deborah: "From Machir came down leaders, / From Zebulun such as hold the marshal's staff [*b'sheivet sofer*]" (Judg. 5:14). Here the word "scribe" has a broader meaning than the person who simply "writes," and covers a much wider role, such as an individual who executes, administers, or leads. As the *Jewish Study Bible* points out, "the [Hebrew] word [*sofer*] suggests commanders, who recorded the number of those going to war."[11]

In the ancient Near East, including Israel, scribes were considered important government officials. We know from many biblical texts, for example, that early kings had their own scribes, not unlike the present-day "secretaries" who are part of cabinets in various governments. David's scribe was Seraiah (II Sam. 8:17; in II Sam. 20:25 he is called Sheva, and in I Chron. 18:16, Shavsha), and Solomon had two: Elihoreph and Ahijah, sons of Shisha (I Kings 4:3). During the reign of Joash, king of Judah (ninth century B.C.E.), the royal "scribe" functioned as a treasury official, a high-level accountant. We are told that he and the High Priest "would come up and put the money accumulated in the House of the Eternal into bags, and they would count it" (II Kings 12:11; see also Neh. 13:13). But we also know that some individuals employed their own scribes to transcribe their messages. A good example is Baruch son of Neriah, who was the scribe of the prophet Jeremiah (Jer. 36:32). In addition, there would likely have been ordinary scribes who wrote letters for individuals, contracts for parties, and religious texts for local sanctuaries.

In the past, scribes were also involved in the preservation of sacred literature; they wrote hymns of glory to the gods on behalf of their master, and frequently copied old myths of national importance, very often for educational purposes in local schools. Some of these myths dealt with the creation of the universe, others with the quest of immortality; many related the dramatic contests between various divine beings. These texts were revered by the general populace and repeated in various versions, because they expressed the foundational beliefs and values of their civilization. In the process of copying, the scribes also adapted, selected, and ultimately fixed them in a prescribed textual form. Israelite scribes must have done the same thing.

In order to study the development of myths or legends in ancient Israel, we first need to find out how and when these writings were put together and how they ultimately became a sacred text in the Jewish community. Some of these narratives are found in the Pentateuch, also known as the Five Books of [or, better, attributed to] Moses (i.e., Genesis, Exodus, Leviticus, Numbers, and Deuteronomy), and it is there that we will begin.

1

Did Moses Write the Torah?

Reni, Guido (1575–1642).
Moses with the Tablets of the Law.
Photo: Mauro Magliani for Alanari, 1998. Galleria Borghese, Rome, Italy.

The Claim

The Hebrew word *torah*, meaning "instruction," often refers to the Five Books of Moses, the Pentateuch. For centuries, Jewish tradition has claimed that Moses was the author of the Pentateuch. After all, the Bible says, "Moses then wrote down all the commands of the Eternal" (Exod. 24:4), and that God dictated the Torah to him: "Write down these commandments" (Exod. 34:27). However, there are many textual and historical challenges to this traditional belief. This chapter will examine these challenges and present alternative possibilities.

Moses as the Author of the Torah

The first-century Jewish historian Josephus affirmed that Moses wrote down the Torah (*Ant.* IV, 8:48), and the Rabbis in the Talmudic period confirmed that belief by stating clearly, "Moses wrote his own book" (BT *Bava Batra* 14b). Even the great medieval Jewish rationalist Moses Maimonides (1135–1204) maintained, "The Torah came from God. . . . We do not know exactly how it reached us, but only that it came to us through Moses, who acted like a secretary taking dictation."[1] In our time, some Jews, who believe that God revealed the Pentateuch verbally to Moses, still hold this position. During the Torah service, after the reading is completed, the Torah scroll is held high, and the reader says, "This is the Torah that Moses placed before the Children of Israel, from the mouth of God and through the hand of Moses."

Many traditional Christians also believe that the Pentateuch is the literal word of God. In 1966, the Fundamental Baptist Information Service stated, "We reject every Bible teacher who claims that Moses did not write the Pentateuch. Regardless of what label such a teacher wears, whether Evangelical or Baptist or Fundamentalist, we reject him as a false teacher and an apostate."[2]

At times, the claim for Mosaic authorship is even buttressed through the use of technology. For example, in his article entitled "Did Moses Really Write Genesis?" Russell Grigg quotes a previous study by Yehuda Radday: " 'After feeding the 20,000 Hebrew words of Genesis into a computer at Technion University in Israel, researchers found many sentences that ended in verbs and numerous words of six characters or more. Because these idiosyncratic patterns appear again and again,' says project director Yehuda Radday, 'it seems likely that a sole author was responsible. Their exhaustive computer analysis conducted in Israel suggested an 82 percent probability that the book has just one author.' "[3]

The question before us is this: can this claim be supported by a critical analysis of the Five Books of Moses or through some ancient Near Eastern texts dealing with biblical Israel? The latter source is totally silent regarding this period. We have no archaeological or historical evidence to prove or disprove anything that happened until the period of the monarchy. The earliest reference to Israel in the ancient Near Eastern texts is found in the Merneptah stele (ca. 1230 B.C.E.)—and the only one in the entire Egyptian corpus—where the Egyptian king boasts that "Israel" has been defeated.[4] This information is not enough to reconstruct the period from Creation to the end of the Mosaic times. We are left only with the evidence that can be culled from the Bible itself.

Textual Difficulties

If the Pentateuch were written by only one person, namely Moses, and if we affirm that it was dictated to him directly by no other than God, we would expect to find a text that is free of blatant inconsistencies, discrepancies, contradictions, or repetitions. Also, it would have to have been redacted before the entry into the land of Canaan, for, as Scripture asserts, Moses did not get into the Land of Israel but died in the land of Moab (Deut. 34:5). However, a critical study of the Five Books of Moses makes it difficult to uphold this assumption. What is the evidence against this traditional claim? By surveying the Pentateuch, we can point out, among many others, the following major textual problems.[5]

Doublets
A survey of the Pentateuch shows that there are a number of doublets as well as virtual repetitions in the text. For example, there are two different stories of Creation (Gen. 1 and 2); God makes two covenants with Abraham (Gen. 15 and 17); the naming of the city of Beersheba appears twice (Gen. 21:22–31 and 26:15–33); Jacob's name is changed twice (Gen. 32:25–29 and 35:9–10); there are two versions of the Decalogue, with considerable variations (Exod. 20 and Deut. 5); the story of the water emerging from the rock at Meribah is told twice (Exod. 17:2–7 and Num. 20:2–13); and the rules about the consumption of forbidden animals are listed twice (Lev. 11 and Deut. 14).

Contradictions
In addition to these doublets and repetitions, we find a number of apparent contradictions in the Pentateuch that have puzzled the commentators for centuries. Among them the following ones are the most blatant:

Order of Creation: The order of Creation in Genesis 1 is very different from Genesis 2. In Genesis 1, animals are created first (1:25) and then humanity (1:27), whereas in Genesis 2, humans (2:7) are created before animals (2:19).

Animals in the Ark: The number of animals entering the ark of Noah are listed in one place as "seven pairs of every pure beast . . . and two of every impure beast" (Gen. 7:2) and in other places as "two of each" (Gen. 6:19, 7:8–9, 7:15).

Moses's Father-in-Law: Moses, we are told, had two wives: Zipporah (Exod. 2:21) and a Cushite woman whose name has not been preserved (Num. 12:1). Yet the Pentateuch gives three names for his father-in-law: Reuel (Exod. 2:18), Jethro (Exod. 3:1, 18:1–6), and Hobab (Num. 10:29).

Levirate Marriage: Levirate marriage occurs when a brother marries the widowed sister-in-law who is left without a child. The purpose is to preserve unity by keeping the patrimony within the family. This is possible only when the first husband dies without fathering a child. It is irrelevant if the marrying brother is already married. He can take on a second wife for his brother's sake. According to Deuteronomy 25:5, this marriage is permissible. According to Leviticus 20:21, it is not.

Knowledge of God's Name: The name of the Israelites' national God was *YHVH* (or, as some scholars spell it, *YHWH*), whose meaning is "being" or "existence" (see Chapter 2). According to Exodus 6:3, Moses was the first to know this name: "I appeared to Abraham, Isaac, and Jacob as El Shaddai, but I did not make Myself known to them by My name *YHVH*." Yet, even before him, Abraham seems to have known it ("I have raised my hand to *YHVH*" [Gen. 14:22]); Laban, the brother of Rebekah, knew it ("Come in, O blessed of *YHVH*, said he" [Gen. 24:31]); Jacob knew it ("I, *YHVH*, am the God of your father Abraham and God of Isaac" [Gen. 28:13]); even Enosh, Adam's grandson, knew it ("Then it was that people began to invoke *YHVH*" [Gen. 4:26]).

Authorship: Who was the actual author of the Five Books of Moses? According to some texts in the Pentateuch, Moses was: "Moses then wrote down all the commands of the Eternal" (Exod. 24:4; see also Exod. 34:28; Num. 33:2; Deut. 31:9). According to other texts, however, it was God: "Upon finishing speaking with him on Mount Sinai, [God] gave Moses the two tablets of the Pact, stone tablets inscribed with the finger of God" (Exod. 31:18; see also Exod. 24:12, 34:1; Deut. 4:13, 5:19, 10:4).

Sinai or Horeb? In Exodus 19:20, we are told that God gave the Torah to the Israelites on Mount Sinai: "The Eternal came down upon Mount Sinai" (see also Exod. 24:16), whereas according to Deuteronomy 5:2, this event took place at Mount Horeb: "The Eternal our God made a covenant with us at Horeb" (see also Deut. 4:10).

Moabites or Midianites? The Book of Numbers reports that the seduction of Israelite men at a place where non-Israelites worshiped Baal-Peor, a local god, was facilitated by Moabite women: "While Israel was staying at Shittim, the menfolk profaned themselves by whoring with the Moabite women"

(Num. 25:1). Yet, a few verses below, this despicable act, we are informed, was done with Midianites: "Just then one of the Israelite men came and brought a Midianite woman . . ." (Num. 25:6; see also Num. 31:1–16).

Post-Mosaic Texts?

The fact that the texts often speak of Moses in the third person argues against Moses as the author: for example, "When Moses had ascended the mountain" (Exod. 24:15) or "Now Moses would take the Tent and pitch it outside the camp" (Exod. 33:7). If Moses were the author, would he have written these passages about himself in the third person? The Book of Numbers describes Moses as being very modest: "Now Moses was a very humble man, more so than any other human being on earth" (Num. 12:3). How likely is it that such a humble person would praise himself in these glowing terms?

Furthermore, the Book of Genesis states, "And these are the kings who reigned in the land of Edom, before a king reigned over the people of Israel" (Gen. 36:31). According to the Bible, Moses lived well before the establishment of the united monarchy in Judah and Israel. It is thus highly unlikely that Moses could have written this verse, because he could not have known of any king reigning over Israel.

At the end of the Book of Deuteronomy we find a reference to Moses's death, and how God buried him in Moab: "So Moses the servant of the Eternal died there, in the land of Moab, at the command of the Eternal. [God] buried him in the valley in the land of Moab" (Deut. 34:5–6). Obviously, a person cannot write about his own death and burial.

Genesis 12:6 reports that "Abram then traversed the land as far as the sacred site of Shechem, as far as the Oak of Moreh. (At that time the Canaanites were present in the land.)" This text implies that Canaanites are no longer there ("were present"). The problem is that when Abram roamed the countryside, the Bible tells us, the Canaanites were indeed part of the historical reality (see Gen. 15:21, 24:3). Later, Joshua fought against them as the Israelites entered the land of Canaan. Whoever penned this verse must therefore have written it after the Canaanites disappeared from the scene, namely, a long time after the Mosaic period.

The Book of Deuteronomy is described as being delivered "on the other side" of the Jordan River: "These are the words that Moses addressed to all Israel on the other side of the Jordan" (Deut. 1:1). The expression "on the other side of the Jordan" (*b'eiver hayardein*) is a geographical term referring to the Transjordan region, east of the river Jordan, as viewed from the perspective of the Land of Israel, a place that Moses never entered (see Deut. 1:37, 3:27). This then is another argument against Moses's authorship.

According to the account in Deuteronomy, God led the Israelites out of Egypt, "to drive from your path nations greater and more populous than you, to take you into their land and assign it to you as a heritage, as is still the case [*kayom hazeh*, literally, 'as it is today']" (Deut. 4:38). The words "as is still the case" most probably mean, now that we live in the Land of Israel. But that took place after Moses, and not during his lifetime.

All these post-Mosaic texts make it highly unlikely that they could come from the hand of Moses.

Confronting the Difficulties

It is difficult to ignore or discard these discrepancies. How can we account for them? Many religious inerrantists, that is, those who claim that the Pentateuch is God's *ipsisima verba*, or literal word, deal with these "apparent" problems in a variety of ways. Some are satisfied by pointing out that the Hebrew Bible states that the Torah is the word of God written by the hand of Moses (e.g., II Chron. 34:14). This divine revelation was verbal and therefore is authoritative and binding. Fundamentalist Christians add the claims of the New Testament about Mosaic authorship (e.g., Matt. 8:4; Mark 7:10; Luke 24:27). Others in this group assert that Moses, as a prophet, could foresee the future and could therefore write about events that took place after his own life. Some scholars contend that archaeology has already proven that writing was known even during pre-Mosaic times, and therefore, it is not inconceivable that Moses could have written these passages using the skills available to him at the time. It is even possible, as some scholars have maintained, that Moses used historical material already in written form that needed editing.

Others, however, are not satisfied with these assertions. For example, the Talmud (sixth century C.E.) recognizes that Moses could not have written about his own death and therefore admits, "Joshua wrote . . . the last eight verses of the Pentateuch" (BT *Bava Batra* 14b). It also maintains that "there is no chronological order in the Torah" (BT *P'sachim* 6b) and that this accounts for some of the texts appearing in a nonsequential pattern. In a bold statement, Rabbi Abraham ibn Ezra of Spain (1092–1167), commenting on the biblical text "At that time the Canaanites were present in the land" (Gen. 12:6), expresses some doubts about the Mosaic authorship: "It appears that Canaan [the grandson of Noah] has acquired the land of Canaan from someone else. If that is not the case, we have a secret here, and let him who understands this keep quiet" (Ibn Ezra, ad loc). Others went even further. In the seventeenth century, both Thomas Hobbes and Benedict Spinoza asserted that the Pentateuch was post-Mosaic.

Taking note of these issues, it became clearer to critical scholars that it is more likely that the texts making up the Five Books of Moses were written, edited, or compiled by different people at different times and places, and were ultimately ascribed to the great leader of the liberation, Moses. In the past, it was not unusual to attribute books to highly respected people who lived long ago. The 150 individual psalms that make up our Book of Psalms were attributed to King David, even though at the end of Psalm 72 we read, "End of the prayers of David son of Jesse"; the Book of *Kohelet* (Ecclesiastes; see 1:1) and the Song of Songs (see 1:1) were attributed to King Solomon; the Psalms of Solomon (a collection of psalms composed about 63–30 B.C.E.) were also attributed to King Solomon. Even the Talmud admits, "The Men of the Great Assembly wrote Ezekiel, the Twelve Minor Prophets, Daniel, and the Scroll of Esther" (BT *Bava Batra* 15a). This would explain the various inconsistencies noted above. The question is whether it is possible to reconstruct the way in which the Pentateuch was put together. A number of theories have been advanced to solve this puzzle. These constitute the basis of what is known as modern biblical criticism.

Various Solutions

Modern textual criticism is said to have begun in the eighteenth century with scholars such as Richard Simon and Jean Astruc. Having noticed that the Book of Genesis employs two different names for God, specifically *YHVH* (pronounced *Adonai* by Jews) and *Elohim*, they claimed that the book was made up of two different sources running parallel to each other. The source using the term *YHVH* was called J (from the German *Jahweh*); the other source was called E (after the Hebrew term *Elohim*).

In the mid-nineteenth century, a new view came into prominence that even the so-called E source was divisible into two sub-sources: E and another one that was interested in priestly matters, therefore called P. In the late nineteenth century, Wilhelm de Wette advanced the idea that the Book of Deuteronomy reflected the reforms of the Judean king Josiah (seventh century B.C.E.; see II Kings 22–23) and therefore represented another source called D. This discovery was highly significant. Once D was placed in its historical context, it became easier to date the other sources. The problem was how to determine the correct sequence.

On the basis of these observations as well as the work of some of his predecessors, the German biblical scholar Julius Wellhausen, in his now famous book, *The Prolegomena to the History of Ancient Israel*, published in 1884, presented the first comprehensive history of the ancient Israelites by putting these sources in a special order. His hypothesis can be summarized as follows: J (ca. 850 B.C.E.) and E (ca. 750 B.C.E.) were combined by a redactor (RJe) about 650 B.C.E. In 621 B.C.E., D was composed and added to the other sources by a redactor (Rd) about 550 B.C.E. The P code, composed in the postexilic period (ca. 500–450 B.C.E.), was combined with the rest of the sources by a priestly writer about 400 B.C.E., thus giving form to the Pentateuch as a whole.

What is the nature of each of the sources? In J, God appears humanlike: God forms the first human being like a potter (Gen. 2:7), makes clothes for Adam and Eve (Gen. 3:21), smells the odor of Noah's sacrifice (Gen. 8:21), and visits Abraham for a meal (Gen. 18:1–8). J calls Moses's father-in-law "Reuel" (Exod. 2:18) and claims that Moses received the Torah on Mount Sinai (Exod. 19:18). The J source has a greater affinity with southern traditions and most likely emerged from areas around Judah.

In the E source, God is more remote and often communicates with humans through dreams (Gen. 20:3), angels or messengers (Gen. 21:17), and prophets (Gen. 20:7). The E source assumes that the sacred mountain is Mount Horeb (Exod. 33:6) and calls Moses's father-in-law "Jethro" (Exod. 18:1). E reflects the northern traditions.

The source called D, Deuteronomy, stands out with its unique hortatory style and vocabulary. In this source, God lives in the heavens, and only the divine "name" dwells on earth (Deut. 4:36, 12:5). The D source cites Mount Horeb as the locus of the Revelation and appears to have a special affinity with the northern traditions. Perhaps it emerged in the north and was brought to the south after the destruction of the Northern Kingdom in the eighth century B.C.E.

P is primarily interested in ritual matters, such as sacrifices, ritual purifications, and festivals, and uses formal and formulaic language to describe the creation of the world (in Gen. 1) and the building of the Tabernacle in the wilderness (Exod. 25ff.). P is marked by precision in details, dates, and places. In the P source, God appears more remote, and is usually manifested through *k'vod YHVH*, "the Presence of the Eternal" (Lev. 9:6).

Critique of Wellhausen's Theory

Many scholars accepted Wellhausen's reconstruction, though some dissented. A few denied that E existed as an independent source, and others put the sources in different order, in particular placing P before D. Some scholars added new sources, such as Morgenstern's K (for Kenite document), Pfeiffer's S (for Seir), and Eissfeldt's L (lay source). Some critics went to extremes by dividing each of the original four sources into a multiplicity of sub-documents. One scholar suggested that J could have been written by a woman. Even though some of these biblical critics proposed a few modifications of Wellhausen's theory, they all worked within the framework of his original hypothesis. It could be modified but not ignored or discarded. Even to this day it remains a working model for many biblical scholars. However, even the proponents of Wellhausen's hypothesis had to confront several major criticisms: (1) Under the influence of Hegelian philosophy, Wellhausen had presumed a rectilinear development in the composition of the Pentateuch, going from the simple to the complicated. We now know that this is not always the case. Nothing in the literary world moves in "rectilinear" fashion, and certainly not always from the simple to the complicated. At times, the simple form follows the elaborate. (2) He argued that short texts, like poems, preceded long texts in prose. The discovery of ancient Near Eastern texts proved him wrong. We now possess longer texts coming from antiquity, such as treaty documents, that are written in prose. (3) He also assumed that the ideas expressed in the texts originated with the texts themselves. Recent studies in the ancient Near East have proved this assumption also wrong. For example, the *Epic of Gilgamesh* went through a number of versions and editions, from the Sumerian to the Akkadian.

The question of how these texts were transmitted is another important part of this discussion. At the beginning of the twentieth century, Herman Gunkel (1862–1932), a German scholar, argued that a large part of the material in the Pentateuch was handed down orally long before any author/editor wrote it up. Therefore, a distinction must be made between the written text and its literary form. Gunkel first distinguished between prose and poetry. Among prose material he placed such literary types as historical narratives, romances, myths, and legends. Among poetic texts he identified secular lyrics, hymns, and oracular sayings. This methodology, known as the form critical method, led scholars to recognize the following: (1) The Bible has had a long and often complicated oral history, with material transmitted orally from generation to generation. (2) The Bible incorporates a number of literary types, each having its own development. Each type arises, develops, flourishes, and at times is combined with others. Some disappear altogether, and others survive. (3) Each literary type originates in a particular "setting in life," such as wedding ceremonies, mourning situations, and work conditions. This setting can be recovered by studying the literary type itself. Using this insight, scholars now debate whether legal statements emerge from real court proceedings or from tribal instructions or even schools. Do priestly injunctions about temple and sacrifice have their origin in real temple procedures, or are they literary constructs?

In our own time, Wellhausen's textual criticism and Gunkel's form criticism have been supplemented by other types of research. Today scholars talk about different approaches to Bible study such as rhetorical criticism, tradition criticism, and redaction criticism. Critics also approach the texts through theological, sociological, psychological, and archaeological points of view in an attempt to understand them. Among them, archaeology plays a major role in discovering the material culture of the past. But it too has its limitations, because it cannot confirm or deny the beliefs recorded in the Bible. Furthermore, finding a stone in a particular place does not mean that, for example, Jacob slept on it (Gen. 28:11), or that a piece of wood discovered in the mountains of eastern Turkey necessarily came from the ark of Noah.

The Canon

The word "canon," originally from Greek, means rule or measure, and often refers to the list of books considered to be sacred and authoritative for a given religious community. In the first century C.E., the Rabbis completed the Hebrew Bible by selecting all the books deemed sacred. Some were left out (such as the books that make up the Apocrypha, which is part of the Catholic Bible but printed separately by the Protestants) and others (like the Book of Jubilees) were rejected because of their sectarian tendencies.

What do we know about the canonization of the entire Bible, called *Tanach* in Hebrew (short for *Torah, N'vi-im* [Prophets], and *K'tuvim* [Writings])? It took a long time for the Hebrew Scriptures to assume the form that it has now. The Pentateuch was probably completed sometime during the postexilic period. The Book of Nehemiah tells us that Ezra, the scribe, read from the "scroll of the Torah of Moses" (Neh. 8:1–3) in 444 B.C.E. Was this the entire Pentateuch? We do not know.

Around the mid-third century B.C.E., the Pentateuch was translated into Greek (the so-called Septuagint) by Jewish scholars in Alexandria, Egypt. The rest of the books were completed sometime during the first and second century C.E. The Septuagint soon became the Bible of the early Christian church.

If the Hebrew Pentateuch started to take shape by the fourth or third century B.C.E., it took much longer to finalize the rest of the *Tanach*. During the second century B.C.E., the Second Book of Maccabees in the Apocrypha already knows of "the Law [namely, the five books attributed to Moses] and the Prophets" (II Macc. 15:9). In the prologue to Ben Sira (second century B.C.E.), another Apocryphal book, there is a reference to other collections as well, without, however, any identification: "The Torah and the Prophets and the others that followed them." In mid-first century C.E., Matthew, in the New Testament, speaks of "the Law and the Prophets" (Matt. 22:40), but toward the end of the century, Luke is familiar with "the Law of Moses and the Prophets and Psalms" (Luke 24:44). Whether or not the word "Psalms" refers to the complete third section of the Hebrew Bible, namely the Writings, or only to the beginning and longest part of Writings is not clear.

According to Jewish tradition, the *Tanach* was finalized by the Rabbis in the city of Yavneh, toward the end of the first century C.E., after the destruction of the Second Temple in 70 C.E. The Second Book of Esdras, dated to the late first century C.E., states that Esdras restored the twenty-four books of the Torah (the number of books in the Hebrew Bible today) that were lost (II Esd. 14:45–47).

It is apparent that even though Wellhausen's reconstruction is not totally accepted by the scholarly community today, we need to work within the framework of his theory, with all the modifications that are necessary. We do not know exactly how the Pentateuch or the Hebrew Bible was finally edited or by whom. However, the critical evidence shows that we must accept the existence of various sources and different ideological schools, at times competing with each other, that make up these texts. Some of this material is based on oral traditions that were slowly concretized over a period of time, and that schools of thought, some of them contemporaneous with each other, like D and P, emerged in different parts of the country or different cultural circles within the same society. These eventually gave rise to texts that were combined by priests or royal scribes, and eventually by the Rabbis, thus becoming sacred in the eyes of the ancient Israelites. Our task today is to attempt to understand the intention and opinions of the authors/editors/collectors within the context of their time. Only then can we grasp the meaning of the material, and begin to evaluate its message.

2

What Is God's Real Name?

Amulet, from Persia.
This amulet was meant to protect mother and child during childbirth.
The name of god, "Shaddai," Almighty, with a crown is encircled
by an invocation against Lilith, an ancient Assyrian female demon.
Parchment watercolor, powdered gold. Israel Museum, Jerusalem, Israel.

The Claim

The Bible claims that the personal name of God, *YHVH (or YHWH)*, was
first revealed to Moses before the Exodus (Exod. 6:3). In this chapter we will
study the mythological context of the ancient Near East out of which biblical Israel created a new concept of the divine, the various names by which
Israel's God was called, and the development of the God concept in Jewish
history as reflected in these names.

Words as Symbols

Linguists who study the function of language have long recognized that
words are mere symbols pointing to some object or idea. For example, the
word "chair" reminds us of an object called "chair," but is not the chair itself.
Furthermore, even though physical objects can be experienced by our five

senses, that is not the case with ideas, values, or concepts. Words such as "love," "democracy," or "beautiful" point to certain images or constructs that are developed as a result of our daily life within the framework of our present culture. Furthermore, the same words, such as "justice," "freedom," or "religion," often mean something different in other societies. Also, as society changes, so does the meaning of the words.

"God" is one of those terms that is difficult to define with precision, because it evokes different images for people around the world. Ultimately, the word stands for that which is most significant in our lives as individuals. Throughout history, people have ascribed different meanings to the term "God" in the process of trying to understand the mysteries of the universe.[1]

God's Existence and Name

Ancient Near Eastern religion was polytheistic, and gods were part of the mythology that attempted to explain existential questions. People gave divine names to almost every natural force in the universe, especially to those forces that dealt with issues of fertility. However, even though biblical Israelites, who were living in the same cultural milieu, used various names for God, towards the end of the biblical period, these multiple nomenclatures reflected only one presumed Master of the universe, because Israelites began to assume that everything in life was placed under the rule of one God alone. Why and how the biblical Israelites came to promote such a monistic view is still a mystery, but it is undoubtedly one of their most significant contributions to Western civilization.

The existence of gods was taken for granted in the ancient Near East. No ancient text ever tries to prove that divine beings were a reality. Acknowledging that death ends human life and that individuals depend on powers greater than themselves for their well-being and prosperity, people simply accepted that gods were ultimately in charge of everything, and required loyalty from their subordinates as well as sacrifices that provided sustenance on a regular basis. In fact, people in Mesopotamia believed that human beings were created in order to care for the gods and do all the menial work involved in this endeavor. For that reason, gods could often be addressed by their personal name.

In the Hebrew Bible, too, the existence of God is a given. According to the Book of Psalms, only "the fool says in his heart, there is no god" (Pss. 14:1, 53:2; see also 10:4). One could complain against God or, like Abraham or

Jeremiah, even argue with God, but there was no doubt in anyone's mind that a supreme being ruled the universe. What concerned the ancient Israelites was not the existence of God, but simply this: "Is the Eternal present among us or not?" (Exod. 17:7). In other words, can we count on God's protection and benevolence or not?

According to the biblical lore, when Moses spoke with God at the Burning Bush, one of his main concerns was to know God's name: "When I come to the Israelites," said Moses to God, "and say to them, 'The God of your ancestors has sent me to you,' and they ask me, 'What is his name?' What shall I say to them?" (Exod. 3:13). The underlying assumption of Moses's question was that if everyone, whether a human or a divine being, has a name, God must have one too. Furthermore, just as we establish a relationship with another person after finding out his/her name, it stands to reason that only by knowing God's proper name could Moses or the Israelites approach God and have a personal relationship with the Divine.

Even though the way the biblical Israelites perceived of God changed through the centuries, going from polytheism (i.e., many gods) to monolatry/henotheism (i.e., God is the God of Israel, but other nations have their own) and finally to monotheism (i.e., one universal God for all humanity), the existence of God was never in question. The attempt to prove the existence of God by using logical arguments came later on during the Rabbinic period, mostly under the influence of Greek thought, and became a major preoccupation for Jewish thinkers during the medieval times. From the perspective of the final redaction of the Bible, and the Jewish theology that was developed by the Rabbis and the later medieval philosophers, God is unique, alone, ineffable, invisible, intangible, and incomparable.

Various Names for Gods in Mesopotamia

In order to understand better the names given to God in the Hebrew Bible, it is important to consider first the larger religious context of the ancient Near Eastern pantheon. In the ancient cultures of Mesopotamia and the Mediterranean basin, the powers of nature were often identified with gods and demons. Thus, for example, in the Sumero-Akkadian religion, in addition to the dominant gods—An, the sky-god; Enlil, the air-god; and Enki, the deity of the sweet waters—there were a number of minor deities that ruled the world: Shamash, the sun god; Sin, the moon god; Ishtar, the goddess of fertility; and Adad, the weather god. There was even a god of pestilence (Nergal) and the god of hunting (Ninurta). Gods were capricious, and their will was not always known. Therefore, the worshipers had no choice but to resort to divination in order to discover the gods' wishes or to use amulets to protect themselves against malicious demons. Consequently, the ancient Near East developed an advanced science of divination and a widespread custom of writing texts to ward off evil powers, as well as an extensive literature on omens.

Gods were frequently graded, from high to low, according to the role they played in the universe, with the major ones having cosmic roles and others becoming household gods that protected the individuals who lived within the same compound. These gods also belonged to a council of gods usually ruled by one supreme being. Worshiped in local temples by their specialized priests, each "deity was considered present in its image."[2] Whenever the image was moved, so did the god.

In the ancient Near East, each country also had a god, and each god had a specific name. For example, Babylon had Marduk, Assyria had Ashur, and the Canaanites served Baal. In the same vein, each city had its own protective deity: Nergal was the patron deity of Cuthah, just as Nabu was the god of the city of Borsippa.

Furthermore, these gods were identified by their specific duties. In the Sumerian "Prayer of Lamentation to Ishtar," the goddess Ishtar is called "the lady of ladies, goddesses of goddesses, queen of all peoples, who guides mankind aright" (*ANET*, 384). In Babylonia, Enlil, the god of air, was "lord of heaven and earth, the determiner of the destinies of the land (*ANET*, 164). Adad, the weather god, was "the lord of abundance, the irrigator of heaven and earth" (*ANET*, 179). Inanna was "the lady of battle and conflict" (*ANET*, 179). Shamash, the sun god, was "the mighty judge of heaven and earth who guides aright living creatures" (*ANET*, 179). Similarly, Baal in Ugarit was the "rider of clouds" (*ANET*, 132; cf. Ps. 68:5).

Things were different in biblical Israel. In the early periods of biblical history, some Israelites worshiped many gods, as evidenced by the fact that the prophets regularly inveigh against this practice (e.g., I Kings 18:20–24; Hos. 3:1; Jer. 9:13). However, this phase gave way to a new conception, called monolatry or henotheism, whereby God was viewed, at least in the official circles, as the protector of the Israelites, without denying the existence of other deities. For example, in Exodus 15:11, we read, "Who is like you, Eternal One [*YHVH*], among the celestials [lit. 'gods']." By the seventh century B.C.E., biblical Israelites considered God in monotheistic terms as being one and unique: "Hear, O Israel! The Eternal is our God, the Eternal alone" (Deut. 6:4). Similarly, during the exilic period, Second Isaiah declares, "I am *YHVH*, and there is none else" (Isa. 45:18). In contrast to the gods of Mesopotamia, the Israelite God does not belong to a divine group as an equal member. Everything in the universe is subservient to the one and only God. God is alone and unique.

During all these periods of Jewish history, the Israelites addressed their God by a variety of names.

El

El is the generic term for "god" in the ancient Near East. Its basic meaning is "power," as when Laban says to Jacob, "It is well within my power [*l'el yadi*] to do you an injury" (Gen. 31:29). In the Bible, the word *El*, referring to the God of Israel, appears sometimes alone (e.g., Num. 23:8, 24:4) and sometimes in compound names, such as *El Elyon* ("Most High God" [Gen. 14:18]), *El Ro-i* (as explained in Gen. 16:13, in reference to Hagar, "Even here I have seen the back of the *One who looks upon me!*"), *El –Beit El* ("God of Beth El" [Gen. 31:13]), *El B'rit* ("God of the Covenant" [Judg. 9:46]), or *El Shaddai* ("God Almighty" [Gen. 17:1]). Often it is part of a proper name, such as Yehezkel (meaning "*El* strengthens") or Immanuel (meaning "*El* is with us").

Elohim

The term *elohim* contains the plural ending -*im* and often refers in the Bible to the gods of other nations (e.g., Exod. 12:12). When this name is ascribed to the God of Israel, it is usually treated as a singular noun, such as "When God [*Elohim*] was about to create [*bara*, a singular verb]" (Gen. 1:1). It is the preferred name in the Elohistic documents that derive from the Northern Kingdom of Israel, as well as in priestly texts. In very few cases, however, it is accompanied by verbs in the plural, perhaps a vestige from the ancient polytheistic view of the divine realm. For example, when Abraham tells Abimelech, king of Gerar, "When God [*Elohim*] made me wander from my father's house" (Gen. 20:13), here the verb "made me wander," *hitu*, is in the plural; similarly, after Jacob built an altar at Beth El, the text reads, "for there, in his flight from his brother, God [*Elohim*] had been revealed [*niglu*, a plural verb] to him" (Gen. 35:7).

In many places in the Bible, a singular vocative[3] form of *Elohim* appears as *Eloah* (e.g., Deut. 32:15, 32:17).

Shaddai

Following the Septuagint and the Vulgate (the Latin translation of the Bible in the fourth century C.E.), the word *Shaddai* is usually translated in English as "Almighty." However, the real meaning is far from clear. Some scholars believe that it is derived from the Akkadian *shadû*, meaning "mountain," and therefore render it as "Mountain God." Others claim it comes from another Semitic root, *shadad*, meaning "to storm," or *Shaddayin*, which were divinities mentioned in old Aramaic texts. In medieval times, Rashi interpreted it homiletically as *she-dai*, that is, "being sufficient" (on Gen. 17:1), meaning that God is the source of all life.

At times, *Shaddai*, as the name of the God of Israel, appears alone (Num. 24:4; Ps. 91:1; Ruth 1:20; and often in Job, e.g., 5:17, 31:35) and, in other cases, in combination with other divine names, such as *El Shaddai* (e.g., Gen. 17:1, 28:3). Sometimes it appears in personal names, such as Zurishaddai (Num. 1:6).

Tz'vaot

The word *tz'vaot* means "hosts" and is usually found in the Bible in compounds, such as *YHVH Tz'vaot* ("*YHVH* of Hosts" [e.g., I Sam. 1:3; Isa. 6:3]), *Elohei Tz'vaot* ("the God of Hosts" [I Kings 19:10, 19:14]), or *Elohim Tz'vaot* ("the God of Hosts" [Ps. 80:8]). Most likely, the reference is to the heavenly council made up of angels or other divine beings that is thought to be assembled under the leadership of the one God. It has also been suggested that it may refer to a God who is identified with all the powers attributed to many gods.[4]

YHVH

This name, transliterated either as *YHVH* or *YHWH*, is known as the Tetragrammaton (from the Greek, *tetra* [four] and *grammaton* [letter]) and occurs more than sixty-eight hundred times in the Bible. It is the distinctive name of the God of Israel favored by the Jahwist documents of Judah (see p. 8): "Eternal One [*YHVH*] is His name" (Exod. 15:3). Though spelled out fully as *YHVH*, it also appears as an abbreviation in the form of *Yah*—"The Eternal [*Yah*] is my strength" (Exod. 15:2)—and as *Yahu* in the names of many Israelites, such as Uziyahu (Isa. 6:1), Yirm'yahu (Jer. 1:1), or, in shortened form, Uriyah (for Uriyahu; II Kings 16:16), as well as in the expression *hal'luyah* (Hallelujah). Its grammatical root could also be related to *Ehyeh*, which is found in God's answer to Moses, "Thus shall you say to the Israelites, '*Ehyeh* sent me to you'" (Exod. 3:14).

Coming from the Hebrew root *hayah*, the name *YHVH*, in its third person masculine imperfect form, can be most accurately translated as "Existence," "He is," "He is present," or even "He causes to be." The origin of the name is uncertain. According to one biblical tradition, it was introduced to Moses before the Exodus: "God spoke with Moses and said to him: "I am the Eternal [*YHVH*]. I appeared to Abraham, Isaac, and Jacob as *El Shaddai*, but I did not make Myself known to them by My name *YHVH*" (Exod. 6:2–3). Yet other sources in the Book of Genesis clearly state that this name was already known before Moses's time, dating back to the time of Enosh, the grandson of Adam (Gen. 4:26; see also 14:22, 24:31). Biblical tradition insists that Moses did not introduce a new God, but reaffirmed the same God who had led the patriarchs in their wanderings, though known to them only as *El Shaddai*.

The earliest reference to this proper name for God is found in the Song of Deborah (Judg. 5:2) and in the Song of Moses (Exod. 15), both coming from about the eleventh century B.C.E. In extra-biblical sources, we find the name *YHVH* in the Moabite Stone of King Mesha of Moab (ninth century B.C.E.): "I took from there the . . . of *Yahveh*, dragging them before Chemosh" (*ANET*, 320). In the sixth century B.C.E., the name also appears in some Israelite texts, such as the Lachish Ostraca:[5] "May *YHVH* cause my lord to hear this very day tidings of good" (Ostracon IV, *ANET*, 322); and in the Arad Ostraca of the sixth century B.C.E.: "May *Yahweh* grant thy welfare" (*ANET*, 569).

However, the name *YHVH* is also found in sources outside of Israel. For example, in a tenth-century-B.C.E. four-tiered cult stand from Ta'anah in northern Syria, *YHVH* is associated with the goddess Asherah.[6] Similarly, the name appears in Phoenician storage jars from Kuntillet Ajrud, in the northern Sinai wilderness (eighth century B.C.E.), in the form of "*YHVH* and his Asherah." This reference gave rise to a theory that at one time *YHVH* may have been conceived of as having a consort.[7] We also have references to "*YHVH* of Samaria" (eighth century B.C.E.) and "*YHVH* of Teiman" (eighth century B.C.E.).[8]

The Bible provides a hint that the name could be of southern, wilderness origin, when it asserts in the final blessing of Moses that "The Eternal [*YHVH*] came from Sinai" (Deut. 33:2). It is possible that the Israelites learned about *YHVH* from some of their neighbors and adopted it as their national God. How this happened, however, is not known. Some scholars argue that Moses learned about *YHVH* from his Midianite father-in-law

Jethro. Others claim that the Israelites learned about it from the Egyptians who had a god by that name. All of these theories, however, are highly speculative. The truth is, we do not know how and when the Israelites first came to view *YHVH* as their God, except for what the Bible states, namely, that *YHVH* was revealed for the first time to Abraham (Gen. 12:1), traditionally considered to be the first "monotheist."

The major problem with the term *YHVH* is that there is no definitive pronunciation for this name. In some ancient Hebrew manuscripts, even though the rest of the biblical texts appear in late Aramaic script, the name *YHVH* is still written in archaic Hebrew letters without any vowels, most likely because of its sacred character. The vowels that came to be attached to this name for God are of later Rabbinic origin.

In ancient times there was a prohibition against misusing *YHVH*'s name. The Ten Commandments clearly state, "You shall not utter the name of the Eternal [*YHVH*] your God in vain [*lashav*]" (Exod. 20:7), most likely because it could be used for magical purposes. However, the meaning of this text is not totally clear (see chapter 9). Later on, the Rabbis also feared that the holy name could be used in magical formulas (JT *Sanhedrin* 28b). Therefore, given the sacred character of the name, they discouraged people from uttering it as written.

During the Second Temple period, the name *YHVH* was pronounced with its proper vowels only by the High Priest during the *Avodah* service on Yom Kippur within the Temple (*Mishnah Yoma* 6:2) and by ordinary priests when they recited the Priestly Benediction in the Temple itself (*Mishnah Sotah* 7:6). With the passing of time, however, the correct pronunciation was lost. In order to preserve the reverence for the divine name, the Rabbis substituted the word *Adonai*, meaning "Master" or "my Master," by applying the vowels of *Adonai* to the name *YHVH*.[9] They taught, "Not as I am written, am I pronounced. I am written *YHVH*, but I am pronounced as *ADONAI*" (BT *Kiddushin* 71a). They further said, "Whoever pronounces God's name according to its consonants has no share in the world-to-come" (*Avot D'Rabbi Natan* 36:6).

In the Septuagint, *YHVH* is translated as *kyrios* (Lord). Theodoret of Cyrus, a fourth-century church father, testifies that the Samaritans used to read it as *Yabe*. In 1278, a Spanish monk named Raymund Martini spelled it as *Yohoua*. In the early sixteenth century, a Catholic priest from Italy, Petrus Galatinus, spelled it as *Yehoua*. The popular name "Jehovah" appears for the first time in 1530 in the English Bible by William Tyndale. Most

---

EPITHETS OF GOD IN THE BIBLE

In the Bible, God is often known by various epithets, reflecting the way in which people conceived of God or related to God. Among them we find *Adon*, "Master" (as in "Master of all the earth," in Josh. 3:13); *Av*, "Father" (Mal. 1:6); *Atik Yomaya*, "the Ancient of Days" (Dan. 7:13); *Tzur*, "Rock" (Deut. 32:4); *Melech*, "King" (Isa. 6:5); *Shofet*, "Judge" (Gen. 18:25); *K'dosh Yisrael*, "the Holy One of Israel" (Isa. 43:3; Ps. 71:22); *Pachad Yitzchak*, "Fear/Terror of Isaac" (Gen. 31:42); *Avir Yaakov*, "the Mighty One of Jacob" (Gen. 49:24); and *Avir Yisrael*, "the Mighty of Israel" (Isa. 1:24).

Israel's God is also viewed, among other descriptions, as *kanna*, "impassioned" or "zealous" (Exod. 34:14); *El zo-eim*, "God of indignation" (Ps. 7:12); *ish milchamah*, "a warrior" (Exod. 15:3); *rachum v'chanun*, "compassionate and gracious" (Exod. 34:6; Jon. 4:2); a shepherd (Ps. 23:1); a healer (Deut. 32:39); a creator (Gen. 1:1; Isa. 40:28); *El emunah*, "a faithful God" (Deut. 32:4); and *tzaddik v'yashar*, "true and upright" (Deut. 32:4)

---

scholars today think that that the correct pronunciation is "Yahveh." However, as one biblical scholar notes, "Most attempts at recovery [of the correct pronunciation] are conjectural."[10]

God's Name in Rabbinic Literature

Based upon biblical teaching, the Rabbis accepted a priori that God existed. For them, the concern was how to defend God's uniqueness against the threat posed by the Persian Zoroastrian dualists of their time and, later on, by the Christian trinitarians. The former claimed that there were, in fact, two gods: Ormuzd, in charge of good, and Ahriman, in charge of evil. The latter maintained that God had three components, namely, Father, Son, and Holy Spirit. Against the Zoroastrians the Rabbis taught, "[Scripture] would not let the nations of the world have an excuse for saying that there are two powers, but declares: 'I am the Eternal your God.' Namely, I am He who was in Egypt, and I am He who was at the sea. I am He who was at Sinai. I am

He who was in the past, and I am He who will be in the future" (*M'chilta, Ba-Chodesh* 4). In medieval times, a denial of possible multiplicity in God's nature is found, among others, in the writings of Maimonides, who taught, "God is one, the cause of all oneness. He is not like a member of a pair, not a series of genus, nor a person divided into many discrete elements" (*Chelek, Sanhedrin* 10).

Though there are no systematic attempts to prove the existence of God in the Bible, the Rabbis, most likely under Greek influence, attempted to do just that. According to one midrash, an unbeliever once came to see Rabbi Akiva and asked him, "Who created the world?" Rabbi Akiva said, "Who made the garment that you are wearing?" The other replied, "Obviously, a weaver!" "Prove it to me," said Rabbi Akiva. The fellow exclaimed, "Don't you know that a weaver makes clothes?" "And don't you know," said Akiva, "that God is the Creator of the universe?" Rabbi Akiva's students, however, were not happy with their teacher's response and pressed him harder. So Akiva said, "Just as a house implies that a builder built it, so the existence of the world implies the existence of its creator, and that is God" (*Otzar HaMidrashim, T'murah, Keta* 7). This "proof" is similar to the "teleological proof" of the existence of God based on design, which was promoted by Greek thinkers and espoused as early as the Jewish philosopher Philo of Alexandria in the early first century C.E. and others later on.

The ancient Rabbis inherited the biblical names ascribed to God, but in order to preserve their sacred character and avoid their misuse by ordinary Jews, they replaced all these names with a general term, *HaShem*, meaning "the Name." They also argued that the difference between *YHVH* and *Elohim* lies in the idea that *YHVH* refers to God's attribute of mercy (*midat harachamim*), as against *Elohim*, which stands for God's attribute of justice (*midat hadin*) (*Sh'mot Rabbah* 3:6). The worshiper hopes that God will deal mercifully with all creation.

In addition to *HaShem*, the ancient Rabbis created a whole list of new terms referring to God. Among them, the following are the most prominent: *HaMakom*, "the Place"; *Shamayim*, "Heaven" (as in *yirat shamayim*, "the fear of heaven"); *HaKadosh baruch hu*, "The Holy One, blessed is He"; *Ribono shel olam*, "Master of the universe"; *Avinu Malkeinu*, "our Father, our King"; *Melech malchei hamlachim*, "the King of all kings"; *HaRachaman*, "the Merciful One"; *Shechinah*, "the Divine Presence"; *HaG'vurah*, "the Power."

The Rabbis, however, stressed the fact that although God has many names, all the names refer to the same one God. Thus, commenting on the biblical verse "And God said to Moses . . ." (Exod. 3:14), Rabbi Abba bar Mamel said, "God said to Moses: You wish to know my name. I am called depending on what I do. When I am judging created things, I am called *Elohim*, and when I am waging war against the wicked, I am called *Tz'vaot*. When I suspend judgment for a person's sin, I am called *El Shaddai*, but when I am merciful toward My world, I am called *Adonai*. For *Adonai* refers to the attribute of mercy, as it is said, 'The Eternal, the Eternal [*Adonai, Adonai*], God, merciful and gracious' [Exod. 34:6]" (*Sh'mot Rabbah* 3:6).

In the later Rabbinic literature, this list of names was expanded by Jewish thinkers of the medieval period, mostly under the influence of Greek and Islamic philosophy, which viewed God as the "mind" or "prime mover." Among them, we find *Ilat ha-ilot*, "Cause of causes"; *Ilah Rishonah*, "First Cause"; *HaBorei*, "the Creator"; *HaShem yitbarach*, "the Name, blessed be He"; and *Shem hamforash*, "the separate Name." In the mystical writings of early kabbalists of thirteenth-century Provence and Spain, the term *Ein Sof* (the Limitless One) appears to describe God who is unknowable and whose existence and thought extend without end. To note the fact that God is beyond human comprehension, other unpronounceable expressions were also used in mystical prayers, such as "In purity I pronounce Your name, You who are One over all creatures," *SBR DR'Y 'DYR DRY'S WHPS DRSYN* (*Maaseh Merkavah* 2:562).[11]

In Modern Times

Under the influence of modern feminism and other contemporary views about God, newer terms continue to make their appearance in the liturgy. For example, Judith Plaskow (b. 1947) argues that in addressing God two items should be stressed. The first of these is the avoidance of anthropomorphic language that involves dominance. Thus, instead of using the term "King" for God, she suggests we should use "Friend," "Fountain of Life," or "Companion." Secondly, she addresses the necessity to invoke images of God as a partner who calls us for responsible action. God, she notes, is encountered in the midst of a community and is experienced as male/female lover, friend, companion and co-creator.[12]

Similarly, the philosopher and poet Marcia Falk (b. 1946) maintains that even though traditional prayers stress "oppositional distinctions" such as space-time and body-soul, in our liturgy today we need to celebrate differences without hierarchy. In her well-received volume *The Book of Blessings*,

THE USE OF THE TERM "G-D"

Many Jews today, in an attempt to avoid uttering the proper name of God, *YHVH*, prefer to use the Rabbinic expression *HaShem* (the Name) or change one letter of the name *Elohim* by saying *Elokim*. Similarly, to avoid erasing the name of God by mistake, many Jews as well as some traditional Christians customarily write "G-D" in place of "God" and "L- -D" for "Lord." In 1963, Rabbi Solomon B. Freehof, a Reform rabbi who was the leading halachist of his generation, dealt with this issue in a well-known responsum, entitled "The Word 'God' Spelled 'G-D.'"

In his "answer," Freehof stated that the Rabbinic prohibition of erasing the name of God is based on the biblical command regarding idolatrous people, "Tear down their altars . . . obliterating their name from that site," which continues, "Do not worship *YHVH* your God in like manner" (Deut. 12:3–4). However, Freehof, added, "the primary prohibition against erasure (by act or neglect) of the name of God applies to the sacred names in the properly written text of the Torah, and even in the Torah itself, those names of God are not sacred unless the scribe sanctifies them with a specifically uttered formula."[13] Besides, the sanctity applies only to the name of God if it is written in the Hebrew language. Consequently, one can spell the English name of "God" in full, without having to place a dash between G and D, and by extension between L and D.

she frequently refers to God as the *eyn hahayim* (source of life) or *ma'yan hayeynu* (the flow or wellspring of life).[14]

In many contemporary liturgies, such as *Mishkan T'filah*, published by the Central Conference of American Rabbis (2007), all references to God's gender are eliminated in the English translation of the prayers. God is addressed in the second person, and Hebrew possessives are ignored (e.g., *asher kid'shanu b'mitzvotav* is rendered as "who hallows us with mitzvot [not '*his* mitzvot']"), thus avoiding the use of "him" or "her." Furthermore, expressions of dominance reflective of past ages are avoided. Thus, for example, *Melech* (King), one of God's attributes, is now rendered as "Sovereign." In many cases, even the biblical proper name of Israel's God, *YHVH* (formerly translated as "Lord") is not only pronounced in Hebrew as *Adonai*, which is appropriate, but also rendered as such in the English translation, for example, "Blessed are You, *Adonai*, our God. . . ."

Struggling how best to call God or how to address the Divine has been one of the great challenges of all thinkers. The ancient Rabbis as well as many philosophers, both ancient and modern, have taught that human language is inadequate to speak of God, who is both transcendent and the ground of our existence. Throughout history, people have tried to give a name to this Source of life without, however, capturing the totality of God's grandeur. Some have conceived of God as a personal God, others as a process or energy. For some God is a reality, for others, an idea. Some concentrate on God's essence, others on what God does. When we call God *YHVH*, *Ein Sof*, or by another name, our attention is drawn to the totality of existence, which is animated by the spirit of an unknowable Power, and to whom/which we owe our life and gratitude, even if we cannot discern God's plan or the way God functions.

Commenting on the biblical text "Walking in all God's ways" (Deut. 11:22), the ancient Rabbis asked, "What are God's ways?" They answered by quoting another scriptural verse: "The Eternal! the Eternal! a God compassionate and gracious" (Exod. 34:6). "So," they taught, "as God is compassionate, you should be compassionate; just as God is gracious you be gracious" (*Sifrei, D'varim, Eikev* 49). We do not know the fullness of God, but we can act like God toward others.

3

Was the Universe Created in Six Days?

Michelangelo Buonarroti (1475–1564).
The Sistine Chapel; ceiling frescos after restoration. The Creation of Adam.
Sistine Chapel, Vatican Palace, Vatican State.

The Claim

People have always been fascinated by theories regarding the creation of the universe. Did it happen as it was described in Genesis? In the year 1650, stringing together all the chronologies in the Bible, James Ussher, an Anglican archbishop of Armagh and vice-chancellor of the Trinity College in Dublin, argued that the world was brought into being in 4004 B.C.E. Around the same time, John Lightfoot, an English scholar at the University of Cambridge, went so far as to claim that this feat took place on October 26, at 9 A.M. Modern science, however, has disproved these claims and maintains that the universe is about four and a half billion years old.

Creation in Genesis

The Bible contains references to Creation in many places, such as psalms (e.g., Pss. 77, 93), prophetic texts (e.g., Isa. 44), and wisdom literature (Prov.

3, 8; Job 40). However, the most extensive as well as the most familiar story is found in the Book of Genesis, as it begins with the following verses: "When God was about to create heaven and earth, the earth was a chaos, unformed, and on the chaotic waters' face there was darkness. Then, God's spirit glided over the face of the waters, and God said, 'Let there be light!'—and there was light" (Gen. 1:1–3).

The Book of Genesis contains two parallel but distinct Creation stories. The first one, Gen. 1:1–2:4a is attributed to priestly writers (P), whereas the second one, Gen. 2:4b–24, is usually assigned to the J source (see chapter 1). There are considerable differences between the two cosmogonies (stories of Creation):

1. The P Account:
   a. The P story conceives of creation in a sequential way, completed in seven days, with the last day being a day of rest. It is written in prose but has a solemn majesty about it. Each day witnesses a new creation. It is repetitious and formal. Usually, there is an announcement: "And God said." This is followed by a command, "Let there be." A report follows: "And it was so." Then there is an evaluation: "It was good/very good." At the end comes the designation of the number of the day: first day, second day, and so on.
   b. In P, God is called *Elohim*. Though this word is a plural noun, the verb that accompanies it is in the singular. In other words, God is one, not many. Creation is by divine word: "God said, 'Let there be light!'—and there was light" (Gen. 1:3). The word itself has creative power, and it is as if God were addressing the emerging universe. The Hebrew verb used for purposes of divine creation is *bara*.
   c. In P, a single human being is created at the end of the process on the sixth day. This human is something like a hermaphrodite, both "male and female," and is made "in the image of God" (Gen. 1:27). The implication of this expression is not clear, but perhaps, based on the Akkadian word *tsalmu*, meaning "image" or "statue," one can argue that humanity was conceived as having "a kingly image" or a "royal stature" vis-à-vis the other creations in order to rule the earth as God's representative. A Bible scholar has argued that here the text may be referring to the "splendor of his bodily form."[1] Jewish tradition, however, sees in this expression a reflection of the intangible qualities attributed to God, namely, compassion, creativity, and morality, and argues that humans too ought to carry out these godly acts.[2]

2. The J Account

The account in J does not have a uniform framework. Instead of the majestic transcendence of P, the language here is more picturesque and flowing. Thus, for example, creation is not carried out in consecutive days. Here, God, referred to as *YHVH Elohim*, appears more immanent, more personal, close. The act of creation is described by the verb *yatzar*, which is related to the word for "potter" (*yotzer* in Hebrew), who fashions things with his hands. There is no creation by word. God fashions first a male and then, from his ribs, a female, not at the end of Creation, but at the very beginning of the process. The text reflects an agricultural perspective on the part of the writer, where Adam appears as a farmer condemned to labor on the soil (Gen. 2:5, 3:17–19).

This critical analysis shows that these two accounts do not come from the same hand, but represent different ideologies. The traditional sources deal with this duplication by stating that the different versions complement one another. For example, Joseph H. Hertz (1872–1946), the former Chief Rabbi of the British Empire, writes in his Torah commentary, "Chapter II is *not* another account of Creation. No mention is made in it of the formation of the dry land, the sea, the sun, moon or stars. It is nothing else but the sequel of the preceding chapter."[3]

What about the duplication in the creation of humanity? Philo of Alexandria (20 B.C.E.–50 C.E.) provides an answer: "The Adam of Genesis 1 was the idea of man, and hence this ideal man never appeared on earth; it was the Adam of Genesis 2, fashioned out of the material dust and immaterial spirit, who was the ancestor of the race."[4] Rabbi Joseph B. Soloveitchik (1903–1993) argues, in his book *The Lonely Man of Faith* (1966), that the two chapters represent two different aspects of Adam. In Genesis 1 we have a majestic Adam, who sees God in the splendor of the universe and shows reverence through science. Genesis 2, however, presents a lonely Adam who craves a personal relationship with God. Even some liberal rabbis take a complementary approach. Thus, for example, for Rabbi Elyse Goldstein, the two stories relate to gender issues: "The first story is women's: one of existential relationship and connection of the interweaving of self and other. The rib story is men's: one of separation and detachment overcome through sexual union."[5] Recognizing the differences between the two accounts, a contemporary non-Jewish biblical scholar writes, "The Priestly editors found no difficulty incorporating the two together. God's magnificent creation of the world in Genesis 1 set the stage for his intimate concern with man and woman in Genesis 2. What God did was awe-inspiring, but it was also very close to us."⁶

Creation Stories of the Ancient Near East

In the ancient Near East, which represents the larger context of many biblical myths, many people, curious about the beginnings of the earth, created cosmogonies that reflected the thinking of their time. Though no standard Creation text has been found among the ancient Egyptian documents, there are various creation stories that circulated in important Egyptian cities with the purpose of exalting the major deity of that city. Each one of these Egyptian narratives has only one creator god who brings into life the world either by word (as later on in the Bible) or, curiously enough, through the semen of the divinity. In ancient Canaan, we find many references to Creation among the Phoenicians and among those who lived in Ugarit, modern-day Lebanon. In these narratives, the creator god is El, and his consort is Asherah. However, the longest Creation stories come from Mesopotamia, either from Sumer or Babylonia. Among them, the most comprehensive Akkadian text is called *Enuma Elish*, "When on High," so named after the first two words of the myth.⁷

This Akkadian myth, written in poetic form between the fourteenth and twelfth centuries B.C.E., appears on seven tablets and relates the following events: In primordial times, the divine assembly consisted of Apsu (fresh water) and Tiamat (salt water). Other gods emerged from them: first Anu, the sky god, and other minor gods called Iggigi. These minor divinities disturbed the primordial pair with their increasing noises, and Apsu planned to destroy them. However, one of the gods, Ea, got wind of the plan and killed Apsu. This caused Tiamat to declare war against all the other gods. Marduk, the principal god of the city of Babylon, was chosen by the other gods to fight on their behalf. During the battle, Marduk killed Tiamat and began the process of Creation:

Then the lord paused to view her dead body,
That he might divide the monster and do artful works.
He split her like a shellfish into two parts:
Half of her he set up and ceiled it as sky. (*ANET,* 67)

Then, as the process of Creation continued:

> In her [Tiamat's] belly he [Marduk] established the zenith.
> The Moon he caused to shine, the night (to him) entrusting.
> He appointed him a creature of the night to signify the days. (*ANET*, 68a)

Once the moon and the sun were created, the wise god, Ea, suggested that one of the rebellious gods be used as material for the creation of a human being. Thus, it was out of Kingu, one of Tiamat's consorts, that the first man was formed:

> States Marduk,
> "Blood I will mass and cause bones to be.
> I will establish a savage, 'man' shall be his name." (*ANET*, 68a)

Marduk and other gods then went to work, and

> Out of his [Kingu's] blood they fashioned mankind.
> He [Ea] imposed the service and let free the [other rebel] gods. (*ANET*, 68b)

After Creation, a lofty shrine was built in Babylon in honor of Marduk, and the gods celebrated with a great feast.

How Is the Biblical Story Different?

There are many similarities between all the ancient Near Eastern Creation stories, including those in the Bible: all speak of a primary chaos; all mention the creation of light; all deal with the forming of the first human being; and, at the end of the process, all stories end up with God resting in celebration after a job well done. However, there are also very important differences between the biblical account and those that come from the rest of the ancient cultures. Following are some of the most important ones.

As one scholar points out, "All the Akkadian creation accounts (and the Sumerian for that matter) show no interest in creation as a historical event in the modern sense but only as validating or exploring present reality."[8] In Babylonia the purpose was political. *Enuma Elish* was recited every year in the springtime, in a dramatic ceremony called Akitu, on the fourth day of the New Year, with the purpose of proclaiming Marduk as the head of the pantheon. The poem was also used to sing the praises of Babylon, which was the city of Marduk, in order to strengthen the claims to supremacy over the entire region.

In the Genesis story we find a religious affirmation of God's sovereignty. However, as another scholar notes, "In the Bible (with the possible exception of wisdom literature) the doctrine of creation does not stand by itself but depends upon and elaborates the redemptive activity of God in history."[9] Genesis was conceived as the first step toward God's self-revelation at Mount Sinai. In this respect, it is viewed only as the beginning of the historical process.

In the ancient Near Eastern texts outside of the Bible, divine beings and the created world are intertwined; they coexist without any differentiation. In the Bible, God creates the world by word or divine hand, but God is independent of the created matter and rules over it.

The priestly authors of Genesis, though most likely familiar with other Creation myths in the region, have demythologized the event. In other stories, we find a conflict among various gods; in the Bible, all creation is subordinated to one creator God. Whereas other ancient Near Eastern texts try to answer the question of how the various generations of gods came into being, Genesis denies that other gods exist and places other "divine beings," such as the angelic hosts in the divine council in Genesis 1:26 ("Let us make human beings . . ."), under God's sole rule. A reflection of this belief is found in the Book of Nehemiah: "You alone are the Eternal. You made the heavens, the highest heavens, and all their host, the earth and everything upon it, the seas and everything in them" (Neh. 9:6). The Creation story may be a myth, but it is devoid of mythology.

In the Mesopotamian texts, the first human being is created from the blood of a minor god. In the Bible, humanity is created by God alone and is made the crown of Creation.

In the Bible, Creation concludes with the Sabbath, which is a day of rest as well as sanctification, an item missing in the other ancient Near Eastern stories. In the biblical texts, the whole creation, even God, rests on the seventh day.

Creation in Rabbinic Literature

The Rabbis inherited the Creation myth from the Bible and accepted it as given. For them, as indicated in the prayer *Baruch She-Amar* ("Blessed is the

One who spoke"), God is "the One who spoke and the world came to be" (BT *Eiruvin* 13b; BT *M'gillah* 13b). Often, they attempted to account for certain discrepancies appearing in the texts. Thus, for example, they noted that in the first Creation story God created "heaven and earth" (Gen. 1:1, 2:4a), but in the second story the order is reversed: "earth and heaven" (Gen. 2:4b). Based on this observation, the school of Shammai argued that the heavens were created first, comparing it to a king who first makes his throne (namely, the heavens) and then his footstool (namely, the earth). According to the school of Hillel, however, it was the earth that was created first, as in the case of a king who builds the foundation and then the upper part of the house. Rabbi Shimon bar Yochai maintained that they were created simultaneously, like a pot and its lid (*B'reishit Rabbah* 1:15).

According to the Jewish calendar, the first day of the first month, Nisan (usually falling between March and April), is not also the first day of the New Year (Rosh HaShanah); this one falls on the first day of the seventh month, Tishrei (usually in September/October). The change from the early biblical calendar that started the year in the fall to the calendar that placed the beginning of the year in the spring had already been made when the Israelites returned from Babylonia in the sixth century B.C.E., bringing with them the Babylonian spring calendar to which they were accustomed in exile. Thus the months were then counted from the first month in the spring, namely Nisan, leaving the New Year to the seventh month in the fall. Against this background, and not knowing exactly when the universe was created, Rabbi Eliezer ben Hyrkanos, in the first century C.E., speculated that Creation took place in the month of Tishrei. Rabbi Y'hoshua ben Hananiah, on the other hand, taught that it occurred in Nisan (see BT *Rosh HaShanah* 10b–11a). There is also an old Jewish tradition that Rosh HaShanah, the day on which "the world was conceived" (*hayom harat olam*),[10] actually celebrates the creation of the first human being, with the forming of the world having taken place six days prior to that, namely on the twenty-fifth of Elul. The book *Seder Olam* (ca. second century) places Creation on October 7, 3761 B.C.E.

The Rabbis also insisted, perhaps in order to counter the reigning dualism of their time, that God was alone when the world was created. God had no partner in the process (*B'reishit Rabbah* 8:9). Furthermore, highlighting the uniqueness of all creation, the Rabbis stressed that nothing brought into life in this world is without a special purpose, and therefore every creature is precious: "Even those things which you may regard as completely superfluous to the creation of the world, such as fleas, gnats, and flies, even they too are included in the creation of the world, and the Holy One, blessed be God, carried out God's purpose through everything, even through a snake, a scorpion, a gnat, or a frog" (*Midrash Rabbah: Genesis,* 10:7, Soncino).

From the creation of the first human being, the Rabbis derived various lessons about the nature and uniqueness of humanity. Thus, they said, God made one human being at the start of Creation in order to teach that "if anyone causes a single soul to perish [from {among the people of} Israel][11] Scripture imputes to him as if he had destroyed the entire world; and if anyone saves alive a single soul [from Israel], Scripture imputes to him as if he had saved the entire world" (*Mishnah Sanhedrin* 4:5).

Creation Out of Nothing

Many philosophers, both Jewish and non-Jewish, have argued that the universe was not created out of preexisting matter. The earliest traces of this *creatio ex nihilo,* "creation out of nothing," can be found in the Apocryphal book II Maccabees, in Hannah's touching words to her son as he was about to die during King Antiochus's persecutions: "I beseech you, my child, to look at the heaven and the earth and see everything that is in them, and recognize that God did not make them out of things that existed" (II Macc. 7:28, RSV). For the early Rabbis this issue was not a major concern, but it became one in later periods, especially during medieval times. Jewish philosophers, under the influence of their contemporary thinkers, fiercely discussed the arguments pro and con about creation versus eternality of the world.

Aristotelians and those who followed them in medieval times believed that matter, hence the world, is eternal, whereas Jewish philosophers, based on the biblical story of Creation, argued that only God is eternal and that matter, hence the world, has its beginning in God's Creation.

The Rabbis asserted God's omnipotence and freedom. It was the will of God, they maintained, to bring about the universe into being, and God did it out of nothing. However, their arguments were not too convincing. Even Moses Maimonides, the great commentator and philosopher of Spain (twelfth century) had to concede that *creatio ex nihilo* could not be proved. Yet he defended Jewish tradition by stating "the foundation of the whole Law is the view that God has brought the world into being out of nothing without there having been a temporal beginning" (*Guide of the Perplexed* 2:30, Pines). On the other hand, the Jewish philosopher Levi ben Gerson (fourteenth century) maintained that the world had an origin in time and that God created it not *ex nihilo*, but from an eternal formless matter that God endowed with form. Later on, Joseph Albo (fifteenth century) in his *Sefer Ha-'Ikkarim* (Book of Principles) took a different approach, declaring, "The Torah does not oblige us to believe in creation *ex nihilo*" (1:50). In the Christian world the principle was set forth during the Fourth Lateran Council of 1215, when it was stated that God "from the very beginning of time by His omnipotent power created out of nothing both the spiritual beings and the corporeal." This has been the dominant position of the church and for many Jewish thinkers for centuries.

In Kabbalistic Teachings

The idea of Creation has occupied the minds of many mystics but created for them a conundrum. This is because one of the basic assertions of Kabbalah is that God is *Ein Sof* (Infinite), namely, a totally transcendent and intangible Deity, without beginning or end, and utterly beyond human comprehension. If, however, nothing else exists outside of God, how did the world come into being? This was not a new philosophical problem and certainly not limited to mystics. Others had dealt with it in the past. For example, Philo of Alexandria (first century C.E.) maintained that God created the world by means of the *logos*, a Greek word meaning "speech" or "word."[12]

Of the many mystics who dealt with this critical issue, Isaac Luria (1534–1572), one of the greatest kabbalists of Safed, came up with a theory that had a tremendous impact on mystical teachings of his time and well beyond into our present days.

According to Luria, Creation occurred in three stages:

1. *Tzimtzum* (contraction): At the beginning of the process of Creation, God "contracted," and into the void that ensued in the middle, God emitted beams of light in order to bring about the world out of nothing. The first act of God, in this view, is not "revelation" as the older mystics had proclaimed, but one of "self-limitation."
2. *Sh'virat hakeilim* (the breaking of the vessels): As divine light flowed into the primordial space, the vessels (*keilim*) that were assigned to shelter the upper "emanations" were broken, and sparks of light spread all over the emerging universe, some returning to their source,

while others fell downward. This created an upheaval in the universe, leaving everything out of place.

3. *Tikkun* (mending): Right after the original shattering of the vessels, God began to mend the world but left its completion to humanity. It is our responsibility, Luria stressed, to bring wholeness to the universe by observing the laws and commandments of the Torah. Only after will the Messiah come, symbolizing the completion of the redemptive process. Out of this Lurianic interpretation of Creation came the concept of *tikkun olam*, or repair of the world. Today this concept is extended to apply to work on behalf on the needy and for the betterment of our world.

Is Genesis Scientific?

In the ancient Near Eastern texts, the world is viewed as a flat disk surrounded by water, both on top and at the bottom. A firmament, like a giant bowl, keeps the upper waters in check, allowing only the rain to come through special holes. The sun, moon, and other stars move in predetermined tracks along the lower part of this bowl. Furthermore, the world stands on stilts built on deep waters underneath, where Sheol, the abode of the dead, can be reached through the graves. This image was dominant throughout the biblical period and even much later, until people began to realize that the world is round. As early as the second century C.E., Ptolemy, a Greek mathematician, advanced this idea, and Copernicus (sixteenth century), Galileo (seventeenth century), and others proposed a sun-centered universe. Today we know that there are various galaxies moving about in the large expanse of the universe.

Today there is a raging debate going on in our society as to whether the biblical story of Creation should be considered "scientific," namely, as the only correct explanation about the way in which the universe came into being. This view, usually referred to as "creationism," has different variations, ranging from "flat earth" to "evolutionary design creationism." Most of the proponents argue that the universe as a whole was created by a supreme being, out of nothing, as an act of free will. They also reject the theory of evolution and the assumption of common descent, which maintains that all organisms have a common ancestor or ancestral pool gene, which diverge through random variations. Furthermore, they insist that the Creation story should be taught in public schools alongside the theory of evolution.

Most modern scientists reject the claims of the "creationists" as being religiously motivated. They argue that Darwin's theory of species (1859) is still the best explanation available regarding the formation of the universe. This theory maintains that all organisms are the end product of a natural process of developments from earlier forms. Similarly, according to the big bang theory, the universe was created billions of years ago from a very small, very hot, and highly dense "singularity," which keeps expanding and cooling.

What is the position of the Rabbis on this issue? Did they take the biblical story of Creation literally? Some Jewish sages said yes. For example, Nachmanides (twelfth century), the medieval Jewish commentator from Catalunia argued (commenting on Gen. 1:3), that the "six days of Creation" were true days composed of hours and seconds, being the same six days of our workday. Others, however, argued, as Philo of Alexandria did in the first century c.e., that Creation was not "in time" and that the expression "six days" merely indicated the most perfect arrangement in existence (see Laws i:2).

Some ancient Rabbis raised questions about the order of Creation and came up with very interesting insights that seem to justify the claim of modern scientists. For example, they argued that before this world was created, God had formed other worlds: "God went on creating worlds and destroying them until God created these [heaven and earth], and then God said: 'These please Me; those did not please Me'" (*B'reishit Rabbah* 9:2, Soncino). They also maintained that before this world was formed, God had created other items first; some were actually carried out, such as the Torah and the Throne of Glory, and others were only contemplated, such as the Patriarchs, the people of Israel, and the name of the Messiah.

In medieval times, the French Jewish commentator Rashi (Rabbi Shlomo Yitzchaki, eleventh century) noted (on Gen. 1:1) that the very first sentence of the Book of Genesis should not be translated "In the beginning God created the heaven and the earth," because the Hebrew word *b'reishit* means "in the beginning of" (as in Jer. 26:1) and, therefore, must be attached to a noun and not to a verb ("created"), as we have it in the biblical text now. The implication of this remark is noteworthy in that it assumes that the first created item was not the heaven and the earth but light itself. Rashi then adds, "The passage [Gen. 1] does not intend to teach us the order of Creation." Based on this insight, Plaut (and many others) now renders the verse as follows: "When God was about to create heaven and earth, the earth was a chaos, unformed, and on the chaotic waters' face there was darkness. Then God's

spirit glided over the face of the waters, and God said, 'Let there be light!'—
and there was light" (Gen. 1:1–3). Furthermore, in the opinion of one biblical scholar, the expression "heaven and earth" cannot be taken literally but
simply means "the totality of cosmic phenomena for which there is no single word in biblical Hebrew."[13]

In some Rabbinic texts, the speculation about the Creation of the universe is clearly discouraged, perhaps because it is beyond human understanding or because it can result in misleading theological positions. For
example, the Rabbis ask, why does Genesis begin with the letter *bet* in the
Hebrew word *b'reshit* (in the beginning)? They answer: "Just as the *bet* is
closed at the sides but open in front, so you are not permitted to investigate
what is above and what is below, what is before and what is behind" (*Midrash
Rabbah, Genesis,* 1:10, Soncino). Similarly, according to the Mishnah, the
events of Creation may not be expounded before two people, only privately
(*Mishnah Chagigah* 2:1). A similar sentiment is expressed in Ben Sira (second century B.C.E.), who advised, "Seek not what is too difficult for you, nor
investigate what is beyond your power" (Ben Sira 3:21, RSV).

The Creation of the universe remains a mystery. Even though many theories have been expounded by scientists and philosophers, the ultimate truth
is most likely beyond our human understanding.

The Biblical Message

Given the conclusion that the Creation myth is not a scientific explanation
of the universe, what lesson can still be derived from the teachings of the
biblical text? A number of contemporary thinkers have pondered this question and come out with some valuable lessons.

In the words of one scholar, "The statements of this chapter [Gen. 1–2]
are not at all intended to be evaluated merely paleontologically. Certainly in
this respect too they present what was thought at that time about the
primeval condition of the world; but since they purport to be statements of
faith, they possess enduring theological interest."[14] Similarly, another scholar
maintains, "Biblical man . . . did not base his views on the universe and its
laws on the critical use of empirical data . . . his thinking was imaginative,
and his expressions of thought were concrete, pictorial, emotional, and poetic. Hence, it is a naïve and futile exercise to attempt to reconcile the biblical accounts of creation with the findings of modern science."[15] From the
approbation formula that sums up the entire story of Creation, "God then

surveyed all that [God] had made, and look—it was very good!" (Gen. 1:31), one theologian derives the lesson that "in God's sight the entire creation is good, in spite of all that seems incomprehensible, cruel, and terrible to human beings. . . . Moreover, this 'goodness' also comprehends beauty (the Hebrew word can mean both 'good' and 'beautiful'); joy in God's creation contains within itself all joy in what is beautiful"[16] This positive attitude to life leads to the realization that life is to be enjoyed, celebrated, and pursued.[17] A contemporary rabbi suggests that a careful reading of the Genesis story could teach us that God is a Force or Power behind everything; that human beings are the highest order of Creation, with more responsibility than any other creation; that life and world are good; and that rest is as important for human life as work.[18] For another contemporary Torah scholar, Genesis "describes not the clarities of origin and cause, but the potentialities of purpose."[19] Similarly, a Chasidic rabbi from Poland insightfully wrote, "The Lord created the world in a state of beginning. The universe is always in an uncompleted state, in the form of its beginning. It is not like a vessel at which the master works to finish it; it requires continuous labor and renewal by creative forces. Should these cease for only a second, the universe would return to primeval chaos."[20]

The Creation story, one of the most powerful foundational myths of the Western world, continues to awaken us to an awareness of our role in the world, our place in society, and our duty to leave for those who will come after us an improved world through the pursuit of peace and well-being for ourselves as well as for others. In theological terms, this pursuit is called "becoming coworkers with God," a lofty if not presumptuous term for our responsibilities as human beings.

4

Did Eve Eat an Apple?

Titian (Tiziano Vecellio) (c.1488–1576).
Adam and Eve, around 1570.
Museo del Prado, Madrid, Spain.

The Claim

The idea that Eve consumed an apple in the Garden of Eden is well entrenched in Western culture, and is reflected in many art forms. In the Renaissance period, a number of masters painted scenes with Eve and the apple. Among them, the most famous are the paintings by the sixteenth-century Italian painter Titian (see above) and almost the same scene depicted by Rubens, the Flemish master, in the mid-seventeenth century. In his book *Paradise Lost* (1667), the poet John Milton too believed that the forbidden fruit was an apple (9:480–90).

In our time, the image of "Eve and the Apple" remains embedded in popular culture. Susanne Back painted "Eve's Apple" in 1945, and Jacques Saint-Surin's nude holding an apple, called "Eve's Apple," was completed in 1998. The city of Windsor, Canada, has a sculpture called "Eve's Apple" in Assumption Park. Jonathan Rosen wrote a book entitled *Eve's Apple* (1997), which deals with anorexia nervosa. For cocktails you can order an "Eve's apple daiquiri," made with rum, or an "Eve's apple," made with vodka, or you can eat an "Eve's apple pudding" for dessert. In Long Island, New York, there is a juice company called "Apple and Eve." And some Canadian travel guides even announce: "Original Sin: Apple Picking in the Monteregian Foothills."

But did, in fact, Eve eat an apple? The Bible is silent about it. So, where did the idea come from?

Adam and the Trees in the Garden

The story of Eve eating the presumed apple takes place in the biblical Garden of Eden, the so-called paradise, the mythical garden where God lives (see Isa. 51:3) and where God places the first humans after Creation in order "to work it and keep it" (Gen. 2:15). The Hebrew word describing the garden, *eden*, is etymologically unclear. The concept of "gods' garden" is of Mesopotamian origin, evidenced by the fact that it is located by the Tigris and Euphrates (Gen. 2:14) and by various references in the ancient Near East going as far back as Sumer, which placed it in Dilmun, a land that is pure, clean, and bright, a land of the living where there is no death or sickness (see, "Enki and Ninhursag," *ANET*, 37–41).

The biblical garden, which is a new location for Adam, contains all kinds of trees, "alluring to the eye and good for fruit" (Gen. 2:9). Among them are two special trees: the "Tree of Life" in the middle of the garden and the "Tree of All Knowledge," literally, "the tree of good [in Hebrew, *tov*] and bad/evil [in Hebrew, *ra*]" (Gen. 2:9).

God then tells Adam—not Eve, who, according to this account, has not yet been created—"You may eat all you like of every tree in the garden—but of the Tree of All Knowledge [*tov vara*] you may not eat, for the moment you eat of it you shall be doomed to die" (Gen. 2:16–17). It is noteworthy that here God does not prohibit eating from the Tree of Life, which would provide immortality, but only from the Tree of All Knowledge, which would be the source of human awareness. It is only later on that God worries that Adam and Eve might eat from the Tree of Life and, living forever, become like God (Gen. 3:22). So, God chases them out of the garden, stationing the cherubim and a fiery sword to guard the gate (Gen. 3:23–24).

One of the linguistic problems we have here is how best to render the Hebrew word *ra*, which could mean either "bad" or "evil." Is the tree "good and evil" or "good and bad"? The text raises serious theological issues, and has direct bearing on the fruit that Eve digested.

Many translators render *tov vara* as "good and evil."[1] Other translators more convincingly argue that it is better to use the phrase "good and bad." As one biblical scholar points out, "The traditional 'good and evil' would restrict the idiom to moral matters.... The broad sense ... is to be in full possession of mental and physical powers."[2] Similarly, for another scholar, *ra* here is not a moral concept (namely, "evil"), but an example of the literary device called merismus, where the totality of something is indicated in different ways, especially by placing the first and last of the series.[3] The same idea is expressed by a theologian who states that the "Tree of Knowledge" is a tree "whose fruit gives omniscience,"[4] and the expression "good and evil/bad," certainly not limited to morality, is therefore "a formal way of saying what we mean by our colorless, 'everything.'"[5] Other translators have accepted this argument and render the expression as "good and bad"[6] or, as Plaut has it, "All Knowledge." Yet, the old translation "good and evil" has remained dominant in our culture.

Eve and the Forbidden Fruit

After Eve is created out of Adam's rib (Gen. 2:22), the Bible tells us, the two of them are without clothes in the garden and not ashamed of their nakedness (Gen. 2:25). During their stay in the garden, the serpent, "the most cunning" (Gen. 3:1) of all the animals, asks Eve, "Did God really say, 'You may not eat of any tree in the Garden'?" (Gen. 3:1), to which Eve replies, "Of any tree in the Garden we may eat the fruit; but God said, 'Of the fruit of the tree in the middle of it do not eat, and do not [even] touch it, or you will die'" (Gen. 3:2–3). Here Eve seems to equate the tree in the middle of the garden with the "Tree of All Knowledge." When the serpent assures Eve that she will not die, she, now realizing that "how good to eat the tree's fruit would be, and how alluring to the eyes it was," takes of its fruit (*mipiryo* in Hebrew) and eats it (Gen. 3:6). She also gives some to Adam. Consequently, their eyes are opened, and they realize that they are naked. To cover themselves, they sew a few fig leaves (*aleih t'einah*) together, and make themselves loincloths (Gen. 3:7).

It is interesting to note that the serpent in this story is viewed only as one of the creatures of God who happens to be shrewd (*arum* in Hebrew). It stands erect and can speak like humans. The serpent is not personified as evil, and it has been shorn of all the mythological baggage that it had in the ancient Near Eastern narratives, where it often appears as a god of healing and fertility (see Num. 21:6–9; II Kings 18:4). The biblical serpent is certainly not the demonic figure of Satan that emerges in later texts and interpretations. That image of the serpent as evil appears for the first time in postbiblical times, in the Wisdom of Solomon, whose author believed that "through the devil's envy death entered the world" (2:24).

Our text does not identify the type of fruit consumed by Eve and Adam. Neither does Josephus in his book, *Antiquities* (I, 1:4). This led to much speculation by the ancient Rabbinic commentators. Thus, we find, in *B'reishit Rabbah*:[7]

> What was the tree thereof Adam and Eve ate?
> Rabbi Meir said: It was wheat . . .
> Rabbi Y'hudah ben Rabbi Ilai said: It was grapes . . .
> Rabbi Abba of Acco said: It was the *etrog* (citron) . . .
> Rabbi Yosei said: They were figs . . .

Other Rabbis, however, have a different take on the subject. So, the midrash continues:

> Rabbi Azariah and Rabbi Y'hudah ben Rabbi Shimon in the name of Rabbi Y'hoshua ben Levi said: Heaven forbid [that we should conjecture what the tree was]! The Holy One, blessed be He, did not and will not reveal to man what the tree was.

Does the Genesis text give us a clue about the nature of the fruit? It does. The context, in fact, suggests that the fruit was a fig. As noted above, Adam and Eve cover themselves with "fig leaves" as soon as they realize they are naked, leading to the possibility that they must have also consumed its fruit.

Jewish tradition supports this idea. In addition to Rabbi Yosei mentioned in the midrash above, we find that also Rashi, in medieval times (twelfth century), noted (on Gen. 3:7) that the tree from which Adam and Eve ate was a fig tree. Similarly, in his collection of Jewish legends, Louis Ginzberg writes, "No sooner had they [Adam and Eve] violated the command given them than the cloud of glory and the horny skin dropped from them, and they stood there in their nakedness, and were ashamed. Adam tried to gather leaves from the trees to cover part of their bodies, but he heard one tree after

A fig leaf

the other say: There is the chief that deceived his Creator. Nay, the foot of pride shall not come against me, nor the hand of the wicked touch me. Hence, take no leaves from me. Only the fig tree granted him permission to take of its leaves. That was because the fig was the forbidden fruit itself."[8]

Figs were one of the seven special species of Israel, along with wheat, barley, grapes, pomegranates, olives, and honey (Deut. 8:8), which made it "a good land" (Deut. 8:7). They symbolized peace and prosperity. We are told, "All the days of Solomon, Judah and Israel from Dan to Beer-sheba dwelt in safety, everyone under his own vine and under his own fig tree [t'einato]" (I Kings 5:5; see also II Kings 18:31; Isa. 36:16). Similarly, the prophet Micah writes that in the ideal future,

> Every man shall sit
> under his grapevine or fig tree [t'einato]
> with no one to disturb him. (Mic. 4:4)

Cultivated extensively in the Mediterranean basin, figs reflect a West Semitic background. An Israelite author/editor would have been more likely to keep this type of fruit in mind when telling the story of Eve in paradise.

Fig leaves are strong and quite large, each almost a foot long, justifying the tradition that Adam and Eve used them for loincloths.

Various Theories

If the Bible is so silent about the nature of the fruit, then where and how did the apple become the favorite one in the Garden of Eden? Biblical scholars have different theories to explain the modern choice of the apple from among the great variety of fruits available in ancient Israel.

According to one scholar,[9] the association of the fruit with the apple stems from an early and mistaken identification of the tree in the Song of Songs 8:5, where we read:

Under the apple tree [*tapuach*] I roused you;
It was there your mother conceived you.

However, there is slight problem with this theory. Even though apples grow in modern Israel today,[10] they are not indigenous to ancient Israel. The word *tapuach* is better translated as "apricot."[11] Even today, in Cyprus apricots are still known as "golden apples."

The other theory is more plausible. The Latin version of the Hebrew Bible, called the Latin Vulgate, in translating the Hebrew expression "the tree of knowledge of good and bad/evil" (Gen. 2:9), used the term *malum*, meaning "evil," for the word "bad." The word *malum* means "evil" as well as "apple,"[12] a popular fruit in Europe. Most likely the influence came from the Greek myth where Eris, the goddess of discord, threw a golden apple of discord into the assembly of the gods, because she was not invited to attend the gathering. It was from that time on that people started to associate the apple with the fruit consumed by Adam and Eve.

In the end, these are only theories. All we have is pure speculation about how the apple came to be identified as the fruit in Genesis 3. What is clear, however, is that the Bible never identifies the forbidden fruit, and it was left to people's imaginations to fill in the gap.

The Banishment

As a consequence of the disobedience committed in the Garden of Eden, God imposes a number of punishments: The serpent is condemned to crawl on its belly, Eve is to suffer pain in childbirth, and Adam is told to toil hard in order to sustain himself (Gen. 3:14–19). Furthermore, once God realizes that humanity has acquired the knowledge of "good and bad" by eating of the forbidden fruit, God fears they will now try to eat from the Tree of Life and become immortal. Therefore God expels Adam (and presumably Eve) from paradise (Gen. 3:22–24).

The quest for immortality is a prominent theme not only in the Bible, but also in the literature of the entire ancient Near East, such as the *Gilgamesh Epic* and the *Myth of Adapa*. In each case, the protagonist tries to defeat death but fails, and is forced to accept his mortality. The same idea is intimated in the biblical text. When God banishes Adam and Eve from the garden, God stations cherubim, legendary beings with wings, to block its entrance. But Adam does not die right away. He lives in exile for a very long time—in biblical terms, 930 years (Gen. 5:5). The Bible is silent about Eve's death and how long she lived.

The biblical narrators did not view as "sin" what Eve did in the Garden of Eden by eating the fruit. In fact, the word "sin" does not appear in Genesis 3 at all. The first occurrence of this word in the Bible is in Genesis 4:7 in connection with Cain, to whom God says, "Sin [*chatat*] is crouching at the door" (the text is unclear; others translate, "Sin is a demon"), meaning Cain has the freedom to choose between good or bad acts, but "sin" is always at the door enticing him to choose the latter.

In Christianity, the disobedience of Adam and Eve is usually considered the source of the "original sin," and their banishment from Eden constitutes "the fall" from the pristine divine grace,[13] requiring faith in Jesus for the ultimate salvation. Furthermore, this "original sin" is transmitted to future generations. Thus the catechism of the Catholic Church (1992) states:

> How did the sin of Adam become the sin of all his descendants? The whole human race is in Adam "as one body of one man." By this "unity of the human race" all men are implicated in Adam's sin, as all are implicated in Christ's justice. Still, the transmission of original sin is a mystery that we cannot fully understand. But we do know by Revelation that Adam had received original holiness and justice not for himself alone, but for all human nature. By yielding to the tempter, Adam and Eve committed a *personal sin*, but this sin affected *the human nature* that they would then transmit *in a fallen state*. It is a sin which will be transmitted by propagation to all mankind, that is, by the transmission of a human nature deprived of original holiness and justice. And that is why original sin is called "sin" only in an analogical sense: it is a sin "contracted" and not "committed"—a state and not an act. (Part I; section 2; 1:7 [#404])

Other Christian scholars, however, disagree with this point of view. For example, Claus Westermann, a German theologian, writes, "The Primal History portrays human existence as created existence in a sequential narrative that attempts to explain the juxtaposition of positive and negative in humanity, the potential and limitation of creatureliness. It does not speak of a 'Fall.' Neither, in the Bible, is sin something that can be inherited."[14]

In Jewish tradition, some sources speak of the fall of humanity. For example, II Esdras, which is part of the Apocryphal books, contains the following statement: "O Adam, what have you done? For though it was you who sinned, the fall was not yours alone, but ours who are your descendants" (II Esd. 7:118, RSV). The ancient Rabbis, on the other hand, maintained that the basic way to human self-realization and the ultimate redemption in the world-to-come is through the observance of various *mitzvot*, commanded religious deeds. For many of them, the banishment from Eden was not a fall. In fact, commenting on the biblical statement that God drove Adam out of the Garden of Eden (Gen. 3:24), Rabbi Shimon ben Lakish believed that God was lenient with Adam (*B'reishit Rabbah* 21:8).

During the medieval times, the Jewish commentator Abravanel (sixteenth century) stated that eating from the Tree of Knowledge was actually beneficial for Adam and Eve, because "the knowledge of good and evil is the perfection of man."[15] However, he added that this eating provided only for bodily needs, instead of for the contemplation of God, which is superior. The commandment against eating of the Tree of Knowledge simply meant "the indulgence in and study of worldly things."[16]

For many contemporary Jewish thinkers, the expulsion from the Garden of Eden was in part a positive turn of events. For example, in *The Torah: A Women's Commentary*, Tamara Cohn Eskenazi points out that in the story of Eve and the fruit, "There is no 'Fall of Man.' Nor does God curse humankind. Rather, the story makes clear that transgression, namely, disobedience, carries consequences."[17] Avivah Gottlieb Zornberg goes further, and notes, "Banishment is a merciful alternative to the finality of immediate death."[18] Rabbi Harold Kushner opines that the story of the Garden of Eden is "not of Paradise Lost but of Paradise Outgrown, not of Original Sin, but the Birth of Conscience."[19] He further states, "The account of Adam and Eve eating the fruit of the Tree of Knowledge of Good and Evil, as I see it, is a mythical description of how the first human beings left the world of animal existence behind and entered the problematic world of being human."[20] For, after eating of the fruit, both Adam and Eve become sexually aware[21] and civilized. Humanity, and with it the capacity for free will, has emerged, specifically because they ate of the forbidden fruit. It is true that "theirs is an act of disobedience and defiance, yet at the same time of growth and liberation."[22]

The myth of the Garden of Eden, containing episodes of "temptation, transgression, and transformation,"[23] continues to be one of the most popular mythic images of our time, because it deals with constant human wants, failures, and accomplishments. Even though the identity of the fruit is not revealed in the biblical text, it stands as a powerful symbol of all types of temptations placed before us in the path of life, and urges us to take responsibility for our acts.

5

Noah and the Ark: History or Myth?

Currier & Ives (19th Century). Noah's Ark.
Hand-colored lithograph.

The Claim

Every so often, the popular media announces that the ark of Noah has been found in remote mountains of Turkey or the greater Middle East. There is tremendous interest in whether or not this dramatic biblical story ever actually happened. This chapter will probe these modern-day claims and in so doing study the mythical content of the narrative emerging from the annals of the ancient Mesopotamian literature, as well as the development of the story in biblical and postbiblical Jewish texts.

Looking for Noah's Ark

"Noah and the Ark" is one of the most well-known myths in the Western world. In addition to scholarly treatises, hundreds of books have been written on this subject, both for adults and for children. There are also numerous games, cartoons, word puzzles, and toys based on this story. In addition, dozens of speculative essays have appeared in print and online. In 1999, NBC's *Noah's Ark* miniseries was viewed by millions around the world. One of America's largest parks, Noah's Ark, is located in the Wisconsin Dells. Similarly, in Jerusalem's Pritzker Children's Zoo, the Ark Sculpture Garden is visited by many people every year. The artist Don Drumm has designed a garden sculpture made of steel called *Noah's Ark Sculpture,* which is well regarded by art connoisseurs. There are even dozens of musical arrangements on the subject of Noah. Michael Sahl wrote an opera in 1978; so did Daniel March in 2000. Children sing a variety of songs on this subject.

The interest in this biblical myth has a long history; even today it continues to fascinate people of all ages with its story line and its characters. The basic outline of the story is as follows: Almost at the beginning of time, God told Noah about the upcoming destruction of the world. Following God's advice, Noah built an ark; brought in his immediate family, a few animals, and food; and survived the devastating Flood. Ultimately the ark landed on Mount Ararat, where everyone got out safely.

For biblical literalists, the story is understood to be historically accurate. Critical scholars, on the other hand, try to find a natural explanation for the disaster in the annals of history. Even an ancient Near Eastern scholar like Efraim Speiser ventured a guess as to how such a deluge could have taken place. He surmised that based on the geological history of Mesopotamia, it is possible that in ages past "waters from the Persian Gulf submerged a large coastland area, owing probably to a sudden rise in the sea level." This, in turn, "could have brought on extremely heavy rains, the whole leaving an indelible impression on the survivors."[1] Yet he was quick to admit that even this reading of the events was only speculation.

For centuries, people have been fascinated by the impact of this story and have looked for clues in order to prove its veracity. For example, a group of people calling themselves "arkologists" constantly collects "evidence" about the ark and its whereabouts. In 1876, Sir James Bryce, a British explorer, found a large piece of hand-tooled wood at the thirteen-thousand-foot level at Mount Ararat, and declared that it came from Noah's ark. It was reported in 1915 that a Russian pilot spotted the ark from the air. In 1953, George Green, a geologist, claimed to have taken six aerial photographs of an object that looked like an ark. The Internet is full of sites that deal with this subject, dedicating extensive coverage to all aspects of this search. Turkey is very supportive of this endeavor, because Mount Ararat is identified with Mount

Agri in eastern Turkey; they have even established the Noah's Ark National Park in order to accommodate all the tourists who travel there regularly.

How true is this story? What part of it could be true? What is the proof? Is this history or literature? In September 2007, Eric H. Cline, a specialist in the ancient Near Eastern studies, decried the fact that "every year 'scientific' expeditions embark to look for Noah's Ark, raising untold amounts of money from gullible believers who eagerly listen to the tales spun by sincere amateurs or rapacious con men; it is not always easy to tell the two apart."[2]

Taken literally, the story of Noah and the ark presents many problems. The miraculous aspects of the episode (e.g., placing all the animals in one boat; the destruction of all humanity with the exception of one couple and their immediate family) strain the credulity of any critical mind. The location of where the ark settled after the Flood cannot be identified with certainty in any of the ancient literary texts we possess. Even the Bible states that the boat rested on "the mountains of Ararat" (Gen. 8:4), not on "the mountain." Where is this place? Ancient Near Eastern sources identify Ararat with Urartu, an old district of Armenia, today in the eastern part of Turkey. Yet, the ancient Rabbis placed it "upon the mountain range of Cordyene" (*al tore kardonya* [*B'reishit Rabbah* 33:4]), in northern Mesopotamia, east of the Tigris, not far from the modern city of Diyarbakir in southern Turkey.[3] Without knowing the ark's location, it is unproductive to turn to archaeology for answers. Even if we did, the mere fact that one finds a piece of wood on a mountain cannot be taken as evidence that it came from an ark, let alone from Noah's ark. Yet, we do have abundant literary evidence about the Flood and the ark in the ancient Near East. By studying these texts, we may be able to understand better the larger context out of which the narrative appears to have derived.

Noah and the Flood

The story of the Flood is told in the Bible in the Book of Genesis, chapters 6–9. The text states that Noah is married to a woman—only one wife is mentioned, but her name is not recorded—and is the father of Shem, Ham, and Japheth (Gen. 5:32, 6:10). He is a righteous (*tzaddik*) and blameless (*tamim*) person who "walked with God" (Gen. 6:9, 7:1). However, because "the earth became corrupt" (Gen. 6:11), God decides to wipe everyone else off the earth, except for Noah and his immediate family.

At God's instruction, Noah builds an ark about 450 feet long, 75 feet wide, and 45 feet high and divides it into three decks. Once the ark is finished, Noah brings aboard his three sons and their respective wives, a number of animals, both female and male, and all the necessary edible food. Then the Flood comes, destroying everything in sight: "[God] wiped out all that existed on the face of the earth—human, beast, reptile, birds of the sky— they were wiped off the earth; there remained only Noah and those with him in the ark" (Gen. 7:23).

After the waters subside, the ark comes "to rest atop one of the mountains of Ararat" (Gen. 8:4). Noah sends out birds to see if they can land. When the last dove fails to return, God tells Noah that it is safe to emerge from the ark. After they all get out, Noah builds an altar in gratitude to God and offers whole burnt offerings. The Eternal One, "inhaling the soothing fragrance" (Gen. 8:21) of the sacrifices, decides never again to put an end to life on earth, even though, as the text states, "the human mind inclines to evil from youth onward" (Gen. 8:21). Then God blesses Noah and his family, telling them, "Be fruitful and multiply" (Gen. 9:1) and adds that they may now eat meat (Gen. 9:3), without, however, consuming its blood (Gen. 9:4). Finally, God establishes a covenant with Noah, placing the rainbow as a sign of God's promise that life will continue on earth: "When the bow is in the cloud, and I see it, I will remember the everlasting covenant between God and all living beings, all that live upon the earth" (Gen. 9:16).

On the surface this appears to be a simple story. In reality the narrative is highly complicated and full of problems. A critical analysis shows that the Bible seems to present two complementary Flood stories, one coming from the P source and the other from J. The two stories are not totally parallel, and some parts of the episode are missing in the other. There are enough similarities, however, to warrant the supposition that there were originally two separate myths that were put together at some point in the history of their transmission.

P appears to have the fuller narrative. Here God is referred to, as in other P texts, as *Elohim*. P announces the Flood in Gen. 6:17 in these words: "I am going to bring the flood-waters upon the earth to destroy all that lives under the heavens, [all] that has the breath of life in it. Everything on earth shall expire." It states that God tells Noah to bring into the ark "two each of every living creature" (Gen. 6:19) and claims that the waters rose over the earth for 150 days (Gen. 7:24) and receded for another 150 days (Gen. 8:3). Finally, God makes a special covenant with Noah, not a covenant of mutuality where each side takes on duties and responsibilities, but what is called a "promissory covenant" (Gen. 9:1–17) by which only God renounces future destructions. At the end of the Flood, God blesses Noah and his children and tells them, "Be fruitful and multiply" (Gen. 9:1). God also gives them permission to eat meat, with the only restriction that they ought to eliminate the consumption of blood from their diet (Gen. 9:4). This is again consistent with other priestly texts in the Bible, in which blood was considered to have a sacral character; blood was a symbol of life, and therefore only God could claim it: "For the life of the flesh is in the blood" (Lev. 17:11, 17:13–14).

On the other hand, the J material refers to God as *YHVH*. Here *YHVH* announces the Flood in 7:4 as follows: "I will pour rain upon the earth . . . and wipe all that exists—all that I have made—off the face of the earth." The J material states that God tells Noah to bring into the ark "seven pairs of every pure beast" and "two of every impure beast" (Gen. 7:2) and of the birds, seven pairs (Gen. 7:3).⁴ It also claims that after seven days, the rains fell for forty days and nights (Gen. 7:4, 7:12). J adds some new elements not found in P—for example, that four times Noah sends out birds to see if it is safe to land (8:6–12). Also in the J material, Noah presents a sacrifice to the Eternal (8:20–21).

The final author/editor chose to combine the two stories to create a continuous narrative in spite of the internal contradictions.

Ancient Near Eastern Flood Stories

The biblical Flood story is not the only myth on this subject that circulated in the ancient Near East. In fact, it was part of a long cultural tradition in the entire region that was familiar with others as well. In 1872, George Smith, an assistant in the Assyrian section of the British Museum, made a sensational discovery. Among the tablets originally found at Kuyuncuk, ancient Nineveh, the capital of Assyria, he identified a text that belonged to *Gilgamesh Epic*, which included a Flood story. This was a seventh century B.C.E. text, but others were found that came from as far back as the nineteenth century B.C.E. In 1914, Arno Poebel, a Semitics scholar, published a Sumerian account of the Flood. A third Babylonian text called the *Atrahasis Epic*, both in its old Babylonian (ca. seventeenth century B.C.E.) and Assyrian versions (seventh century B.C.E.), was discovered in various sites in ancient Mesopotamia and Syria; it too contains a story of the Flood. We now have a Sumerian, an Akkadian, but also a Hittite, a Hurrian, an Indian, and a biblical version. It is apparent that there was a Flood myth that was very popular in the entire ancient Near East, perhaps based on a local flood, that left a deep impression on the imagination of the people who lived in the area.

A careful examination of the background of the biblical story of Noah and the ark shows that it is primarily Mesopotamian, not Canaanite, in origin. Among the factors taken into consideration in coming to this conclusion are the following:

1. Flooding occurs often in Mesopotamia, whereas most of Canaan is hilly and dry.
2. The ancient Hebrews were not well practiced in the arts of seafaring and building boats, whereas the Mesopotamians were.
3. The mountains on which the ark allegedly rested after the Flood is one of the Ararat Mountains, located in Anatolia.
4. Just as the ancient Sumerian king list makes a distinction between those kings who reigned before and after the Flood, in the Bible too, the Flood story is set between Creation and Abraham—ten generations apart. In Genesis, Noah appears as a second Adam. Adam and Noah represent humanity in general.

Ancient Near Eastern Versions

In the Sumerian version (*ANET*, 42–44), dating from about 1700 B.C.E., of which so far only one tablet has been recovered, Ziusudra, a pious king of the city of Shuruppak, modern Fara, hears from a god that the assembly of gods will send a flood. When it finally arrives, it rages for seven days and seven nights. After "the huge boat had been tossed about by the windstorms on the great waters" (*ANET*, 44), Utu, the sun god, comes out, and Ziusudra offers sacrifices to him. Afterwards Ziusudra becomes god.

In the *Gilgamesh Epic* (*ANET*, 93–97), which contains the longest of all the Flood stories, the deluge represents only one scene in the life of Gilgamesh, the legendary Sumerian king of Uruk (ca. 2650 B.C.E.). In the eleventh tablet, Utnapishtim, the hero of the Flood story, recounts to Gilgamesh how he escaped the general destruction when the great gods of the ancient city of Shuruppak resolved to destroy humanity by a flood. At the suggestion of the god Ea, the god of fresh water and wisdom, Utnapishtim builds an ark looking like a cube, about two hundred feet long, wide, and high, with six decks, and he brings inside all his family members, as well as craftsmen, and prepares for the Flood to arrive. The Flood arrives with a vengeance:

> [The wide] land was shattered like [a pot]!
> For one day the south-storm [blew],
> Gathering speed as it blew, [submerging the mountains],
> Overtaking the [people] like a battle.
> No one can see his fellow,
> Nor can the people be recognized from heaven.
> The gods were frightened by the deluge. (*ANET*, 94)

The terrible storm lasts six days and six nights, and on the seventh day the boat rests on Mount Nisir (the location is unknown, but it is thought to be in northern Iraq). Utnapishtim sends three different kinds of birds to test if the land is dry. When the last bird does not return, presumably because it lands safely, Utnapishtim and everyone else emerge from the ark. He then offers a sacrifice to the gods:

> The gods smelled the sweet savor,
> The gods crowded like flies about the sacrifier. (*ANET*, 95a)

Afterwards, the text continues:

> Hitherto Utnapishtim has been but human.
> Henceforth Utnapishtim and his wife shall be like unto us gods. (*ANET*, 95b)

In the *Atrahasis Epic* (*ANET*, 104–6, 512–14), the other Mesopotamian Flood myth, we are told that at the beginning of time, there were divine warriors and elders in the divine assembly. At some point the young warriors revolt and refuse to do the work assigned to them, which is to run the affairs of the world. The god Ea-Enki devises a scheme with them by which human workers would be created to dredge the canals. But even these workers revolt against the divine assembly, refusing to do their job. After gods use a drought and a famine to subdue these workers, the gods finally decree a flood, in order to destroy the world. Ea, one of the gods, then advises Atrahasis to build himself an ark:

Destroy the house, build a ship,
Renounce (worldly) goods,
Keep the soul alive! (*ANET,* 105a)

[The god added]:
Enter [the ship] and close the door of the ship.
Aboard her [bring] thy grain, thy possessions, thy goods,
Thy [wife], thy family, thy relations, and the craftsmen.
Beast of the field, creatures of the field, as many as eat herbs. (*ANET,* 105b)

After the devastation, which lasts seven days, Atrahasis and his family disembark, and he offers a sacrifice to the gods in gratitude for his survival. To control the growth of population, the god Enlil decides that, from now on, one-third of the women would not give birth successfully, and priestesses would not be allowed to bear children.

We do not know which myth in the ancient Near East emerged first, because the stories were copied many times, and along the way underwent numerous changes.

Similarities and Differences

There are great similarities and remarkable differences between the biblical story and its ancient Near Eastern parallels. The basic structure of the myth seems to be the same. Almost all the ancient versions contain the following elements: the command to build an ark, taking people and livestock aboard, landing of the ark on a mountain, sending out birds to scout whether the earth is dry, building an altar, and offering a sacrifice of gratitude.

However, there are some noteworthy differences between the biblical and ancient Mesopotamian stories:

1. In the Bible only one God decrees the Flood. In the ancient Near-
   ern myths, there is a multiplicity of divinities.
2. The *Gilgamesh Epic* does not tell us why the gods brought about the
   Flood. It simply says, "When their heart led the great gods to produce
   the flood . . ." (*ANET,* 93a). In the *Atrahasis Epic,* however, we have a
   rationale: the Flood occurs because people were so noisy that they
   were depriving the god Enlil of his sleep:

The land became wide, the people became numerous,
The land *bellowed* like wide oxen.
The god was disturbed by their uproar.
[*Enlil*] heard their clamor
(And) he said to the great gods:
"Oppressive has become the clamor of mankind.
By their uproar they prevent sleep." (*ANET,* 104b)

In the Bible, the reason for the Flood is the depravity of the human race: "The earth became corrupt before God; the earth was filled with lawlessness [*chamas* in Hebrew]" (Gen. 6:11). The nature of this "lawlessness" is not identified here. The Jerusalem Talmud interprets this to mean that people were cheating one another (JT *Bava M'tzia* 4:2). For Rashi, this implied robbery.

3. In the *Gilgamesh Epic,* the warning appears in a dream while Utnapishtim is asleep in a reed hut. In the Bible, God communicates directly with Noah (Gen. 6:13).

4. In the *Gilgamesh Epic,* the ark is divided vertically into six decks. In Genesis, the ark contains three stories and numerous cells.

5. In the *Gilgamesh Epic,* the protagonist brings into the ark "the seeds of all living things" (*ANET,* 93a) and the "beasts of the field" (*ANET,* 94a), all the members of his family as well as boatmen and craftsmen. In *Atrahasis* the list is even longer, including grain, possessions, goods, and beasts of the field, as well as craftsmen. In the Bible, Noah brings in his wife, his three sons, the wives of his sons, animals, and edible food of every kind, but no craftspeople.

6. There is a different order in the bird scene. In the *Gilgamesh Epic,* three birds make attempts to find land: a dove, a swallow, and a raven. In the Bible, there are four: a raven, a dove, and then two more doves.

7. In the *Gilgamesh Epic,* Utnapishtim becomes a god. In the *Atrahasis Epic,* both Atrahasis and his wife become divine. In the Sumerian text, to Ziusudra, "life like (that of) a god they gave him" (*ANET,* 94b). In Genesis, however, Noah remains human, even though he lives for 950 years.

8. In the *Gilgamesh Epic,* the hero is chosen for no explicit reason. In the Bible, Noah is selected because he is deemed righteous.

9. The biblical text rejects two underlying assumptions of the *Atrahasis Epic:* (a) that the fertility of human beings and their annoying

noises displease the gods, and (b) that the problem of overpopulation is resolved by non-marrying women, barrenness, and even stillbirth. On the contrary, in the Bible, God promises never again to bring doom upon the world and commands that human beings should be fruitful and multiply and fill the earth (Gen. 8:21–9:1, 9:7).

Noah in the Rabbinic Literature

In Rabbinic literature, Noah receives mixed reviews. Commenting on the biblical assertion that Noah was "a righteous man in his generation" (Gen. 6:9), the ancient Rabbis came up with contradictory evaluations. In the second century C.E., there was a difference of opinion on this subject between Rabbi Y'hudah bar Ilai and Rabbi N'chemyah. The former said, "Only in his generation was he a righteous man [by comparison]; had he flourished in the generation of Moses or Samuel, he would not have been called righteous" (*Midrash Rabbah: Genesis*, 30:9, Soncino). Rabbi Y'hudah illustrated his opinion by quoting a proverb: "In the street of the totally blind, the one-eyed man is called clear-sighted." Rabbi N'chemyah took a totally different position and said, "If he were righteous even in *his* generation [namely, in spite of his corrupt environment], how much more so [had he lived] in the days of Moses." He, too, gave an example: "He might be compared to a tightly closed phial of perfume lying in a graveyard, which nevertheless gave forth a fragrant odor; how much more then if it were outside the graveyard!" (ibid.).

Some Rabbis viewed Noah in positive terms, seeing him as a comfort to himself and to the world at large (*B'reishit Rabbah* 30:5). He fed and provided for all those in the ark the whole twelve months (*B'reishit Rabbah* 30:6). He invented the plow, the scythe, the hoe, and other implements for cultivating the ground (*Tanchuma B'reishit* 11).

Others were not so generous toward Noah. Rabbi Y'hudah said, "His [spiritual] strength was feeble" (*B'reishit Rabbah* 30:10). Rabbi Yochanan opined that Noah lacked faith: "Had not the waters reached his ankles, he would not have entered the ark" (*B'reishit Rabbah* 32:6). When he got out of the ark, the Rabbis say, he should have planted something useful, such as figs or olives; instead he planted a vineyard (*B'reishit Rabbah* 36:3). He then "drank immoderately, became intoxicated, and was thus put to shame" (*Midrash Rabbah: Genesis*, 36:4, Soncino).

According to one midrash, Noah did not care for his contemporaries. Thus we are told:

> After the flood, Noah opened the ark and looked out. He saw the earth desolate, forests and gardens uprooted, corpses visible everywhere. There was no grass, no vegetation; the world was a wasteland. In pain and dismay, he cried out to God: Sovereign of all creation, in six days You made the earth and all that grows in it: it was like a garden, like a table prepared for a feast; now You Yourself have brought the work of Your hands to nought, uprooting all that You planted, tearing down all that You built. Why did You not show compassion for Your creatures? God then replied: O faithless shepherd! Now, after the destruction, you come to Me and complain. But when I said to you: Make an ark for yourself, for I am going to flood the earth to destroy all flesh, you did not plead for your neighbors! How differently Abraham will act; he will pray on behalf of the people of Sodom and Gomorrah. And Moses, when his people anger Me with their calf of gold, will offer his life for them. But you—when you saw that judgment was about to strike the world—you thought only of yourself and your household, while all else perished by fire and water!
>   Then Noah understood that he had sinned.[5]

In medieval times, Rashi (eleventh century) made a distinction between Noah, who walked *et*, "with," God (Gen. 6:9), and Abraham, who walked *l'fanav*, "before," God (Gen. 24:40). Noah needed some help; he had not reached his potential, whereas Abraham paved the way for others.

Rabbinic texts contain various legends about Noah. According to one legend, the generation of Noah was so sinful that God exhorted the people for 120 years to amend their ways and threatened to bring down a flood, but it was to no avail. Even when Noah started to build the ark, his contemporaries would ask him what he was doing. In spite of his warnings, people did not repent, and when the floods came, it was too late (*Tanchuma Noach*, 5). Another legend adds a few more details, as for example, Noah acquired all the necessary wisdom to build the ark from a book given to Adam by the angel Raziel. Once Noah built the ark, he brought into it his wife Naamah (she now gets a name), the daughter of Enosh, and the rest of his immediate family. One of the biggest problems he encountered was how to provide food for one whole year to all the animals in the ark. When the flood came to an end, Noah refused to leave the ark, fearing that God would bring another flood upon the earth. He disembarked only after God swore that never again would there be another disaster like that.[6]

Noachide Laws

The ancient Rabbis taught that Jews must keep the commandments of the Torah but all human beings must observe some universal laws given by God to Adam and Noah.[7] They are known as the Seven Noachide Laws (BT *Sanhedrin* 56a) and apply to all people as the foundation of a civilized world. These laws were loosely based (see BT *Sanhedrin* 56b) on Gen. 2:16, which states, "God commanded Adam." For the Rabbis, here the word "Adam" refers not only to the first human being, but to humanity in general. These universal laws include laws against idolatry, incest, cursing the divine name, robbery, murder, and eating a limb from a living animal, as well as requiring obedience to local civil law (or setting up courts of law) (*B'reishit Rabbah* 34:9). Other Rabbis added a few others, such as laws against sorcery, emasculation, crossbreeding, and witchcraft (BT *Sanhedrin* 56b; *B'reishit Rabbah* 34:8). According to the Rabbinic Sages, anyone who abides by these "seven" laws is considered a "righteous gentile" and is assured a place in the world-to-come (BT *Sanhedrin* 105a; Maimonides, *Mishneh Torah*, Kings 8:11).

Many non-Jews, even in our time, have declared themselves as *b'nei Noach*, "descendants of Noah," and have assumed a discipline inspired by the Torah. Among them, one of the most prominent was Aimé Pallière (1868–1949), a French writer and theologian, and the author of a celebrated book, *The Unknown Sanctuary* (1928). He adopted the Noachide Laws at the suggestion of his mentor and teacher, Rabbi Elie Benamozegh, an Italian rabbi and philosopher, but never formally converted to Judaism.

The Message

The analysis of the old myth of Noah and the ark, as recorded in the Bible and elaborated on in the Rabbinic literature, shows clearly that we are not dealing here with an historical event that took place at the beginning of time, but with the attempt of some authors/editors in ancient Israel to teach a lesson of morality based on a widespread belief about a Flood story in antiquity. As Nahum M. Sarna, a biblical scholar, notes, "Popular imagination has been at work magnifying local disastrous floods into catastrophes of universal proportion."[8]

Without a doubt, the narrators of Genesis were familiar with the prevalent myth of the Flood but placed it within a moral context: the floods came in because of lawlessness. After the Flood, God reaffirmed the notion that human beings were made in the image of God (Gen. 9:6; see Gen. 1:26). One interpretation of this statement is that among all the creatures, only human beings carry the stamp of royalty among all creatures, and thus stand for God's presence on earth.

What is the message that the Bible wishes to impart through the myth of Noah? On this matter various biblical scholars stress the following: For some, the story is a vehicle to tell about "1) God's judgment on sin, which had so affected Creation; 2) God's concern to preserve what was begun at Creation; and 3) God's reaching out to humankind in covenant." [9] In the opinion of another scholar, "the Narrators used ancient popular traditions as a vehicle to express a fundamental conviction of Israel's faith: God's inescapable judgment in human affairs." [10] One contemporary biblical expert argues that it promotes the idea that "law and the sanctity of human life are the prerequisites of human existence upon the earth." [11] For another critic, in the story of Noah, "the Torah aims at warning humans of every generation of what could happen to them if they, too, allowed *chamas* ["violence" or "lawlessness"; see Gen. 6:11, 6:13] to become their way of life." [12] It is also possible to maintain that the biblical text teaches that unrighteousness is destructive, that society must be built on justice, and that human life is inviolable.

Contemporary thinkers continue to debate the implications of the Flood myth regarding the role that God plays in the universe. For some, the Flood represents a total failure by God, who ends up destroying the world; for others, it shows that through the cooperation of human beings, God stands by a commitment to renewing all creation and to preserving it through eternity. The biblical text tells us that after the Flood, God established a covenant with Noah and his descendants, setting up the rainbow as the sign of this covenant, and assuring humanity of continuous life on the earth (Gen. 9:12–17).

The story of Noah and the ark, though an old myth, still reminds us of God's covenant and of our responsibility to avoid corruption in society and to pursue wholeness in life as creatures made "in the image of God."

6

Did Moses Have Horns?

Michelangelo Buonarroti (1475–1564). Moses.
Detail of Head. From the tomb of Julius II. 1513–1542.
S. Pietro in Vincoli, Rome, Italy.

The Claim

In one of his most famous sculptures, Michelangelo placed two horns on the head of Moses. It is assumed that he did so on the basis of a common misreading of Exodus 34. This idea of Moses having horns led to the demonization of the Jews for many centuries. This chapter will examine related texts in order to deal with how this interpretation arose, as well as other ways that the biblical text can be understood.

The Statue

In 1503, Pope Julius II commissioned the famous Renaissance artist Michelangelo (1475–1564) to design a magnificent mausoleum for him. After the pope died in 1513, his tomb was placed in the Church of St. Peter in Chains, in Rome, the pope's titular church, even though his body was interred in St. Peter's Basilica.

The most celebrated piece of art in St. Peter in Chains is Michelangelo's *Moses,* a large marble sculpture, almost eight feet high, created between 1513 and 1515. Moses is seated, flanked by Jacob's wives, Rachel and Leah, holding the tablets of the Torah under one arm, and stroking the coils of his long beard with the other. His head is turned aside with what appears to be a wrathful expression. His eyes are fixed, his face is tense, and on his head are two protruding hornlike extensions. This depiction is puzzling. Did Moses have horns? Where did Michelangelo get this idea?

Over the centuries other artists have portrayed Moses with hornlike bulges on his forehead.[1] In one of the magnificent windows of the Cathedral of Chartres in France, Moses appears with horns. The same portrayal of Moses is seen in the work of the Jewish painter Marc Chagall (1887–1985) who has depicted Moses in several paintings with "bulges," though it is not clear if Chagall meant by them rays of light or simple horns coming out of Moses's head. The modern sculptor Joseph Kiselewski (1901–86), in his 1965 terracotta *Moses,* also showed him with horns.

The image of Moses with horns has long contributed to the dehumanization of the Jew in Western society. These depictions have led people to believe that all Jews, like Moses, have horns on their heads. In order to understand the derivation of this idea, we need to look first at the biblical text from which it was mistakenly derived.

The Man Moses

There are various portraits of Moses in the Bible, but they all describe him as a giant of a person who led the Israelites out of Egypt, who received the Torah on Mount Sinai/Horeb, and who brought his people to the edge of the Holy Land. The Pentateuch speaks glowingly about this great leader: "Now Moses was a very humble man, more so than any other human being on earth" (Num. 12:3), and "Never again did there arise in Israel a prophet like Moses—whom the Eternal singled out, face to face" (Deut. 34:10).

Regrettably, there are no references to Moses outside of the Bible, and archaeology is not helpful. The only known material about Moses is the biblical text itself, and that is mostly legendary in nature. We do not know when he was born or when he lived. Scholars place him somewhere between the fifteenth and thirteenth centuries B.C.E. Even his real name is unknown. The

Egyptian princess who found him called him *Mosheh* "Moses," because, as the text says, "I drew him out [*meshitihu*] of the water" (Exod. 2:10). However, to be grammatically correct, his name should have been the passive participle of the verb *mashah*, namely *mashui*, "drawn out," whereas the word *Mosheh* is an active participle, meaning "drawing out." In reality, the name Moses, like Tuthmosis ("Toth is born") or Rameses ("Re is born") stems from an Egyptian verb meaning "to give birth." Most likely "Moses" was part of another name, which has not been preserved.

What does the Bible tell us about Moses? He was of a Levitical family that lived in Egypt; his father was Amram (Exod. 6:20; Num. 26:59), and his mother Yocheved (Exod. 6:20). He had one brother, Aaron, and one sister, Miriam. Nothing is known about his youth or education. Adopted by the Egyptian princess, he probably grew up in the palace. One day he killed an Egyptian when he saw him attacking a Hebrew, "one of his kinsmen" (Exod. 2:11). Escaping to Midian, he married Zipporah (Exod. 2:21), the daughter of Jethro, a Midianite priest, with whom he had two sons, Gershom (Exod. 2:22) and Eliezer (Exod. 18:4). Later there is a reference to him possibly taking another wife, "a Cushite woman" (Num. 12:1). What further complicates the picture is that, though Moses had two wives, the Pentateuch records three names for his fathers-in-law: Jethro (Exod. 3:1, 18:1), Reuel (Exod. 2:18), and Hobab, son of Reuel (Num. 10:29). We are told that Moses had a speech impediment (Exod. 4:10), even though the nature of it is unclear.

It is not known how long Moses lived in Midian with his new family. According to a tradition recorded in the Christian Bible, Acts 7:30, it was forty years, a round number meaning a long time.

At some point in his life, Moses had a vision of God, who told him to go to Egypt to rescue his people: "Come, therefore, I will send you to Pharaoh, and you shall free My people, the Israelites, from Egypt" (Exod. 3:10). With the help of Aaron, his brother, who acted as his spokesperson, he confronted the Pharaoh a number of times. After the ten plagues fell upon Egypt, the Israelites were let free to go out of Egypt amid wondrous signs. In the wilderness, Moses received the Torah at Mount Sinai/Horeb and lived with his contemporaries for 40 years. He died before entering the Holy Land at the age of 120 in the land of Moab. The Bible admits, "No one knows his burial place to this day" (Deut. 34:6). If these numbers are reliable, then Moses was 80 years old during the Exodus from Egypt.

Though it is not possible to prove definitively that Moses lived, it is also difficult to accept that he was merely a product of someone's imagination.

Like other great leaders of history, many legends were attributed to Moses, including that he had horns on his head. But these reinforce the belief that he must have played a pivotal role in the life of the Israelites at the beginning of their history, even though many of the details in his life were never recorded.

The Biblical Story

According to the biblical story in Exodus 32–34, after receiving the Decalogue on Mount Sinai, Moses discovers that the Israelites in the camp below are worshiping the Golden Calf fashioned by his brother Aaron. In anger, Moses smashes the tablets of the Ten Commandments and reprimands his fellow Israelites. God severely punishes the culprits, but then asks Moses to ascend the mountain once again, to get a second set of the tablets. There, upon Mount Sinai, he spends forty days and forty nights, rewriting the terms of the covenant on new tablets. The biblical text continues:

> So Moses came down from Mount Sinai. And as Moses came down from the mountain bearing the two tablets of the Pact, Moses was not aware that the skin of his face *karan*, since he had spoken with God. Aaron and all the Israelites saw that that the skin of Moses's face *karan*; and they shrank from coming near him. But Moses called to them, and Aaron and all the chieftains in the assembly returned to him, and Moses spoke to them. Afterward all the Israelites came near, and he instructed them concerning all that the Eternal had imparted to him on Mount Sinai. And when Moses had finished speaking with them, he put a *masveh* over his face. Whenever Moses went in before the Eternal to converse, he would leave the *masveh* off until he came out; and when he came out and told the Israelites what he had been commanded, the Israelites would see how *karan* the skin of Moses's face was. Moses would then put the *masveh* back over his face until he went in to speak with God. (Exod. 34:29–35)

There are two significant problems that need to be resolved in this text. How should the verb *karan* be translated, and what is a *masveh*? Figuring this out will help with the examination of Moses and his alledged horns.

The Meaning of the Verb *Karan*

In biblical Hebrew, *karan* is a denominative verb coming from the root *keren*, which basically means "horn," like "the horn of a ram" (see, for example, Gen. 22:13; I Sam. 16:13; I Kings 22:11). The verbal form, *makrin*, is found in Psalms 69:32, "That will please the Eternal more than oxen, than bulls with horns [*makrin*] and hooves." However, *keren* can also be used as a symbol of strength and power, as in "my horn of redemption" (*keren yishi* [II Sam. 22:3; Ps. 18:3]), "my horn [*karni*] is high, because of the Eternal" (I Sam. 2:1), or "his horn [*karno*] shall be exalted through My name" (Ps. 89:25). Additionally, the verb *karan* is found in association with light: Speaking of God, the prophet Habakkuk tells us that God is a "brilliant light that gives off rays [*karnayim*] on all sides" (Hab. 3:4).

The problem, then, is this: Does *karan* in our text, Exodus 34:29–35, mean "to grow horns" or "to shine"? On this issue traditions differ. Traditional Jewish sources, including the Aramaic translations, render *karan* as "shining." The Septuagint, the early Greek version of the Bible created by Jews, also understands it as "radiate" and translates the phrase as "The skin of his face had become glorious." So does the Christian Bible, when Paul says, "The people of Israel could not gaze at Moses's face because of the glory of his face" (II Cor. 3:7, NRSV). The *Tanchuma*, a ninth-century Rabbinic midrash, specifies that the "horns" were "rays of majesty" (*Tanchuma Ki Tisa*, #37; see also *Sh'mot Rabbah, Ki Tisa*, 47:6). In medieval times, Rashi notes that *keren* is like *karnayim* (in Hab. 3:4) "because light radiates and protrudes like a type of horn." Modern Jewish translations of the Bible follow the same trend. JPS (1917) has "sent forth beams." NJPS (1985) renders it "his face was radiant." Everett Fox translates it as "the skin of his face was radiating."[2] Nahum Sarna comments, "The awe-inspiring radiance emitted by Moses' face may be understood as the afterglow of the refulgent splendor of the Divine Presence."[3]

However, when the Bible was translated by Aquila into Greek (second century C.E.) and by Jerome into Latin (the so-called Vulgate, ca. 425 C.E.), the word *keren* was translated literally as "horn." For example, in the Latin Vulgate we find the expression *cornuta esset facies sua*, namely "his faced was horned." Today, even though most non-Jewish translations of the Bible follow the Jewish understanding,[4] two of the old versions include the literal meaning: both the Douay (1635)–Rheims (1582) Bible and the Wycliffe Bible have "his face was horned."

It is clear, therefore, that in ancient times there were different understandings of the text. Some even tried to come up with a "naturalistic" explanation of the episode. Abraham ibn Ezra (1092–1167), the famous medieval Jewish Torah commentator from Spain, believed that the verb *karan* meant "shining." In his commentary, there is a reference to a Jewish heretic by the name of Hiwi al-Balki, an Afgani, who lived in the ninth century. Rejecting al-Balki's reading of the text, Ibn Ezra writes, "May the bones of Hiwi,

Rembrandt Harmensz van Rijn (1606–1669).
Moses Destroying the Tablets of the Law. 1659.
Oil on canvas. Photo by Joerg P. Anders.
Gemaeldegalerie, Staatliche Museen zu Berlin, Berlin, Germany.

the sinner, be pounded into dust who said that it was because (Moses) did not eat bread (on Mount Sinai) that his face dried up as hard as a horn."[5]

In late medieval times, the famous Dutch painter Rembrandt (seventeenth century), perhaps sensitive to Jewish concerns of his time, painted Moses coming down from the mountain with two tablets in his hands. Two remarkable items in the painting, called *Moses Destroying the Tablets of the*

Law (1659), draw our attention: unlike other paintings of the time, the tablets contain real Hebrew letters (and not gibberish signs), and Moses displays not horns or rays of light, but a lock of hair at the top of his head. Where Rembrandt got the idea of placing hairs on Moses's head is not known, but it represents yet another interpretation of the biblical text.

Modern scholars have suggested various theories as solutions to this puzzle. According to one, the horned image of Michelangelo's *Moses* is a vestige of an older and now suppressed tradition that claimed that Moses was a god, the offspring of the horned moon god, Sin of Sinai. Another one maintains that the glowing face of Moses is a sign of his elevation to a semi-divine status. Yet, a third one argues that what we have in our text is a case of disfigurement, like keratosis, a wartlike growth on the face that emerges as a result of exposure to radiation.[6]

There is, however, no need to resort to such extreme explanations. The idea of a "glowing face" or "having horns of glory" is grounded in the traditions of the ancient Near East. According to A. Leo Oppenheim, in ancient Mesopotamia, "Kingship was of divine origin. The sanctity of the royal person is often said to be revealed by a supernatural and awe-inspiring radiance or aura, which . . . is characteristic of deities and of all things divine. In Akkadian this was called *melammu*, 'an awe-inspiring luminosity.'"[7] This glow was a proof of the king's legitimacy.

Horns, as indications of divine power, adorned many of ancient kings' and leaders' headgear. Both Alexander the Great and Attila the Hun are described as wearing "horns." In fact, in Islam, Alexander appears as "the two-horned Alexander" (*al-Iskandar Dhu 'l-qurnayn*). This image results from the passage on "the two horned" (*Dhu 'l-qurnayn*) in Sura 18:82–97 ("the Cave") of the Qur'an. Also, in the victory stele of Naram Sin (2300–2200 B.C.E.), the grandson of Sargon the Great, and the fourth king of the Semitic dynasty of Akkad (now at the Louvre in Paris), we see Naram Sin climbing the mountain at the head of his troops with his helmet bearing the horns symbolic of divine power. In the Bible, according to the author of the Book of Daniel, powerful monarchs have symbolic horns. God tells Daniel, "The two-horned [*hakarnayim*] ram that you saw [signifies] the kings of Media and Persia" (Dan. 8:20).

The idea that horns were a symbol of strength and power is also found in a remarkable Rabbinic midrash. After the death of Abel, the Bible tells us, God provided Cain with a protective "sign" (Gen. 4:15) but does not specify its nature. In discussing what kind of "sign" this was, Rav said that God provided him with a dog. But Abba Yosei claimed that God made a horn to grow out of his head (*B'reishit Rabbah* 22:12).

It is therefore highly possible that neither Aquilas nor Jerome, in rendering *keren* as "horns," meant it literally. It is, on the other hand, most likely that they were referring to Moses's might, splendor, and honor.

The eleventh century in Christian Europe was a turning point for the interpretation of this concept. This was the era of the Crusades (the first one was in 1096), when Jews were maliciously charged with "blood libels" and "desecrating the host." It is from this period on that Europe saw the emergence of a new and distorted description of the Jew, who bore horns, just like Satan. The Jew was transformed into the "devil-Jew." Jews were considered serfs of royal powers, which, on the one hand, provided them with some protection, but at the same time left them at the mercy of kings and church leaders. As the historian Ben-Sasson writes, "When the diabolic nature of the Jews had pervaded the Christian imagination, stonemasons and painters began giving the demons and wicked angels whom they carved and painted the appearance of contemporary Jews."[8]

Jewish commentators vainly tried to stem this tide by pointing out the mistake in the biblical interpretation among Christian thinkers. For example, Rashbam (Rabbi Samuel ben Meir of Northern France, 1085–1174) writes, "Anyone who connects *keren* in this verse [Exod. 34:29] to the meaning of 'horns' as in the biblical phrase, 'He has horns like the horns of the wild ox' [Deut. 33:17] is a fool."[9] However, the trend was too powerful. In fact, in 1267, the ecclesiastical synod of Vienna ordered all Jews to wear the *pileum cornutum*, a cone-shaped headdress, or a horned hat.

It is within this context that one can place the European images of Moses wearing "horns." The earliest known illustration of this image is found in the Paraphrase of the Pentateuch and Joshua by Aelfric (ca. 955–1020), a monk of the old monastery of Winchester.[10] It is thus likely that when Michelangelo carved the statue of Moses and placed two "horns" on Moses's head, he was reflecting the thinking of his time, using the Latin Vulgate's literal rendition. Regrettably, the image of the Jew wearing horns is still prevalent in some ignorant quarters around the world today.

The Meaning of *Masveh*

As noted above, according to the biblical narrative, Moses covered his face with a *masveh*, except when he spoke with God and when he addressed the Israelites. What does this word mean, and what was its function?

The word *masveh* occurs three times only in our text. The Brown-Driver-Briggs *A Hebrew and English Lexicon of the Old Testament* derives it from the root *s-v-h* and defines it as "veil." According to Rashi, the word means "a garment [*beged*] that is placed in front of the face, and covering the eyes."[11]

The function of this "veil" is not at all clear, and therefore theories about it abound. For some, the veil was understood as a cultic mask worn by priests. For others, the biblical tradition, which did not conceive of Moses becoming a deity, was resisting the ancient Near Eastern use of the shaman by having Moses speaking with the people without a face covering. There are those who argue that the veil was only a symbol of Moses's reaffirmed authority. Some say the veil was used for purposes of humility and modesty. It looks like the entire pericope of Exodus 34:29–35 was written in order to explain the use of the enigmatic tradition of "Moses's veil," even though its origin or actual purpose still evades us.

In the biblical text, the term "horn" most likely was used equivocally in order to stress that the true mediator between God and the people of Israel was Moses, and not the horned Golden Calf that was created in Moses's absence by Aaron and others.

Modern Expression: "Horned"

In many modern languages, a naïve husband whose wife has committed adultery is called "horned." In Italian, the expression is *cornuto*, from *corna*, meaning "horn." In Spanish, it is *poner los cuernos*, and in French, *porter des cornes*. To show visually that a man has been cuckolded, one stretches the index finger and the little finger, holding down the middle ones and the thumb. In French literature, Molière, in his comedy *L'Ecole des Femmes* (1662), tells the story of a man who mocks cuckolds but "wears the horns" himself at the end. Geoffrey Chaucer's *Canterbury Tales* (1372–77) contain the story of "The Miller's Tale," describing the life of a cuckold. Shakespeare, in his *Much Ado About Nothing*, speaking of blind love, has the indignant Benedict saying, "Pluck off the bull's horns and set them in my forehead" (act 1, 254–59).

There may, in fact, be a connection between being "horned" and the biblical use of the word "horn," inasmuch as horns represent power and authority. According to one explanation, when the Roman legionnaires returned from war, they were given horns as a prize. But in the case of a cuckold, the joke would be on him: he was victorious in battle but not in his home. Others trace the custom to Greek mythology, to Minotaur, a fierce creature born of Queen Pasiphae and a white bull, who is betrayed by the king Minos of Crete. For some, the custom goes back to a legend whereby the hapless husband was forced to wear antlers on his head as symbol of the infidelity of his wife. To put the horns on a husband is to become his sexual surrogate, to reduce him to be a passive and ineffectual husband.

Conclusion

The point of view that horns represent a symbol of authority and splendor appears to be the best explanation for the enigmatic image of Moses coming down from Mount Sinai with his face aglow in light and, at times, covering it with a veil. Based on a number of textual renditions that are more literal, in combination with the deteriorating image of the Jew in the medieval times, Michelangelo and others like him were influenced by their culture and prejudices, ascribing to the biblical text meanings that were foreign to it.

Regrettably, the idea that Jews have horns still lingers even in our time in some communities. A good friend of mine, Edward Ginn of Natick, Massachusetts, reported the following account to me:

> I was an officer in the Judge Advocate Generals Corps of the U.S. Army (legal corps). It was in the fall of 1963 in Saluda, South Carolina, when a civilian secretary assigned to the U.S. Army Swift Strike III Claims Maneuver office, where I was stationed, was surprised when I said I was going to be out for the Jewish holidays, as she said I did not look Jewish. She asked if she could feel my head. She did it and said, "Where are your horns? I thought," she added, "all Jews had horns!"

7

Did the Israelites Escape Through the Sea?

Chagall, Marc (1887–1985). © ARS, NY. The Crossing of the Red Sea. 1955.
Oil on canvas. AM1988-80. Photo by Gérard Blot.
Musee National message biblique Marc Chagall, Nice, France.

The Claim

The Torah recounts a powerful and miraculous story of the Israelites' escape from Egypt. God parted the waters, and the Israelites passed through to safety. The Egyptians, following them in chariots, were drowned in the sea. The recent reports (e.g., *WorldNetDaily*, June 21, 2003) that Egyptian chariot wheels were found in the Red Sea has sparked a new discussion of the reliability of the Exodus story. Did the story really happen as described? Is it possible that at least some elements of the story are true? In this chapter we will study these claims and discuss the lessons derived from this foundational myth in Jewish thought.

The Legend of the Crossing

The story is told of the youngster who came home from Sunday school, having been taught the biblical story of the crossing of the Red Sea. His mother asked him what he had learned in class, and he told her, "The Iraelites got out of Egypt, but Pharaoh and his army chased after them. They got to the Red Sea, and they couldn't cross it. The Egyptian army was getting closer. So Moses got on his walkie-talkie, the Israeli Air Force bombed the Egyptians, and the Israeli Navy built a pontoon bridge so the people could cross." The mother was shocked. "Is that the way they taught you the story?" "Well, no," the boy admitted, "but if I told it to you the way they told it to us, you'd never believe it."[1]

This story is amusing, but its underlying assumptions represent a major challenge to all readers of the Bible. How did the ancient Israelites manage to cross the sea? Did the sea, as is popularly recounted, miraculously split into two, allowing the Israelites to go through? Is there a natural explanation for the so-called miracle at sea? Or, is there another interpretation of this event?

Critical scholarship acknowledges today that the entire episode of the Exodus from Egypt is shrouded in mystery. A fundamental epic in the self-understanding of the biblical Israelites, it has, in the last two millennia, been embellished by so much legendary material that it is impossible to verify exactly what happened during the departure from Egypt. We have no contemporary extra-biblical evidence about it in any of the ancient Near Eastern texts. Even the Bible itself contains various accounts regarding the Exodus. We don't know when or how the ancient Israelites[2] got out of Egypt, what happened during the crossing of the sea, and which route they took in their wilderness trek.

After the devastating effect of the plagues, the Bible reports that an unnamed Pharaoh, perhaps Rameses II (thirteenth century B.C.E.), finally consented to the departure of the Israelites from Egypt. After leaving the city of Rameses with six hundred thousand men, plus women, children, and other Egyptians who joined them (the Bible calls them "a mixed multitude" [Exod. 12:38, cf. Num. 11:4]), as well as animals, the text states, "Now when Pharaoh let the people go, God did not lead them by way of the land of the Philistines, although it was nearer; for God said, 'The people may have a change of heart when they see war, and return to Egypt.' So God led the people round about, by way of the wilderness at *yam suf* [sea of *suf*]" (Exod. 13:17–18).

This chapter will discuss two major issues: (1) Which sea did the people cross? (2) What happened during the crossing? The analysis of the relevant texts will show the importance that the early Israelites gave to this transformative event in their history, even though most of details are beyond recovery.

Locating the Sea of *Suf*

There is a long tradition claiming that the crossing took place at the Red Sea. In fact, the Septuagint identifies this body of water as *eruthra thalassa*, which means "Red Sea." Similarly, the Latin Vulgate has *mare rubrum*, again meaning "Red Sea."

The Red Sea is the northwestern arm of the Indian Ocean, separating Arabia on the east from Africa on the west. In the north is the Sinai Peninsula, with the Gulf of Suez on the west and the Gulf of Aqaba/Eilat on the east. The Red Sea is about 1,200 to 1,400 miles long and roughly 190 miles wide.

Based on the tradition that the deliverance at the sea took place at the Red Sea, many Bible translations render the "sea of *suf*" as "Red Sea."[3] However, if this were the case, it would place the crossing way too far, at about 120 miles south of Goshen, located in the northeastern part of Egypt, in the Nile River Delta, where the Israelites lived during their captivity (Gen. 47:27). Also, the Red Sea is too wide for any crossing; the narrowest cross-point is roughly 21 miles in length.[4] Furthermore, as one scholar has noted, it would have taken a path half a mile in breadth in the sea for a column of one thousand abreast, and two thousand in depth for all the people of Israel, along with those who joined them in the departure, plus all the animals, to cross in less than two hours.[5] These observations make the Red Sea an unlikely place for the Exodus crossing.

There is another translation possible. In biblical Hebrew, the word *suf* refers to "reeds," not "red." For example, when the mother of Moses could no longer hide her son at home, the text tells us, she put him in a wicker basket and "placed it among the reeds [*basuf*] by the bank of the Nile" (Exod. 2:3; see also 2:5). Similarly, in a psalm inserted in the Book of Jonah, the poet exclaims, "The waters closed in over me, / The deep engulfed me, / Weeds [*suf*] twined around my head" (Jon. 2:6). It is thus more likely that the people crossed the "Sea of Reeds" and not the "Red Sea." This is also the understanding of Rashi, who says that *suf* refers to "a marsh where reeds grow."[6]

In addition to the long distance between Goshen and the Red Sea, we encounter a great difficulty if the crossing is placed at the Red Sea. Reeds need fresh water to grow; the Red Sea, being saline, does not have reeds. Therefore, it is not likely that the crossing was done through the Red Sea. So, many recent translations now render the "Sea of *Suf*" as the "Sea of Reeds"[7] or the "Sea of Rushes."[8] But where is this sea located?

The text teaches that God led the people by the way of the wilderness, even though the "way of the land of the Philistines" (Exod. 3:17) would have been nearer. It is worth noting that there is an historical problem with this expression. The Philistines did not arrive on these shores before 1200 B.C.E., so the Exodus, being of Mosaic period (ca. 1250 B.C.E.), occurred before this highway could have been called by this name. But assuming that the story was written after the fact, we still need to ask, where was this particular main road located? Most likely, it is the route that borders the Mediterranean Sea, the so-called northern route, which leads to Megiddo, and from there to Mesopotamia or Asia Minor. The Egyptians called it "Ways of Horus"; the Romans, *Via Maris*. But it was heavily fortified by Egyptian troops that monitored the traffic in and out of Egypt. Taking this northern route would have led the fleeing Israelites right into the hands of the enemy once more. So, the people marched south.

Where could they have gone? The Reed Sea can be placed in at least three locations: the Gulf of Suez, the Gulf of Aqaba/Eilat, or an unknown "Sea of the Exodus." The biblical expression *yam suf* can refer to any of these three.

The Book of Numbers identifies the different sites where the ancient Israelites camped during their wanderings in the wilderness. In one section, we are told that "they set out from Elim and encamped by the Sea of Reeds. They set out from the Sea of Reeds and encamped in the wilderness of Sin. . . . They set out from Alush and encamped at Rephidim" (Num. 33:10–11, 33:14). We do not know where Elim or Alush is located, but Rephidim was most likely in the Sinai Peninsula, not too far away from the Suez Canal.[9] It is possible, therefore, that the Reed Sea was located close to it, in the Gulf of Suez.

On the other hand, the expression "Sea of Reeds" can also refer to the Gulf of Aqaba/Eilat. For example, according to the Book of Kings, "King Solomon also built a fleet of ships at Ezion-geber, which is near Eloth on the shore of the Sea of Reeds in the land of Edom" (I Kings 9:26). The location of Eloth (or Elath) is not known, but the references to Ezion-geber and the "Sea of Reeds in the land of Edom" clearly places the Reed Sea by the Gulf of Aqaba/Eilat (see Num. 14:25; Jer. 49:21). Similarly, in the Genesis Apocryphon, an Aramaic text found among the Dead Sea Scroll material, the patriarch Abraham tells us, "I continued walking along the shore of the Red Sea until arriving at the branch of the Sea of Reeds which issues from the Red Sea, and continued towards the South until I reached River Gihon (21:17–18)."[10] This text too convincingly places the Reed Sea by the Gulf of Aqaba/Eilat.

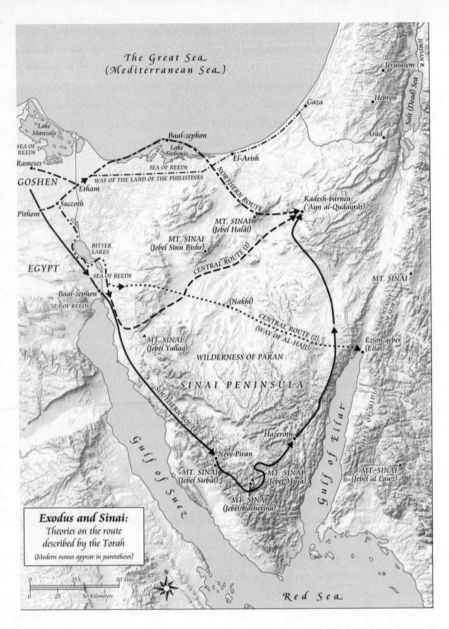

Exodus and Sinai:
Theories on the route
described by the Torah
(Modern names appear in parentheses)

The Reed Sea may have also been located at a third location that is somewhere within the Sinai Peninsula, closer to the city of Rameses, perhaps in one of the lagoons near the shore of the Mediterranean Sea. Scholars have suggested a variety of small lakes or marshes in that area, such as the Ballah Lakes or Lake Sarbonis, though without any definite success.[11]

It appears that the expression "Sea of Reeds" was used loosely to cover the entire network of lakes and marshes that skirted the wilderness in the Sinai Peninsula, from the Delta region in the north to the southern gulfs of Suez and Aqaba/Eilat. The context of the Exodus story, however, urges us to look for a place near the city of Rameses and perhaps in one of the marshes in the northern region.

Instead of pinpointing the exact location of the crossing, some scholars have argued that the origin of the term *yam suf* may have been irrelevant to the storyteller trying to convey a message. For example, one scholar has argued that the Exodus narrative derives it from later traditions that are based on the editors' knowledge of Egypt at the time of the writing/editing.[12] For others, the reference is not to the sea of *suf*, meaning "reed," but to the "sea of *sof*," meaning "end." Thus, for example, another scholar notes, "what we call the Red Sea came to be known as the *yam suf* because it was regarded by the ancestors as the sea at the end of the world."[13] This interpretation was also known to Abraham ibn Ezra, the twelfth-century medieval Jewish commentator, who considers it a mistake. For him, *yam suf* is a proper name and means a definite place close to Egypt.[14] Other Bible specialists see in the word *yam* ("sea") echoes of the original myth involving the primeval battle during the creation of the universe between chaos, represented by "Sea" (*Tiamat* in Akkadian, *Yamm* in Ugaritic), and order, and therefore see in the story of the crossing vestiges of the belief in the formation of the people Israel as a creation almost equal to the creation of the universe.[15]

The evidence so far suggests that it is not possible to locate the exact spot of the crossing of the Reed Sea. However, according to tradition, it must have taken place somewhere in the Sinai Peninsula, perhaps in a marsh closer to Egypt.

The Deliverance

In relating significant events, the Bible often provides parallel texts; usually a prose narrative is followed by a poetic rendition of the same episode. For example, the prophetess Deborah's victory over Sisera is related first in prose (Judg. 4) and then in poetry (Judg. 5). Scholars maintain that the poetic form is the earlier. Similarly, when the Israelites crossed the sea, the deliverance is told in two different forms: the prose version in Exodus 13–14 and the poetic version in Exodus 15.

How did the Israelites cross the sea? Contrary to popular belief, the Bible provides various images. The earliest account, found in Exodus 15, the so-called Song at the Sea, is usually assigned to the J source in the Bible. Here God is the main character; there is no mention of the splitting of the sea, and the sea itself is always referred to fully as the "Sea of Reeds." God drives back the Reed Sea with a strong east wind ("At the blast of your nostrils the waters piled up" [Exod. 15:8]; "You made Your wind blow, the sea covered them" [Exod. 15:10a]), and the Egyptians, perhaps in ships, overtaken by a storm, ultimately sink to the bottom of the sea ("They sank like lead in the majestic waters" [Exod. 15:10b]).

In one of the most well-known passages, usually assigned to the P source in the Bible, Moses is the main character, and the sea is always referred to as "the Sea," never the "Reed Sea." We read: "Then Moses held out his arm over the sea and the Eternal drove back the sea with a strong east wind all that night, and turned the sea into dry ground. The waters were split, and the Israelites went into the sea on dry ground, the waters forming a wall for them on their right and on their left. And the Egyptians came in pursuit after them into the sea" (Exod. 14:21–23). Then at the command of God, Moses held out his arm over the sea, and the waters returned to their normal state, destroying the Egyptian army in it (Exod. 15:27–28).

Yet, in a verse assigned to another P version, the crossing is described differently: "At the morning watch, the Eternal looked down upon the Egyptian army from a pillar of fire and cloud, and threw the Egyptian army into panic. [God] locked the wheels of their chariots so that they moved forward with difficulty" (Exod. 14:24–25).

These three stories cannot be reconciled. As one biblical scholar aptly argues, "If the Egyptians were already on the floor of the sea, as in P, then they could not sink like a stone or like lead. If they were on the sea's surface, as in Exodus 15 suggests, their chariots are irrelevant."[16]

Scholars have tried for centuries to solve this puzzle by offering their own interpretations of these events. Some, like Rashbam (Rabbi Samuel ben Meir, b. 1085 in northern France) followed the traditional line and argued, "God acted in the usual way, for the winds dry up and coagulate the rivers."[17] Others, wishing to justify the biblical text, resorted to so-called naturalistic explanations, including the claim that a volcanic eruption on the island of Santorini produced a tidal wave and parted the Red Sea, or that the crossing was really done during a low tide, or even that a tsunami caused the parting of the sea. None of these, however, can be substantiated.

Other traditional Jewish sources provide us with different images. According to Psalms 77:18, "clouds streamed water; the heavens rumbled." Josephus, the first-century C.E. Jewish historian, intimated that Moses chose his route by means of clever calculations. Pointing to the "strangeness of the narration," he expressed doubts "whether it happened by the will of God or whether it happened of its own accord" (*Ant.* II, 16:64). In the Wisdom of Solomon, a first-century-B.C.E. apocryphal book, the deliverance was the work of personified wisdom: "A holy people and blameless race wisdom [lit., she] delivered from a nation of oppressors. . . . She brought them over the Red Sea and led them through deep waters" (Wisd. of Sol. 10:15, 10:18, RSV). For Philo, a first-century-C.E. Jewish philosopher from Alexandria, the entire episode is an allegory: "God cast to utter ruin and the bottomless abyss the four passions and the wretched mind mounted on them. This is practically the chief point of the whole Song."[18]

Great legends attract further elaborations. The Book of Psalms mentions a rebellion at the sea: "Our forefathers in Egypt did not perceive Your wonders; they did not remember Your abundant love, but rebelled at the sea, at the Sea of Reeds" (Ps. 106:7). Josephus clarifies: this means they forgot all the miracles and turned against Moses (*Ant.* 2:327), based on a comment on Exodus 14:11–14, which tells us that the people, afraid of the advancing Egyptian army, complain to Moses that they are about to die. Moses urges them to march on, assuring them that God will fight for them. The people then take their anger out on Moses. The Aramaic *Targum Neophyti* (ca. first century C.E.) even suggests that the Israelites formed four different groups debating the viability of the move into the sea.[19] Philo remarks that some people even planned to commit suicide.[20]

In the Rabbinic literature, the episode of rebellion elicits further comments. In the Talmud, Rabbi Meir opines that when the Israelites stood by the sea, the tribes contended (*mitnatzehim*) with one another, each one eagerly wanting to jump in, and the tribe of Benjamin took the first plunge. On the other hand, Rabbi Y'hudah suggests that no one wanted to get into the water first until Nachshon ben Aminadab, of the tribe of Judah, went in with his tribe (BT *Sotah* 36b).[21] Similarly, according to another Rabbinic source, the sea was not split until all the Israelites stepped into it, indeed until the waters reached up to their very noses (*Sh'mot Rabbah* 21:10). Commenting on the verse "Tell the Israelites to go forward" (Exod. 14:15), another Rabbinic teacher taught that God said to Moses, "My children are in distress, the enemy is in pursuit and you stand there praying away! There is a time to be brief. Tell the Israelites to move!" (*Sh'mot Rabbah* 21:8).

Other texts highlight the various miraculous events during the deliverance. The Book of Deuteronomy speaks, in the plural, of "signs and deeds" (Deut. 11:3); Nehemiah mentions "signs and wonders" (Neh. 9:10); the Book of Psalms recalls "the awesome deeds at the Sea of Reeds" (Ps. 106:22). For the prophet Isaiah, the Reed Sea was even made as dry as a wilderness (Isa. 63:13). In the Rabbinic period, the Mishnah mentions the "ten miracles" that happened to the Israelites at the Sea (*Pirkei Avot* 5:4),[22] deduced apparently from various verses taken from Exodus 15.

The deliverance at the sea was a great victory for the Israelites, but it also came at the expense of the death of the Egyptians. Though some Jewish legends state that God brought upon them far more excruciating pain than the ten plagues,[23] there are other voices in the literature that decry their death. For example, in the Talmud, according to Rabbi Yochanan, God does not rejoice in the downfall of the wicked (BT *M'gillah* 10b). Also, the text continues, when the ministering angels wanted to chant a song on the occasion of the rescue, God rebuked them by saying, "The work of my hands is being drowned in the sea, and you chant hymns?" Furthermore, according to one Jewish tradition, even though all the Egyptians drowned at sea, the pharaoh escaped. As Louis Ginzberg puts it, "Pharaoh never dies, and never will die."[24] As a symbol of tyranny, he is destined to remain at the portal of hell rebuking those who enter by saying, "Why didn't you learn from me?"

The Message

If after all this analysis we are forced to assume that the details of the redemption at the sea and, in fact, of the entire episode of the Exodus cannot be verified by independent testimony of extra-biblical material, are we compelled to accept that the whole story is unreliable and, worse, the imaginary creation of later-period Judaism? Some thinkers, mostly those belonging to the so-called biblical minimalist historians of the Copenhagen school, have actually claimed and argued that because there is no corroboration from external sources, it must be assumed that the Exodus is purely mythic in character. The maximalists, on the other hand, follow more or less the biblical outline. But archaeology, history, and critical study of texts do not support their claim. Yet, there is a third position, one in between, which assumes the presence of a kernel of truth with layers of legends built on it. The story of liberation may not have occurred exactly the way the Bible relates it, but a reasonable reconstruction is possible. For example, as Michael D. Coogan has suggested, "Under the leadership of Moses, a small group of Hebrew slaves (probably a few hundred at most) escaped from their forced labor in the eastern Nile delta. They headed for one of the swamps or wetlands in the vicinity, pursued by their guards. Because they were on foot, the escapees were able to make their way through the swamp, but the Egyptians, in chariots, got bogged down and gave up the pursuit, so that the Hebrews got away. This event would have been relatively inconsequential to the Egyptians, but for those who escaped it was nothing short of a miracle."[25]

One scholar notes, "A grand miracle deserves a grand setting."[26] Irrespective of the belief that the rescue at the sea may or may not have been a miracle, there is no doubt that the Exodus in general and the deliverance during the crossing in particular have left an indelible imprint in the historical views of the ancient Israelites. Historians have found that many people went in and out of ancient Egypt. For the Egyptian royal scribes, these movements may have been insignificant, but for the Israelites the departure was monumental. They viewed it not as a simple escape but as the freedom brought about by no less than God. For centuries after that they were told to remember it as a transforming event in their national identity: they were slaves and they became free. Thus, for example, in the Ten Commandments, God appears not as Creator but as Liberator: "I the Eternal am your God who brought you out of the land of Egypt, the house of bondage" (Exod. 20:2; see also Lev. 25:38; Num. 15:41; Deut. 24:18). The Exodus became the rationale for the injunction not to wrong the "resident alien" (*ger*): "The strangers who reside with you shall be to you as your citizens; you shall love each one as yourself, for you were strangers in the land of Egypt: I the Eternal am your God" (Lev. 19:34). It even became a paradigmatic event that set the pattern for others. Second Isaiah, for example, looked back to the original Exodus and predicted that the second one, this time back from Babylonia, would be even more magnificent: "Every valley shall be raised, / Every hill and mount made low" (Isa. 40:4). Even though during the Exodus the Israelites had to leave from Egypt in haste (Exod. 12:11), the prophet assured his contemporaries during the exile that the return from Babylon would be leisurely: "You will not depart in haste; / Nor will you leave in flight" (Isa. 52:12); the return will even be a happy one: "You will leave in joy and be led home secure" (Isa. 55:12).

Because the redemption from slavery has left a lasting impact among Jews, for the last two thousand years or so they have celebrated the first Exodus from Egypt on Passover in the springtime with a ritualized meal at home called the seder. This festival originally marked two distinct holy days: the first, Chag HaPesach, was a semi-pastoral spring feast, probably of pre-Mosaic times, and characterized by the slaughter and consumption of the paschal animal on the fourteenth day of Nisan (Exod. 34:25; Lev. 23:5); and the second, Chag HaMatzot, the Festival of Unleavened Bread, reflecting an agricultural setting, was probably taken over from the Canaanites after the conquest. It marked the beginning of the grain harvest and took place on the fifteenth of Nisan (Exod. 23:15, 34:18; Lev. 23:6; Deut.16:16). At some point these two were combined, because of the proximity of dates, and eventually connected with the escape from Egypt. It was after the biblical period, perhaps in early Rabbinic times, that the message of the redemption at the sea was applied to every Jew. In the traditional Passover Haggadah, we are told, "In every generation one is obligated to see oneself as if he/she came out of Egypt. . . . Not only did God redeem our ancestors alone, but us as well with them" (see *Mishnah P'sachim* 10:5).

A transformative event like this, which left a deep impression in the consciousness of the ancient Israelites, and among all Jews, is hard to invent. It is remarkable that the story of Israel's liberation goes against the grain of many ancient civilizations that derive their origin from the realms of the gods (e.g., the Babylonians, the Greeks). Only the people of Israel has claimed that their history is rooted in slavery. One biblical scholar remarks, "The deliverance from Egypt and the rescue at the Red Sea found their way into Israel's confession of faith—indeed, they actually became Israel's earliest confession, around which the whole Hexateuchal [the Pentateuch plus Joshua] history was in the end ranged."[27]

The escape from Egypt represents the beginning of Jewish peoplehood. The patriarchal period is full of legendary material about the succession of three generations (i.e., Abraham, Isaac, and Jacob) within a small family. After the Exodus, the Israelites looked back to the liberation from Egypt as God's special redemptive act, and in gratitude they bound themselves to a discipline of Torah. Even today, as a foundational myth about the beginnings of the Jewish people, the Exodus from Egypt continues to play a major role in the self-identity of the modern Jew. At the same time, the Exodus from Egypt also teaches Jews to appreciate freedom and to work against slavery and oppression. These lessons are embedded in what the Exodus has meant for Jews throughout history, as it promotes the revolutionary idea of freedom for all people.

8

What Happened at Mount Sinai?

The Sinai Range (shortly after sunrise). View from Mount Sinai.
On Mount Sinai, God gave Moses the Law.
Photo by Erich Lessing. Mount Sinai, Sinai Desert, Egypt.

The Claim

One of the fundamental teachings of Judaism is that the Ten Commandments were given on Mount Sinai. The Torah tells of Moses ascending Mount Sinai and descending with the tablets in his hands. The narrative is compelling and dramatic. But is it historically true? This chapter will probe that assumption, and point to the complexity in unraveling the format and content of the Revelation as reflected in our sacred texts.

Geography

Sinai is a triangular peninsula that sits between the Mediterranean Sea to the north and the Red Sea to the south. It borders the Suez Canal on the west and the Gulf of Aqaba/Eilat to the east, covering an area of about sixty thousand square kilometers. It was somewhere in this peninsula that, the Israelites believed, God revealed the Torah. In the Rabbinic literature, this is called *matan Torah*, "the giving of the Torah."

According to the biblical narrative, when the ancient Israelites left Egypt, they wandered through the wilderness for forty years (e.g., Deut. 8:2; Neh. 9:21) and settled in Kadesh-barnea (Num. 33:36; Deut. 1:19). In this transitional period, God's Revelation took place during an awe-inspiring theophany on top of a holy mountain. It was also there that God established a covenant with the people of Israel. The Pentateuch tells us this momentous event took place at a place called Mount Sinai, but sometimes known as Mount Horeb. Historians and archaeologists have been searching for the location of this famous mountain for centuries.

Christian tradition assumes that Mount Sinai is Jebel Musa ("the mountain of Moses") in the southern part of Sinai where St. Catherine's Monastery is located. The problem with this assumption is that this tradition goes back only to the fourth century C.E., when a small chapel was built there by Christian monastic groups to mark the place they thought was the location of the "Burning Bush" as experienced by Moses (see Exod. 3).

In the sixth century C.E., the Byzantine emperor Justinian built a fortress around this religious site. Its original name was the Monastery of the Transfiguration. It did not become known as St. Catherine's Monastery until the eleventh century, when it was renamed in memory of a martyr who was beheaded by the Romans. According to legend, after her death, her body was transported by angels to the top of the mountain that now bears her name.

St. Catherine's Monastery is built between two mountain ranges, Jebel Musa and Ras es-Safsaf, and is located on the northwestern foot of Jebel Musa, which is 7,495 feet high (about 2,285 meters). However, as one critic notes, "Whether Ras es-Safsaf or Jebel Musa is the sacred mount, or whether both are involved in the tradition, cannot now be decided, and is relatively unimportant. Christian tradition thinks of the former as Horeb and the latter as Sinai, though the latter is some three miles distant from the plain."[1]

Biblical and Postbiblical References

God's Revelation of the Torah, the text reiterates, took place on the "mountain of God" (Exod. 3:1; see also I Kings 19:8). As noted previously, the Bible, which is the only source available on the subject, gives us two different answers about the name of this mountain. According to the J strand, it is "Sinai" (Exod. 19:20). The P source also calls it "Sinai" (Exod. 24:16). However, E (e.g., Exod. 3:1) and D (e.g., Deut. 4:10, 5:2) refer to it as "Horeb." It is not clear how these two places are related to one another.

One possibility is that they are two different mountains: One is Mount Horeb located in the area called Midian, in the northeastern part of the Gulf of Aqaba/Eilat. It was in Midian that Moses spent forty years (*B'reishit Rabbah* 100:10; see also Acts 7:29, 30) living with his wife Zipporah and his father-in-law Jethro, and it is also the location of his encounter with the Burning Bush (Exod. 3:1). The other one is Mount Sinai, which is located in the Sinai Peninsula, although its exact location has still not been identified. Another option is to consider "Sinai" as the mountain range, with Horeb being one of the peaks. The reverse is also possible—namely, Horeb is the mountain range, and Sinai is one of the peaks. A third possibility is that the Bible recorded two different traditions about where the actual Revelation took place and wove the different stories together. We have no way to verify any of these options. It appears that by the time the stories about the giving of the Torah were consolidated, the exact location was already forgotten.

The only other reference to Mount Horeb in the Bible is found in the stories about the prophet Elijah (ca. ninth century B.C.E.): "He [Elijah] arose and ate and drank; and with the strength from that meal he walked forty days and forty nights as far as the mountain of God at Horeb" (I Kings 19:8). Here Elijah appears like a second Moses, perhaps even molded after his image.

In the Rabbinic literature, references to other mountains such as "the Mountain of Bashan," "the Mountain of Peaks," "Mount Moriah," "the Wilderness of Zin," "the Wilderness of Kedemot," and "the Wilderness of Paran" (see *Sh'mot Rabbah* 2:4; *B'midbar Rabbah* 1:8; BT *Shabbat* 89a) are all interpreted midrashically as substitutes for Sinai. The Talmud, playing on the words "Sinai" and *sinah* (meaning "hostility"), records the opinion of two sages who state that it was called "Sinai" because hostility toward idolaters descended upon them on account of their rejection of the Torah (BT *Shabbat* 89a).

In the postbiblical period, Sinai and Horeb were considered synonymous. According to the Book of Sirach (second century B.C.E.), it was the prophet Elijah "who heard rebuke at Sinai, and judgments of vengeance at Horeb" (Sir. 48:7, RSV). The uncertainty about the exact location of the Revelation continued to be argued well into the Talmudic period (BT *Shabbat* 89b). In medieval times, Rabbi Abraham ibn Ezra (1092–1167) seemingly resolved the issue by saying, "Horeb is Sinai."[2]

The Route

The location of the "mountain of God" is closely related to the question of the route that the Israelites took in the wilderness before entering the land of Canaan. Here, neither history nor archaeology can provide definitive proof. The Bible offers only a few clues. For example, the text states that after the Exodus, God led the people not "by way of the land of the Philistines" (Exod. 13:17) but "round about, by way of the wilderness at the Sea of Reeds" (Exod. 13:18). It also adds that "it is eleven days from Horeb to Kadesh-barnea by the Mount Seir route" (Deut. 1:2). Furthermore, it states that the wandering through the wilderness (not "desert" like the African Sahara, because there was enough vegetation to sustain them) was extremely difficult: "We set out from Horeb and traveled the great and terrible wilderness" (Deut. 1:19). This information is hardly enough to establish the route through the Sinai.

In contrast, the Book of Numbers gives us a detailed list of each of the locations where the ancient Israelites rested, even if only for a short period of time. The text states that the people went from Rameses to Succoth (Num. 33:5), then to Etham (Num. 33:6), then to Migdol (Num. 33:7), until they finally reached Kadesh-barnea (Num. 33:36). Of all the places mentioned in the Bible, only two sites can be identified with a modicum of certainty: The first is Ezion-geber (Num. 33:35; Deut. 2:8), which, the text says, is "on the shore of the Sea of Reeds in the land of Edom" (I Kings 9:26). Archaeologists locate it at Tel el-Kheleifeh, near modern-day Eilat. The second one, Kadesh-barnea, is in the eastern part of the Sinai wilderness, about fifty miles south of Beer-sheba, at a place now called Ein Qudeirat.

Given the lack of information on this subject, historians have proposed at least four different possible routes that the ancient Israelites could have taken as they crossed the Sinai wilderness.

The first, called "the northern route," bordered the Mediterranean Sea. The Book of Exodus calls it "the way of the land of the Philistines" (*derech eretz P'lishtim*) (Exod. 13:17). This is what the ancient Egyptians called "the way of Horus," and the Romans, *Via Maris*.

Going toward the south, the next suggestion is the "way of Shur" (*derech Shur*), which the Patriarchs used as they went down to Egypt (Gen. 16:7; 25:18, "which is near Egypt"). According to Exodus 15:22, when the Israelites left the Sea of Reeds, "they went on into the wilderness of Shur." However, the same place is called "Etham" in Numbers 33:8. "The way of Shur" was probably an old caravan route that went from Egypt to Hebron.

A third option is the "Way of Seir Mountain" (*derech Har Seir*). According to the Book of Deuteronomy, "It is eleven days from Horeb to Kadesh-barnea by the Mount Seir route" (Deut. 1:2). The term "Seir" refers to Edom, which is located between the southern end of the Dead Sea and north of the Gulf of Aqaba/Eilat.

Scholars have also pointed to the most southern route called "the way to the hill country of the Amorites" (*derech har ha-Emori*) that leads from Horeb to Kadesh-barnea (Deut. 1:19).

With the multitude of options to date, no agreement has been reached by critics about the exact route taken by the Israelites during the Exodus. The location of Mount Sinai, which is within this trajectory, therefore, remains an enigma.

Biblical scholars have proposed various sites within the Sinai Peninsula that could be identified as the "mountain of God." At least ten such sites have been suggested.[3] Yet, of all the alternatives, the best option is to locate it somewhere in the lower part of the Sinai Peninsula. For, as one biblical archaeologist convincingly argues,[4] only in this part of Sinai is there a reasonably adequate water supply that could sustain a group of wanderers. Also, this is the only part of the peninsula that was beyond the hegemony of the Egyptian powers. But even this suggestion is not without its problems: no remains of human occupation in the late Bronze Age (ca. 1500–1200 B.C.E.)—the period accepted by most scholars today regarding the Exodus—have been found in this area.

The Covenant

The Pentateuch asserts that during the theophany at the summit of the mountain, God singled out the Israelites from among all peoples, proclaiming them to be God's "treasured possession" (*s'gulah* in Hebrew; Exod. 19:5), and destined them to become "a kingdom of priests and a holy people" (Exod. 19:6). Furthermore, as part of this new relationship, God established a special covenant (*b'rit* in Hebrew) with the people that included mutual obligations and responsibilities (Exod. 24:4–8; see also Deut. 4:13). This momentous event is now celebrated on Shavuot ("Weeks"), one of the Three Pilgrimage Festivals, which originally marked the midsummer grain harvest, and eventually became associated with the giving of the Torah on Mount Sinai/Horeb.

The form of many biblical covenants or treaties was influenced by the literary patterns of the ancient Near East. In the covenant of Sinai, God

---

COVENANT

A "covenant" is a contract or a treaty signed between two parties. In the ancient Near East, it was customary for countries to sign treaties with one another in order to establish their mutual responsibilities. There were two basic kinds of covenants: (1) "treaties of mutuality" were signed between equals, such as the famous treaty concluded between Rameses II, king of Egypt, and Hattusilis III, king of the Hittites (ca. 1280 B.C.E.); (2) "suzerainty treaties" were imposed by a mighty king upon vassals, such as the numerous vassal treaties of Esarhaddon, king of Assyria (seventh century B.C.E.).

These legal documents followed a specific format, and were accompanied by prescribed rituals. For example, the Hittite treaties of 1400–1200 B.C.E. usually included the following components: (1) identification of the covenant giver; (2) a historical prologue indicating how the suzerain's acts benefited the vassal; (3) the stipulations, the rules and regulations that bound the vassal; (4) a provision for deposit of the document in the temple and the requirement for periodic reading; (5) the list of witnesses, including various gods but also heaven and earth or mountains and rivers; (6) blessings and curses to ensure implementation of the treaty; (7) a ratification ceremony through the sacrifice of an animal, implying a self-curse (i.e., if I do not comply with the stipulations of the treaty, may this happen to me!).

---

promises to take care of the Israelites, and in exchange the people voluntarily submit to God's laws and commandments when they declare, "All that the Eternal has spoken we will do!" (Exod. 19:8, 24:3, 24:7).

The Broader Context

Exodus 19 sets the stage for the Revelation on Mount Sinai: The Israelites arrive in the wilderness of Sinai three months after leaving Egypt (Exod. 19:1) and remain there for almost another three months (Num. 10:11). Once the Israelites are within Sinai, God, through the mediation of Moses, reveals the Torah to them and establishes a covenant with them. The Israelites enthusiastically accept the terms of the covenant even before they know the details (Exod. 19:8; see also 24:7). But when Moses comes down from the mountain, he finds the Israelites worshiping the Golden Calf (Exod. 32). Furious over the incident, Moses breaks the tablets of the Torah (before sharing the content with the people), destroys the idol, punishes the culprits, and then ascends once more to plead forgiveness from God. Subsequently, God tells Moses to carve two more tablets of stone, on which God, at the summit, inscribes the words that were on the first tablets (Exod. 34:1).

Though this broad outline is culled from several sources in the Bible, the details are extremely difficult to establish. There are several texts that intrude between Exodus 19 and Exodus 34, when the story more or less resumes, such as the Book of the Covenant (Exod. 20:19–23:19), the instructions about the Tabernacle and the consecration of priests (Exod. 25–31), and Moses's request to "see God's face" (Exod. 33). Some Jewish medieval commentators, like Rashi (eleventh century), commenting on Exodus 24:1, had to admit that certain parts of the Revelation (e.g., Exod. 24, which was recorded after the Decalogue and the Book of the Covenant) should have been placed right after Exodus 19. The Rabbis maintained, however, "there is no chronological order in the Torah" (BT *P'sachim* 6b).

The Preparation

The preparation for the theophany as told in Exodus 19 is loaded with problems. For example:

1. Moses goes up (vv. 3, 8, 20) and down (vv. 7, 14, 25) the mountain three times.
2. In one part of the text, people appear fearful of approaching the mountain (v. 16), yet in another, a warning is issued against their encroachment (vv. 12–13, 21–23).
3. It is not clear if the authors/editors conceived of God as living in the heavens (Exod. 20:19) or on the mountain (Exod. 19:3). Nehemiah combines both points of view: "You came down on Mount Sinai and spoke with them from the heaven" (Neh. 9:13). Rabbinic literature presents another image: God "lowered the upper heavens down to the top of the mountain and still spoke to them from the heavens" (*M'chilta, BaChodesh,* #9).

4. The names of God in Exodus 19 fluctuate between *YHVH* (vv. 3b, 7–11, 20–24) and *Elohim* (vv. 3a, 17, 19).
5. Two different conceptions of the theophany are mixed in the chapter: did it take place through volcanic smoke (Exod. 19:18; see also 24:17) or through cloud and thunders (Exod. 19:16, 19:19)?

These inconsistencies cannot be easily reconciled. It may be that we have a number of sources that have been combined through the centuries, making the narrative confusing to the reader.

The Format

According to the Book of Exodus, after the people prepare to receive the Torah, they assemble at the foot of the mountain (Exod. 19:17). Then, during an awesome display of nature's power (i.e., thunder, lightning, and smoke), God reveals the Torah. However, it is not clear how this took place.

The narratives in both Exodus 19 and Deuteronomy 5 specify that the people of Israel could not handle the impact of the Revelation and ask that Moses act as a mediator (Exod. 20:16–17; Deut. 5:24). Moses declares, "I stood between the Eternal and you at that time to convey the Eternal's words to you" (Deut. 5:5). Yet, in Deuteronomy 5:4 (cf. 4:12, 5:21) we are told, "Face to face the Eternal One spoke to you [the people] on the mountain out of the fire." Furthermore, the Book of Deuteronomy insists that the Israelites heard a "voice" (Deut. 4:12, 4:36, 5:19, 5:22) but perceived "no shape [of God]" (Deut. 4:12, 4:15). The discrepancy between these statements is glaring. One biblical critic also suggests that the people heard only the "voice" but not the distinct words, and that Moses told them the rest afterwards.[5] Another scholarly explanation is that Deuteronomy 5:5 represents an older tradition.[6]

Exodus 24:9–11 contains a different version of the Revelation: "Then Moses and Aaron, Nadab and Abihu, and seventy elders of Israel ascended; and they saw the God of Israel—under whose feet was the likeness of a pavement of sapphire, like the very sky for purity. Yet [God] did not raise a hand against the leaders of the Israelites; they beheld God, and they ate and drank." Here God is not hidden; we do not have smoke or clouds on the mountain. Unlike the instructions recorded in Exodus 24:1–2, Moses goes up with the others; they eat and drink together. Here, Moses does not play a separate role.

The Content

Just as the format of the Revelation is unclear, so is the content of the Revelation. What exactly was given to the Israelites on Mount Sinai/Horeb? According to Exodus 19:25, "Moses went down to the people and spoke to them." This statement comes just before the Decalogue. It implies that what was revealed at the summit were the Ten Commandments, written on "two stone tablets" (Exod. 24:12; Deut. 5:19) either by God (Exod. 24:12) or by Moses as dictated to him by God (Exod. 24:4; Deut. 5:19). In fact, the latter claim is supported by the Book of Deuteronomy, which states right after the giving of the Decalogue, "The Eternal One spoke those words—those and no more—to your whole congregation at the mountain. . . . [God] inscribed them on two tablets of stone and gave them to me" (Deut. 5:19; see also 4:13).

Yet, Exodus 24:7 seems to refer to a much longer document, for it states that after the theophany, "He [Moses] took the record of the covenant [*sefer hab'rit*] and read it aloud to the people." Did this "record" contain not only the Decalogue but also the Book of the Covenant in Exodus 21–23? Also, according to Exodus 24:12, God said to Moses, "Come up to Me on the mountain and wait there, and I will give you the stone tablets with the teachings and commandments [*v'hatorah v'hamitzvah*], which I have inscribed to instruct them" (see also Neh. 9:13). These appear to be much longer than the two relatively short ten injunctions that could be carved on two stones.

It is interesting to note that neither Psalms 105 or 106 nor Joshua 24, which contain historical retrosprectives on the early biblical period, make any reference to the Decalogue as being revealed on Mt. Sinai, implying perhaps that the traditions about the giving of the Ten Commandments at Sinai/Horeb circulated among other (competing?) intellectual circles or ideological centers in ancient Israel.

Several postbiblical texts attempt to fill in the gaps in order to explain the content of the Revelation. The Book of Jubilees (ca. second century B.C.E.) claims that at Sinai God gave Moses not the text of the Decalogue but taught him the specific details regarding Jubilees' sectarian calendar, namely, "the divisions of the years—from the time of creation—of the law and of the testimony of the weeks of the Jubilees" (1:29). On the other hand, according to Philo, the Decalogue, which was uttered by God alone, comprised "general legal categories," while the commandments uttered through Moses were specific laws.

The exact content of the Revelation at Mt. Sinai remains unclear, and, throughout history, people have ascribed different texts to this momentous event.

The Meaning of "Torah"

The idea that God gave the Torah on Mount Sinai/Horeb to the people of Israel is affirmed by many biblical texts. But what did the Israelites mean by the word "Torah," and how did the idea develop?

The word "Torah" comes from the Hebrew root *yarah*, meaning "to throw," "to point out," and, therefore, "to direct" and "to instruct." The ancient priests used to give authoritative direction to the people, namely "Torah" (e.g., Lev. 10:11; Deut. 33:10), by using the Urim and Thummim. These were sacred lots, perhaps in the shape of dice, which were "thrown" in order to determine the will of God. During the monarchy, the word "Torah" assumed a wider meaning and often referred to specific priestly injunctions, such as the "Torah of the meal offering" (Lev. 6:7) or the "Torah of the Nazirite" (Num. 6:21). It was the responsibility of the priests to teach and to impart Torah (Lev. 10:11; Deut. 24:8; Jer. 18:18). Their role continued into the postexilic period (sixth century B.C.E.), when the returnees gathered around Ezra, the priest, to study the teachings of the Torah with priests and Levites (Neh. 8:13).

In the biblical wisdom literature, Torah was identified with *hochmah*, "wisdom," but that is human wisdom, the teachings of the wise sages. Here the word simply means parental instruction: "Hear, my son, the discipline of your father, and do not forsake the instruction [*torah*] of your mother" (Prov. 1:8). In time, the word came to mean "teaching" and "instruction" in general, and divine teaching in particular, covering all the biblical and Rabbinic material.

The Rabbinic View of Revelation

The Rabbinic literature creates an alternative description of what happened at Sinai. According to the midrash, "When God gave the Torah no bird twittered, no fowl flew, no ox lowed, none of the Ophanim stirred a wing, the Seraphim [both Hebrew words refer to angels or divine beings] did not say 'Holy, Holy,' the sea did not roar, the creatures spoke not, and the whole world was hushed into breathless silence and the voice went forth: I am the Eternal your God" (*Sh'mot Rabbah* 29:9, adapted from Soncino).

This Torah, the Rabbis taught, was given freely in the wilderness not only to the Israelites, but also to all the nations of the world. Another legend states that God's voice split into seventy voices, in seventy languages, so that all nations could comprehend it clearly (*Sh'mot Rabbah* 5:9). Even though the other nations rejected the Torah, Israel accepted it right away (see *M'chilta* 2, *BaChodesh, Yitro*).

In all these texts, the giving of the Torah is viewed positively. However, in a separate Rabbinic source, Torah is viewed as a burden to the Israelites, who had no choice but to accept it. Most likely this attitude echoes the reality of the teacher who lived at a time of persecution. According to this Talmudic text, God overturned the mountain of Sinai, like an inverted cask, and said to the Israelites, 'If you accept the Torah, it will be well; otherwise, you will be buried underneath'" (BT *Shabbat* 88a; BT *Avodah Zarah* 2b–3a).

The diversity of images reflected in our sacred texts, whether biblical or Rabbinic, regarding the Revelation has led many Jewish thinkers to doubt that the details of the momentous events at Mount Sinai could ever be recovered with certainty. The first-century Jewish historian Josephus, for example, admitted, "As to these matters, every one of my readers may think as he pleases; but I am under a necessity of relating this history as it is described in the sacred books" (*Ant.* III, 5:2). Other sages simply gave up on trying to figure out how it happened. The philosopher Judah Halevi (b. ca. 1080), concerned about the anthropomorphic images emerging out of the episode of God's Revelation states, "We do not know how the intention became corporealized and the speech evolved which struck out our ear, nor what the new thing God created from naught, nor what existing thing He employed."[7]

The Twofold Torah

Even though the exact way in which the Torah was given to the Israelites could not be ascertained, the Rabbinic concept of *Torah min hashamayim* (Torah revealed from heaven) remained a basic principle of Jewish theology for centuries. One of the cardinal assumptions of Pharisaic Judaism is that during the Revelation at the mountain, God gave to Moses, and through him to the entire people of Israel, two complementary Torahs (BT *Shabbat* 31a): the Written Torah (*Torah Shebichtav*), namely the Pentateuch; and the Oral Torah (*Torah Shebal Peh*), which includes all the interpretations and conclusions that Rabbinic sages later on deduced from the Written Torah, as well as all the regulations instituted by them (cf. BT *Yoma* 28a–b and Rashi).

This Oral Torah comprises the entire traditional teaching in the Mishnah, the *Tosefta*, and the halachic midrashim. The basic teachings of the Oral Torah were finally compiled by Rabbi Y'hudah HaNasi at the beginning of the third century because of the fear that all those teachings would otherwise be forgotten. This new compilation became known as Mishnah. The *Tosefta* and halachic midrashim were also subsequently written down.

Based on the assumption that God gave the twofold Torah on Mount Sinai/Horeb, Rabbinic sages went on to enlarge the scope of the specific texts that they believed were part of the Revelation in order to increase the sanctity of these texts. The Talmud asks, "What is the meaning of the verse: 'I will give you the stone tablets with the teachings [*v'hatorah*] and commandments [*v'hamitzvah*] which I have inscribed to instruct them'" (Exod. 24:12)? And it answers: "'Stone tablets' means the Ten Commandments. 'The teaching' means the Pentateuch. 'Commandments' means the Mishnah. 'Which I have inscribed' means the Prophets and the Writings. 'To instruct them' means the Gemara. All these texts were given to Moses on Sinai" (BT *B'rachot* 5a).

Some medieval commentators were more precise. For Abraham ibn Ezra (twelfth century) the word "teachings" (in Exod. 24:12) refers to the Written Torah, whereas "commandments" refers to the Oral Torah. He adds that all the commandments were given to Moses while he stood at Sinai. In his comment on Exod. 24:12, Rashi states that this verse refers to all the 613 mitzvot given at the summit, and this constitutes the entire code of Jewish lore. By attributing the entire Torah, both the Written and the Oral, to God, the Rabbis were able to establish a discipline that was binding on Jews for all time.

In the late Rabbinic times, most likely under the influence of Greek thought, it became unacceptable to maintain that God could be described in human terms and that God would speak actually using human language. So, the Sages tried to avoid all types of anthropomorphism from their theological discourse. We find this approach reflected as early as the Talmudic period. Thus, the Gemara states that only the first two commandments were revealed directly by God to the people; Moses mediated the rest (BT *Makkot* 23b–24a).

During medieval times, Maimonides (twelfth century) argued, "Speech was addressed to Moses alone." As for the Israelites, "they heard the great voice, but not the articulation of speech" (*Guide of the Perplexed* 2:33, Pines). The attempt to distance God from every type of anthropomorphism continued through the ages. According to Rabbi Mendel of Rymanov, a Chasidic master

who lived in the late eighteenth century, not even the first two commandments were revealed directly to the whole people of Israel. All that Israel heard
was the *alef*, namely the silent first letter of the Ten Commandments, which
starts with the Hebrew word *anochi*. For the existentialist Franz Rosenzweig
(1886–1929), the only thing the people experienced at the summit was God's
overwhelming presence. The words themselves came from Moses and received
their variant expressions in time. For Martin Buber (1878–1956), the soul of
the Decalogue is to be found in the word "you." Therefore, it can be heard at
any time, not only by those at Sinai, but also by those who feel they are being
personally addressed at all times. Furthering this thought, Abraham Joshua
Heschel argued, "Revelation is but a beginning, our deeds must continue, our
lives must complete it."[8] For Mordecai Kaplan (1881–1983), a naturalist, Revelation is basically a "discovery," and Sinai refers to "the original prophetic discovery of the moral law as the principal self-revelation of God."[9] Eugene
Borowitz maintains that Revelation is based on relationship and begins in
awareness of personal intimacy with God.[10]

The Eternal Torah

The Israelites believed that the Torah given to them at Mount Sinai/Horeb
and the covenant contained within it was intended for all generations to
come. As the Book of Deuteronomy asserts, "The Eternal our God made a
covenant with us at Horeb. It was not [only] with our ancestors that the
Eternal made this covenant, but with us, the living, every one of us who is
here today" (Deut. 5:2–3). It adds, "I make this covenant . . . with those who
are standing here . . . and with those who are not with us here this day"
(Deut. 29:13–14). This was understood as referring to all future generations.[11] The Torah was given by God and now belongs to all Israel for all
time, and Israel is obligated to preserve and transmit it future generations.
Deuteronomy proclaims, "Moses charged us with the Teaching [Torah] as
the heritage of the congregation of Jacob" (Deut. 33:4).

In Rabbinic times, *matan Torah* became a firm principle of the Jewish
belief system: Moses received the Torah at Mount Sinai and handed it to
Joshua; from Joshua it was passed down to the elders, then to the prophets,
and finally to the sages of the Sacred Assembly (*Pirkei Avot* 1:1). The concept
of *matan Torah* even entered the liturgy: at the beginning of the Torah reading in the synagogue, a Jew blesses God, "who has chosen us from among all
nations and has given the Torah."

Even though the Torah was given to the Israelites in the wilderness period, the Torah itself, the Rabbis believed, existed as an entity beforehand. In some sources, the early Rabbis suggested that Torah existed even before Creation. There is a Rabbinic teaching that God consulted with the Torah in order to create the world; the Torah was God's handmaid and tool by which God set the foundations to the deep, assigned functions to sun and moon, and formed all nature (*Tanchuma B'reishit,* # 1). Even after Creation, Torah remains as one of the three pillars of civilization, the other two being worship (sacrifices, during the Second Temple period) and good deeds (*Pirkei Avot* 1:2).

The pursuit and study of Torah are among the most important duties of all Jews. "The teachings of the Eternal [*torat YHVH*]," writes the Psalmist, "is his delight, and he studies that teaching [*uv'torato*] day and night" (Ps. 1:2). The Talmud emphasizes, "The study of Torah is equal to the sum total of all other mitzvot" (BT *Shabbat* 127a).

In modern times, the concept of Torah still plays an important role in Jewish identity. For example, the 1999 "A Statement of Principles for Reform Judaism" proclaims, "Torah is the foundation of Jewish life. We cherish the truths revealed in Torah, God's ongoing revelation to our people and the record of our people's ongoing relationship with God . . . . We are called by Torah to lifelong study in the home, in the synagogue and in every place where Jews gather to learn and teach. Through Torah study we are called to *mitzvot,* the means of which we make our lives holy."[12]

The Message

From the observations above we may conclude that the ancient Israelites believed that something transformative happened at the summit. Regardless of the contradictions or inconsistencies of the biblical texts regarding the Revelation of Torah, something very important took place in the wilderness of Sinai, which turned the people of Israel into a covenantal community. For centuries, Jews have looked back to that event with awe and gratitude. Like many other fundamental historical assertions of the Bible, the story of the giving of the Torah at Mount Sinai most likely contains a seed of historical accuracy underneath multiple layers of tradition. We do not know where and how it happened. We can only propose a possible scenario. Perhaps, those Israelites who came out of the Egyptian oppression decided to create a new national identity based on freedom and mutual responsibility, and covenanted themselves to their newly discovered God, *YHVH*, assuming a new discipline of life considered worthy of divine sanction. The details of the Revelation have been forgotten or became very elusive, but the event left an indelible impact on the Jewish memory. Sinai/Horeb became a concept. As Maimonides writes, "The true reality of that apprehension and its modality are quite hidden from us, for nothing like it happened before and will not happen after" (*Guide of the Perplexed* 2:33, Pines).

Reform Judaism has consistently made Revelation an ongoing process. As people of Israel, we look back to that mythical moment with pride and gratitude, but we open ourselves to new discoveries as we interact with nature and one another. Maybe Martin Buber's acknowledgment is a message we can all live with. In his book, *The Eclipse of God*, he writes:

"My own belief in revelation . . . does not mean that I believe that finished statements about God were handed from heaven to earth. Rather it means that the human substance is melted by the spiritual fire which visits it, and there now breaks forth from it a word, a statement, which is human in its meaning and form, human conception and human speech, and yet witnesses to Him who stimulated it and to His will. We are revealed to ourselves—and cannot express it otherwise than as something revealed."[13]

Thus, the question for us is not necessarily what happened at Sinai, but whether Sinai is in us and whether we are capable of responding to it.

9

Do the Ten Commandments Stand for "God and Religion"?

Marc Chagall (1887–1985), © ARS, NY. Moses, 1956.
Musee National message biblique Marc Chagall, Nice, France.

The Claim

The Ten Commandments, also known as the Decalogue, are one of the most familiar texts in the Hebrew Bible but also one of the least understood. People have many mistaken assumptions about it, such as that it stands for religion in general, that it prohibits "lying," that it contains the command "to love your neighbor as yourself." This chapter will discuss some of these issues by subjecting the texts to a critical examination in light of ancient Near Eastern material as well as other biblical texts. Whenever necessary, Rabbinic insights will also be used to elucidate some of the critical points.

The Decalogue

A close analysis of the Decalogue shows that it does not deal with "lying," even though it prohibits using the name of God in vain and false witnessing. Furthermore, only in the Christian Bible is the command "to love one's neighbor" (a quote from Lev. 19:18) placed together with some of the prohibitions of the Decalogue (see Rom. 13:8–10).

The greatest misconception about the Decalogue is that it stands for "God and religion." It is this misunderstanding that is the background of many of the modern controversies regarding the display of the Ten Commandments in public places in the United States. For example, in 2001, Chief Justice Roy S. Moore put a 5,280-pound monument containing the Ten Commandments in the lobby of the state supreme court in Alabama. In August 2003, the federal district court ruled that the monument violates the "separation of church and state" clause of the Constitution, and asked that the Decalogue be removed from public display. Judge Moore responded angrily, saying, "It is a sad day in our country when the moral foundation of our laws and the acknowledgment of God has to be hidden from public view."[1] When the associate justices of Alabama's Supreme Court asked him once again to remove the monument, Judge Moore became defiant and said, "I must obey God." Finally on August 20, 2003, the supreme court rejected Moore's appeal, and on November 13, 2003, a special ethics panel ousted the judge from his position.

The ancient Rabbis seem to have encountered a similar challenge by people who claimed that the Decalogue stood for the whole Torah. The Mishnah (*Tamid* 5:1) tells us that originally the Ten Commandments were included in the daily worship service during the Second Temple period. However, at some point in time, the Rabbis refused to adopt the recitation of the Decalogue outside of the Temple on account of the *minim* (heretics) who said that only these commandments were divinely revealed. Many critics assume that the reference to the "heretics" here is some early Christian group, but there is no way to prove it. The Rabbis' objection was based on their belief that the Decalogue was not more important than any other law in the Torah, because they were all commandments by God. So, the Ten Commandments, though extremely important, did not represent the totality of the Jewish religion and hence did not have a privileged position in Judaism.

Today, the lack of centrality usually assigned to the Decalogue is questioned by many biblical scholars who have yet to agree on the function that the Decalogue played in ancient Israel (see the end of this chapter). However, the Decalogue does have a major place in the Hebrew Bible inasmuch as it is *sui generis*; there is nothing else like it in the entire ancient Near East.

Uniqueness

To date, no collection of laws has been found in the ancient Near East that reads like the Decalogue, namely, a short set of directives formulated in terse language, covering both moral and religious matters. Scholars have looked for similar formulations in the literature of other cultures, but they have not found any exact parallels.

One contrasting example is from the Egyptian literature; it is a list found in the *Book of the Dead,* in which an individual declares his innocence before the tribunal of the god Osiris. This confession, formulated in the first person, is one of the most important sources of Egyptian social norms, and it reads in part, as follows:

> I have not committed evil against men.
> I have not mistreated cattle.
> I have not committed sin in the place of truth.
> I have not blasphemed a god.
> I have not defamed a slave to his superior. . . . (*ANET,* 34)

Though this list of infractions deals with some of the topics of the biblical Ten Commandments, the content and form of these declarations are very different from the biblical Decalogue, which lists ten commands directed to an individual.

In ancient Babylonia, the king made a similar declaration of innocence during the New Year festival:

> I have not sinned, O Lord of lands, I have not been negligent in respect to your godhead;
> I have not destroyed Babylon; I have not ordained (anything) to disrupt it;
> I have not disturbed Esagila [the temple complex in Babylon], I have not been oblivious of its rites;
> I have not smitten the cheek of the people under (your) protection,
> I have not occasioned their humiliation;
> I have cared for Babylon, I have not destroyed its walls.[2]

This text, too, is formally different from the Ten Commandments: it is formulated in the first person and deals primarily with cultic issues.

Additionally, there are some Mesopotamian incantations (in Akkadian called *shurpu*) that refer to a variety of sins, including murder, adultery, false oaths, and talebearing, and are intended to free an individual from every imaginable sin. These wrongdoings are formulated in the third person and pronounced by the priests. For example, "He entered his neighbor's house, had intercourse with his neighbor's wife, shed his neighbor's blood."[3] These too have been compared to the Decalogue, but in terms of form and content, this list of wrong deeds is different from the Ten Commandments because the statements do not read like directives addressed to individuals.

We are left to conclude that no other culture in the ancient Near East has produced a set of commandments that reads like our Decalogue. How and why these injunctions found their way into the Hebrew Bible is still unknown.

Terminology

In the Bible, the Ten Commandments are called *Aseret HaD'varim*, "the Ten Words" (Exod. 34:28; Deut. 10:4). In the Talmud, we find the expression *Aseret HaDib'rot* (BT *B'rachot* 12a; BT *Shabbat* 86b), where the word *dibeir* becomes a technical term for divine speech (see also Jer. 5:13).

The English word "Decalogue" comes from the Greek *deka* (ten) and *logos* (word). It was first applied to the text by a Greek church father by the name of Clement of Alexandria, about 200 C.E. However, why these commandments were numbered "ten" is unknown. In fact, if one were to count all the verbs in the text implying commandments, it would become clear that there are many more than ten in number.

In the Bible, the number ten, along with the numbers three, seven, and forty, has literary and cultural significance. In biblical times, a group of ten people appears to constitute a legal court. Thus, for example, in order to resolve the issue of inheritance, Boaz requests the presence of "ten elders of the town" (Ruth 4:2) to sit at the gate, which was the commercial and administrative center of any ancient Israelite town. Later on, based on this verse, a quorum (*minyan*) of ten men was required by Rabbinic law for public worship (BT *K'tubot* 7b). With regard to the Decalogue in the Bible, it has even been suggested, facetiously perhaps, that because we have ten fingers, it becomes easier to remember a group of ten commandments.

The Text

There are two main versions of the Decalogue in the Pentateuch: Exodus 20:2–14 and Deuteronomy 5:6–18. There are considerable differences between the two versions.

The Decalogue was given to the people of Israel during God's self-revelation on Mount Sinai/Horeb three months after the departure from Egypt (Exod. 19). Some scholars argue that the "Ten Words" in Exodus 34:28 originally referred to the so-called Yahwist Decalogue (where God is referred to as *YHVH*) in Exodus 34:10–26, which deals with some cultic matters and festivals, and only secondarily to the Ten Commandments found in Exodus 20, even though it is difficult to identify a distinct set of "ten words" in Exodus 34.

Following is the text of the Ten Commandments as they appear, in parallel, in Exodus 20 and Deuteronomy 5 (the boldface font indicates the differences):

Exodus 20	Deuteronomy 5
I the Eternal am your God who brought you out of the land of Egypt, the house of bondage.	*I the Eternal am your God who brought you out of the land of Egypt, the house of bondage.*
You shall have no other gods besides Me: you shall not make for yourself a sculptured image, or any likeness of what is in the heavens above, or on the earth below, or in the waters under the earth; you shall not bow down to them or serve them—for I the Eternal your God am an impassioned God, visiting the guilt of the parents upon the children, upon the third and upon the fourth generations of those who reject Me, but showing kindness to the thousandth generation of those who love Me and keep My commandments.	*You shall have no other gods beside Me. You shall not make for yourself a sculptured image, any likeness of what is in the heavens above, or on the earth below, or in the waters below the earth. You shall not bow down to them or serve them. For I the Eternal your God am an impassioned God, visiting the guilt of the parents upon the children, upon the third and upon the fourth generations of those who reject Me, but showing kindness to the thousandth generation of those who love Me and keep My commandments.*
You shall not swear falsely by the name of the Eternal your God; for the Eternal will not clear one who swears falsely by God's name.	*You shall not swear falsely by the name of the Eternal your God; for the Eternal will not clear one who swears by God's name.*
Remember the sabbath day and keep it holy; six days you shall labor and do all your work, but the seventh day is a sabbath of the Eternal your God: you	***Observe*** *the sabbath day and keep it holy,* **as the Eternal your God has commanded you.** *Six days you shall labor and do all your work, but the*

shall not do any work—you, your son or daughter, your male or female slave, or your cattle, or the stranger who is within your settlements—for in six days the Eternal made heaven and earth and sea (and all that is in them) and then rested on the seventh day; therefore the Eternal blessed the sabbath day and hallowed it.

Honor your father and your mother, that you may long endure on the land that the Eternal your God is assigning to you.

You shall not murder.

You shall not commit adultery.

You shall not steal.

You shall not bear false witness against your neighbor.

You shall not covet your neighbor's house: you shall not covet your neighbor's wife, nor male nor female slave, nor ox nor ass, not anything that is your neighbor's.

seventh day is a sabbath of the Eternal your God: you shall not do any work—you, your son or your daughter, your male or female slave, **your ox or your ass,** or any of your cattle, or the stranger in your settlements, **so that your male and female slave may rest as you do. Remember that you were a slave in the land of Egypt and the Eternal your God freed you from there with a mighty hand and an outstretched arm; therefore, the Eternal your God has commanded you to observe the sabbath day.**

Honor your father and your mother, **as the Eternal your God has commanded you,** that you may long endure, **and that you may fare well,** in the land that the Eternal your God is assigning you.

You shall not murder.

You shall not commit adultery.

You shall not steal.

You shall not bear false witness against your neighbor.

You [men] shall not covet your neighbor's wife. Likewise, none of you shall **crave** your neighbor's house, **or field,** or male and female slave, or ox, or ass, or anything that is your neighbor's.

Versions and Form

Even though the two texts in Exodus 20 and Deuteronomy 5 are very similar, they also contain significant differences. For example the fifth commandment dealing with the Sabbath begins with "remember" in Exodus but with "observe" in Deuteronomy; the rationale for keeping the Sabbath in Exodus is *imitatio dei*, whereas in Deuteronomy it is social and historical; and the last commandment in Deuteronomy adds to the list of coveted items a "field" not mentioned in Exodus.

The text of the Ten Commandments must have been very well-known in the past. Outside of the two versions that appear in the Pentateuch, the Decalogue is also found in the Samaritan Pentateuch (with a slightly different text); in the Nash Papyrus (ca. second century B.C.E.), where it is closely related to the Septuagint version of Exodus; and in a fragment among the Qumran material (ca. first century C.E.).

The traditional explanation of the discrepancies between the two texts is that God simultaneously uttered both of them in a manner incomprehensible to humans (see BT *Sh'vuot*; 20b; BT *Rosh HaShanah* 27a). Many modern thinkers, however, maintain that this repetition resulted from the work of scribes and redactors over a period of time.

Originally, the Hebrew Bible contained only consonants. Later on vowels were added to help the reader. Finally, special notes were added to allow one to chant the sacred text. In the case of the Decalogue, we have two different cantillation systems: The "lower" one, recognized by special symbols placed under the consonants, divides the Hebrew text into twelve regular verses. The "higher," attached to the top of the consonants, identifies each commandment as a unit, thus dividing the text into ten verses. Usually the "upper" system is used for public reading, while the "lower" one is reserved for private study.

The commandments vary among themselves with regard to their formulation as well:

1. At the beginning, God speaks in the first person, whereas in the rest of the statements, God is spoken of in the third.
2. Some commandments are short, and others are rather long.
3. Some carry motivational clauses, such as the one about the Sabbath (includes a rationale) and honoring parents (includes a promise); whereas others are formulated as simple direct orders: "You shall not."
4. Only two of the commandments are expressed in the positive form (i.e., Sabbath and honoring parents); the rest are in the second person negative form: "You shall not . . . ."

In the Pentateuch, God promulgates the text to the people as a whole (Exod. 19:25; Deut. 5:4). Using the second person singular masculine form in the Hebrew, God directs the commands to every individual, thus placing the responsibility on the shoulders of every single person.

Division

Historically there have been different ways of dividing the text into "ten" distinct commands, based on theology and tradition. The normative Jewish division is indicated in the parallel texts on pages 101–102.

Some scholars, including the philosopher Philo of Alexandria (20 B.C.E.–50 C.E.), the historian Josephus (first century C.E.), some Rabbinic sages such as Rabbi Yishmael (see *Sifrei* on Num. 15:31), and John Calvin (1509–64), the Protestant Reformer, consider "You shall have no other gods" as the first and "You shall not make for yourself" as the second commandment.

Conversely, St. Augustine (354–430 C.E.), the Catholic Church, and the Lutheran Church view "You shall have no other gods" and "You shall not make for yourself" as the first commandment; view "You shall not swear falsely" as the second; and divide the last one into two different commandments, "You shall not covet your neighbor's house" and "You shall not covet your neighbor's wife. . . ."

In traditional Jewish sources, the set of the "Ten Words" are also divided in terms of their content, the first half dealing with relations "between God and human beings" (*bein adam laMakom*) and the second "between one person and the other" (*bein adam lachavero*), with the commandment regarding honoring the parents playing the role of a bridge between the two sets.

Dating

It is not known when the Ten Commandments were originally formulated. The Bible attributes them to the wilderness period during the days of Moses. Scholarly views on the subject vary. Some place it in the Mosaic period (fourteenth to twelfth century B.C.E.), and others in the exilic period after the destruction of the First Temple (sixth century B.C.E.).

The Decalogue appears to be quoted by some of the prophets who date from the eighth and seventh centuries B.C.E. (e.g., Amos 3:1–2; Hosea 4:2; Jer. 7:9) and by the Psalmist (Pss. 50:7, 81:9–10), which shows that at least by the eighth century B.C.E., the Decalogue was known in some fashion as a set of norms.

The word "house" used in Exodus 20:14 and Deuteronomy 5:18, which would imply a sedentary background, could be understood as a physical house and, therefore, datable to the period after the entry into Canaan when the Israelites settled and built permanent homes rather than living as semi-nomads in the wilderness. Alternately, the term "house" could also refer to "household," and thus it could apply to any time, even during the Sinai period. As one scholar wrote, "There is no proof that the Ten Commandments are older than any other laws in the Torah. . . . Just as there is no proof of the special antiquity of the Decalogue, so are there no grounds for postdating it."[4] It is possible, however, that later editors expanded the various motive clauses that accompany some of the commandments.

Exegesis

One of the great misconceptions about the Decalogue is that the text is clear and the meaning of the original indisputable. The following analysis will show that the Decalogue contains a number of problematic references that make the understanding highly questionable.

First Commandment (Exod. 20:2; Deut. 5:6): One God
In Hebrew, the verb "to be" is rendered only by the personal pronoun "I" (not by "I am"), "you" (not "you are"), and so on. Logical subordination is often indicated by placing two sentences next to one another, with the first missing a verb. A good example is found in this commandment. It can be translated either as "I [am] the Eternal your God" or "[Since] I [am] your God . . . ." Here the second option is better because the first sentence does not have a verb, whereas the second does (i.e., "you shall have"). Thus the text should be understood as "Since I, the Eternal, am your God who brought you out of the land of Egypt, the house of bondage, therefore, you shall have no other god . . . ." However, in Jewish tradition this introductory statement is considered a commandment in its own right, establishing the basis for the belief in the existence of one God and the source of all divine commandments.

In this "word," God appears not as the Creator of the universe but as the Redeemer of the people of Israel. The text stresses that God is involved in human history and, as such, interested not only in the workings of nature but in the lives of individuals and nations as well. As it reads, the text does not claim that there is only one God; only that it is God who redeemed Israel from slavery.

Second Commandment (Exod. 20:3–6; Deut. 5:7–10): No Idolatry or Apostasy
The second commandment stresses God's absolute transcendence. God is incorporeal and requires exclusive worship. Cultic images made of stone, wood, or metal are prohibited. The fear is that an Israelite would identify the "image" or "statue" of God with the invisible Israelite God, *YHVH*, or, through a prescribed ritual, would venture to animate the idol and worship it. The explanation for this commandment seems to find a clear expression in Deut. 4:15: "since you saw no shape when the Eternal your God spoke to you at Horeb out of the fire."

The implication of the Hebrew expression at the end of the first verse, *al panai*, is not at all clear. Does it mean "in My presence," that is, at the Temple; or does it mean "in defiance of me," namely, "in addition to Me"? The question is whether we have here a monotheistic concept where God is alone and unique, or henotheism, which is the belief in one single god among many others. An argument can be made for both positions.

In the text, God is described as "an impassioned God," who requires exclusive worship from the Israelites. God's kindness is extended to the "thousandth generation," that is, forever. The guilt of one generation is visited upon another until "the third or fourth generation" (Cf. Ex. 34:6–7; Num. 14:17–18). This idea of inherited guilt was repudiated by the later prophets, who spoke of individual responsibility (Jer. 31:29–30; Ezek. 18:20; cf. Deut. 24:16).

Third Commandment (Exod. 20:7; Deut. 5:11): Misuse of God's Name
Ancient Israelites, like their neighbors, considered a name as part of the being that carried it. Knowing a name adds intimacy and helps form a relationship. Thus, when Moses wants to know God, he asks for God's name (Exod. 3:13). The third commandment forbids this misuse by stating *lo tisa*. What do these words mean? Literally, they can be rendered as "you shall not lift," that is, "utter [God's name]."

The last word in the verse, *lashav*, can be translated either as "in vain" (see Jer. 2:30; 4:30) or as "falsehood" (see Pss. 144:8, 144:11). What is the prohibited act here? Is it the frivolous use of God's name ("in vain"), or is it perjury ("swear falsely")? The answer is not clear. Therefore, various translations have been offered: "swear falsely by" (NJPS, Plaut), "not make wrong use of the Name" (NEB), "not utter the Name to misuse it" (JB). In traditional Jewish sources this commandment is understood to mean taking a false oath (see Ps. 24:4; Lev. 19:12).

The original idea may have been to guard against using God's real name, *YHVH* (which we do not know how to pronounce because of the lack of vowels in ancient Hebrew [see chapter 2]), in sorcery or magic. In Jewish traditional sources, this prohibition has been extended to unnecessary blessings (BT *B'rachot* 33a) and the casual use of God's name in written form. Some people unnecessarily write "G-D" or "L--d," even though the prohibition refers only to the name *YHVH* and applies only when it is used in a sacred context[5] (see Chapter 2).

Fourth Commandment (Exod. 20:8–11; Deut. 5:12–15): The Sabbath
This is the only commandment in the Decalogue dealing with a cultic issue. The text in Exodus differs considerably from the one in Deuteronomy. The motivational clause in Exodus is *imitatio dei*, that is, one is expected to rest on the Sabbath just as God rested after Creation. In Deuteronomy, two reasons are given. The first is humanitarian: "so that your male and female slave may rest as you do." The second is historical: redemption from Egypt. Also, in Exodus the command begins with *zachor* (remember); in Deuteronomy, with *shamor* (observe).

The origin of the Sabbath is unknown. Even though in the ancient Babylonian calendar certain days during the month, such as the seventh, were considered "evil days," the Israelite Sabbath is independent of the lunar/solar cycle and occurs every seventh day. The ideas of rest, joy, sanctity, and the sign of the covenant, which characterize this day, make the Sabbath unique in the ancient world.

The Sabbath commandment is one of the two that is formulated in the positive. Some scholars argue that the original wording was "Do not perform any labor on the Sabbath." This main prohibition, labor, is not defined in great detail in the Bible, even though some examples are given, such as not plowing and reaping (Exod. 34:21), not lighting a fire (Exod. 35:3), not gathering wood (Num. 15:32–36), and not doing ordinary work (Isa. 58:13). Rabbinic literature, however, provides a long list of thirty-nine main categories of work that are to be avoided on this day (BT *Shabbat* 7:2). The question as to what constitutes "labor" is still being debated in our own day.

Fifth Commandment (Exod. 20:12; Deut. 5:16): Honoring Parents
This commandment is formulated positively. In order to bring it in line with the other negative commands, some scholars have suggested that the origi-

nal text may have read: "You shall not despise/treat with contempt/curse your father or mother." However, there is no strong argument in favor of that hypothesis.

Exodus 20 and Deuteronomy 5 place "father" before "mother." There does not seem to be an intention of upgrading one against the other. In Leviticus 19:3, we find the reverse: "You shall each revere your mother and your father . . . ." It is interesting to note that these texts do not speak of "love," but rather of "honor" and "reverence."

The Deuteronomy text adds the words "as the Eternal your God has commanded you" and "that you may fare well." In this commandment a promise of well-being is given, rather than a reason for observing it.

Who is being addressed here? For some, the commandment is of a general nature and is directed to children of all ages. Others have argued that the purpose of the commandment is to foster respect for aging parents as well as to ensure that, even after their death, they would be honored by having someone care for their graves.

Sixth Commandment (Exod. 20:13; Deut. 5:17): Spilling Innocent Blood
This commandment stresses the sanctity of life. The rationale for the injunction may be derived from Genesis 9:6:

> The shedder of human blood,
>   that person's blood shall be shed by [another] human;
>   for human beings were made
>   in the image of God.

The Hebrew verb used in this commandment, *ratzach*, can be translated both as "kill" (e.g., Deut. 19:4) and "murder" (e.g., I Kings 21:19). Thus, the command can be translated as both "You shall not kill," and "You shall not murder." Even though *ratzach* covers accidental as well as deliberate killing, it is preferable to render it here as "murder" because biblical law does not prohibit the application of the death penalty or waging wars. Some scholars have argued that the original meaning of the command was to prohibit blood revenge on the part of a family member.

In medieval Rabbinic literature this law was applied, for example by Ibn Ezra, not only to cases of physical violence but also to talebearing, based on the argument that gossip is tantamount to murdering a person's reputation. On the other hand, the Rabbis affirmed the idea of self-defense, with some limits.

Sixth Commandment (Exod. 20:13; Deut. 5:17): Adultery
Marital loyalty is at the basis of this commandment. In biblical times, a man could marry more than one wife, but he was not allowed to engage in a sexual relationship with a married or betrothed woman. If he did, both were considered adulterers and punished by death (Lev. 20:10; Deut. 22:22). Thus, if a man, whether married or not, lay with a single woman, he did not commit adultery.

The reason why such a heavy penalty is imposed upon the perpetrators of adultery is because adultery is viewed as an affront to God and a direct violation of God's will (see Gen. 20:6, 39:7–9; II Sam. 12:13).[6] There are, however, no examples in the Bible of any adulterer or adulteress actually being put to death. In the Christian Bible, adultery is applied even in cases of intention to commit it (Matt. 5:28; Mark 10:11).

In Rabbinic literature, this prohibition is at times extended to include immoral speech, immodest conduct, and even association with people who scoff at the sacredness of family purity.[7]

Eighth Commandment (Exod. 20:13; Deut. 5:17): Stealing
This commandment affirms the right of possession. Even though some biblical (e.g., Gen. 40:15; Exod. 21:16) and Rabbinic sources (e.g., BT *Sanhedrin* 86a; *M'chilta*, Yitro 8; *Sefer Hahinnuch*, #36) limit the scope of this law to kidnapping other humans, the prohibition appears to be of a general nature and applies to all illegal appropriations—humans, animals, and goods.

No penalty is indicated here. In the ancient Near East, the death penalty was applied for stealing property (e.g., Laws of Hammurabi 22). In the Bible, however, this harsh penalty was used only in cases of kidnapping humans (Exod. 21:16) or stealing religious objects (Gen. 31:30–32). Stealing animals or objects carried monetary payment rather than death (Exod. 21:37, 22:3, 22:6–8; Prov. 6:30–31).

In Rabbinic law, this prohibition was extended to cover illegal acquisition of property by cheating, embezzlement, or forgery.

Ninth Commandment (Exod. 20:13; Deut. 5:17): Bearing False Witness
This prohibition deals with making false accusations, thus safeguarding the validity of the judicial process. According to biblical law, two witnesses are needed to convict the criminal (Num. 35:30; Deut. 17:6, 19:15). The penalty for making false accusations is not included in this text, but from other

sources (e.g., Deut. 19:16–21) we know that it was severe and included the death penalty.

In later Jewish sources, this law was applied to all forms of slander, defamation, and misrepresentation.

Tenth Commandment (Exod. 20:14; Deut. 5:18): Coveting
This commandment bans unchecked greed. There are a few notable differences between the texts in Exodus and Deuteronomy. First, not only is the order of the coveted objects reversed, but also Deuteronomy adds "field" to the list. Second, the meaning of the commandment is far from clear: whereas Exodus prohibits the act of *chamad* (covet) in both of its clauses, Deuteronomy has *chamad* in the first clause but *hitaveh* (crave) in the second. Are they the same? Some people make a distinction and state that even thinking about taking something away from another (namely, *hitaveh*) is punishable. Others maintain that the difference is only stylistic, and the two verbs mean essentially the same thing. It is also possible that *chamad* in Exodus means, "coveting and taking" (cf. Josh. 7:21; Ex. 34:24), and that the text in Deuteronomy is an interpretation by clarifing that *chamad* should only be understood as *hitaveh* ("simple craving in one's heart"). The Bible does not specify a penalty in cases of coveting.

In Rabbinic law, *chamad* requires action (*Mechilta, Bahodesh*, 8; *Sefer Hahinnuch*, #38). In other words, in order to be punished for "coveting" something, one has to act and do it. Simple desire does not constitute a punishable act.

Function of the Decalogue

The Ten Commandments represent the basic legal and moral foundations of Judaism. They do not replace or substitute for the rules and regulations that governed the Israelite society during the biblical times and beyond. They do not cover all the contingencies of daily life. For that, it is necessary to turn to other legal collections in the Bible, such as the Book of the Covenant (Exod. 21–23), the Holiness Book (Lev. 17–26), the laws in Deuteronomy (Deut. 12–27), and the entire collection of laws in Rabbinic texts—and even these are not comprehensive. Yet, the Decalogue in the Pentateuch stands alone as a remarkable collection of fundamental rules.

What role did it play in biblical times? Because of the paucity of reliable and clear sources in Scripture, scholars have offered differing views on this subject. Among them are the following: The Ten Commandments constituted Israel's pre-exilic criminal law; they were a series of prohibitions against entering a Yahwist sanctuary; they represented an educational and ethical ideal by which the individual Jew may be trained; they were the minimal imperatives essential to the maintenance of an ordered and wholesome society; they were the basic conditions for inclusion in the community of Israel; they composed the stipulations of the covenant between God and Israel. This diversity of opinions demonstrates that the function of the Ten Commandments is unknown.

The observation that the Decalogue did not include any penalties has led some scholars to argue that these statements represent moral injunctions rather than law. Furthermore, the content matter of these orders makes prosecution very difficult, if not impossible. For example, how does one bring a perpetrator to justice for "coveting"? What is the limit of "honoring" one's parents? The Bible does not offer details.

The thinking that would separate morality from law is foreign to biblical mentality. Even though Roman law makes a distinction between *jus* (human law) and *fas* (divine law), and ancient Mesopotamia contained separate collections for laws, wisdom sayings, and priestly handbooks, the Hebrew Bible does not distinguish between secular and religious law. All divine pronouncements are authoritative and binding, whether they are formulated as moral instructions or tribal orders. Thus, even though the Decalogue lacks the penalty clause, it is considered "divine law" simply because it is issued by God.

In Jewish tradition, the Decalogue is often viewed as the center pillar of the mitzvah system by which every Jew should live. As Rashi, the great medieval Jewish commentator (eleventh century) has indicated, "All the 613 commandments are included in the Decalogue" (on Exod. 24:12).

The "Ten Words," a foundational text in Judaism, remain a major building block of the moral structure of Judaism and, in fact, of the entire Western world. Even though they do not stand for "God and religion," and it is not always easy or possible to understand all the nuances of the injunctions, they will continue to be studied, analyzed, and applied to everyday life as important norms that govern modern societies.

10

Did the Israelites Really Conquer Canaan?

Raphael (Raffaello Sanzio) (1483–1520). (School of):
The Fall of Jericho. From the story of Joshua.
Fresco. Logee, Vatican Palace, Vatican State.

The Claim

The Bible claims that the land of Canaan was conquered by the Israelites after the Exodus from Egypt. The conquest is described in detail. This ragtag band of former slaves is able to perform wondrous acts of military daring in order to take control of the land. Can any of this narrative be supported by historical research? This chapter will examine the conquest texts from the Bible and explore the views of contemporary scholarship regarding their accuracy.

The Conquest of Canaan

The story of the conquest of the land of Canaan is told primarily in the biblical Book of Joshua. This book is divided in two parts: the first few chapters

(1–12) deal with the conquest, and the last chapters (13–24) cover the apportionment of the land to the twelve tribes of Israel.

After the death of Moses, Joshua, his assistant and successor, entered the land of Canaan from the eastern part of the Jordan River, conquered it militarily, and allotted territory to all the twelve tribes. The Book of Joshua reports: "Joshua conquered the whole country: the hill country, the Negeb [the region south of Judah], the Shephelah [the region next to the highlands of Judah], and the slopes, with all their kings; he let none escape, but proscribed everything that breathed—as the Eternal, the God of Israel, had commanded" (Josh. 10:40; see also 11:16, 21:43).

How did this incredible feat take place? After crossing the Jordan River, the Israelites established their first camp at Gilgal. Though this location has yet to be identified by archaeologists, the Torah places it "on the eastern border of Jericho" (Josh. 4:19). There they prepared to take over the country. The military campaign had three prongs: The first move was westward and included the destruction of the cities of Jericho and Ai. The second was toward the south; after defeating a coalition of kings led by the king of Jerusalem, the Israelites moved further and conquered other city-states, including Makkedah, Libnah, Lachish, Eglon, Hebron, and Debir. The third was toward the north and ended up with the destruction of the city of Hazor. These military intrusions were accomplished quickly, within five to seven years of entering the land (Josh. 14:7, 14:10).

Biblical historians are divided about the veracity of this account. Some accept it as is and argue that the political conditions were right for such a military conquest. They point to the following facts: In the thirteenth century B.C.E., the Assyrians were weak, and the Egyptians halted the Hittites of Anatolia at the Battle of Qadesh on the Orontes River (modern Syria) approximately 1275 B.C.E. At the same time, Egypt was being attacked by the "Sea People" from Crete and Greece, some of whom were known as Philistines, who established a beachhead in the southeastern part of the land. In Canaan there was great dissension among small city-states. It is under these circumstances that the Israelites entered the land. Furthermore, biblical historians argue that the military victory was gained through good planning and appropriate strategies. As one scholar wrote, "The Israelites strove to avoid frontal assaults upon Canaanite fortifications and, wherever possible, relied on deception, military cunning and diversionary maneuvers rather than open confrontation."[1] What they lacked in resources, they made up for in strategy.

Other scholars, however, have great difficulties with Joshua's narrative. First of all, it seems hard to imagine that the Israelites, who just came out of slavery and endured forty years in the wilderness with very little military experience, would have been able to attack and defeat strongly fortified cities as those mentioned above. Secondly, the internal biblical contradictions about the conquest (see below) make it highly improbable that it happened as described in the Book of Joshua. How does one decide between these two contrasting scenarios? Unfortunately, we do not have extra-biblical texts to consult for further elucidation. Our only source is the biblical account, and it is unreliable because of the conflicting information it contains about this subject. Not even archaeology can be of help to us, because most of the locations sited in the biblical text cannot be identified as yet, and those that have been located with certainty yield incompatible results.

Inter-biblical Problems

The Bible is not always consistent regarding the story of the conquest of Canaan. Though it provides a great deal of information, it is almost impossible to put all the data in historical sequence relative to their date of occurrence. A critical study of the relevant texts reveals a number of inconsistencies that have puzzled scholars for many years.

Among these inconsistencies are the following:

1. According to Joshua 10:36–37, Joshua destroyed the city of Hebron. Yet, according to Judges 1:10, the city was conquered by Judah.
2. Joshua 10:38–39 tells us that Joshua took Debir. However, according to Joshua 15:13–17 (see also Judg. 1:11–15), it was Othniel the Kenizzite who did it.
3. The capture of Jerusalem is recorded in Judges 1:8 and attributed to the people of Judah. Yet, II Samuel 5:6–7 states that it was David who conquered Jerusalem many years after that.
4. The Book of Joshua creates the impression that the entire country was conquered during a short period (see Josh. 10:40). Other biblical sources, however, indicate that it took much longer. In fact, the Book of Judges opens with the following query: "After the death of Joshua, the Israelites inquired of the Eternal, 'Which of us shall be the first to go against the Canaanites and attack them?'" (Judg. 1:1). This implies that the attack had not yet occurred. Even the Book of Joshua is com-

pelled to admit that when Joshua was "advanced in years . . . very much of the land still remains to be taken possession of" (Josh. 13:1), including Jerusalem (15:63), Gezer (16:10), Beth-shean, Dor, Taanach, and Megiddo (17:11).

5. The city of Shechem is not listed among the many cities conquered by Joshua (see Josh. 12:9–24). Yet, in chapter 24, we find a major covenant-renewal ceremony that took place in this city, with Joshua playing a key role. How did Joshua get into Shechem? This remains unclear.

6. The land that Joshua is said to have captured appears to be much smaller than the land he distributed among all the twelve tribes. How could this be?

These and other textual problems require us to rethink the entire sequence of the story of the conquest of Canaan. For this we need to turn to other disciplines such as archaeology as well as anthropology to help us recreate a possible scenario of the entry into or the emergence of the Israelites in the land of Canaan.

The Evidence from Archaeology

Most scholars place the conquest in an archaeological period called the Late Bronze Age, which spans circa 1550–1200 B.C.E. Assuming the Exodus from Egypt occurred approximately 1250 B.C.E., Joshua's military assaults would have occurred around 1200 B.C.E.

During the Late Bronze Age a number of cities were destroyed within Canaan. Among them are Lachish, Hazor, and Bethel, even though we are not told that Joshua took the last one. Some say that it must have been the Israelites who caused this destruction. This, however, is an assumption that does not rely on hard proof. In other words, archaeologists have so far not been able to find a document or material that states, "This place, called such and such, was conquered by the Israelites during the days of Joshua." Thus, we are left only with textual hints that the conquest took place as described by Joshua. These hints do exist, but they are few in number, and most of them unreliable. With the biblical texts offering conflicting information, researchers then turned to archaeology for possible answers. They, too, fell short.

The town of Hazor is a case in point. Yigael Yadin, the foremost Israeli archaeologist (1917–84) who excavated Hazor in the 1960s, wrote that the city was "suddenly destroyed and set on fire in the 13th century, no later than about 1230 B.C. On the thick debris of the mound of the destroyed Canaanite city, we found a new settlement, unfortified, poor and obviously semi-nomadic character."[2] He claims that the victors were Israelites. As to the date, he argues that Mycenean III B pottery, reflecting the presence of non-Israelites in the city, was found in the destruction layer but that this type of pottery was not used after 1230 B.C.E. Therefore, he assumes that the Canaanite city of Hazor must have been destroyed in the thirteenth century. But all these are assumptions, not clear proof.

Things are not so clear with regard to Lachish. David Ussishkin, who excavated this site in the late 1970s, states that the sudden destruction of Lachish, which would correspond to the period of Joshua's conquest, took place around 1150 B.C.E., or slightly later. But if this were the case, then Hazor and Lachish would have been destroyed almost a century apart.[3]

The capture of Jericho presents even greater historical difficulties. One of the oldest cities in the world and, at 670 feet below sea level, the lowest, Jericho is situated at Tell es-Sultan, by the Jordan River, north of the Dead Sea. According to the biblical story, the Israelites, coming out of Shittim, moved out in force. Having previously received important inside information from a Canaanite woman by the name of Rahab, they crossed the Jordan "on dry ground" (Josh. 3:17)—reminiscent of the crossing of the Reed Sea—and circled around the city seven times, the priests blowing horns as they marched. On the last day, the Bible tells us, "the people shouted when the horns were sounded. When the people heard the sound of the horns, the people raised a mighty shout and the wall collapsed. The people rushed into the city, every man straight in front of him, and they captured the city" (Josh. 6:20).

How did this incredible event take place? Setting aside for the moment the miraculous aspect of the legendary story, Abraham Malamat, an Israeli scholar, points to a similarity in military strategy in Roman sources. Citing Frontius, a Roman military expert of the first century B.C.E., Malamat relates that "a Roman general marched the troops regularly around the walls of a well-fortified city in northern Italy, each time returning them to camp; when the vigilance of the defenders had waned, he stormed the walls and forced the city's capitulation."[4] Malamat suggests a comparable approach in the case of Jericho.

Archaeological proof of the conquest of Jericho is difficult to find. John Garstang, a British archaeologist who worked in Jericho in the 1930s, concluded that the city corresponding to the period of Joshua was destroyed by fire about 1400 B.C.E. Kathleen Kenyon, another British archaeologist from the 1950s, dated the destruction of that level to 1550 B.C.E. Bryant G. Wood, an American archaeologist, argues that Garstang's assertions were correct. Based on newly found pottery on location, he maintained that the city was destroyed and its walls collapsed, perhaps by an earthquake, in the 1400s B.C.E.[5] However, the problem still remains: Joshua could not have conquered Jericho because the fortified city did not exist then.

The same argument applies to the city of Ai, about ten miles west of Jericho, which according to the Bible was captured by Joshua (see Josh. 8). Archaeologists claim that by this time, the city was already in ruins. It was destroyed about 2400 B.C.E. (The Hebrew word *Ai* means "ruin.") Yadin's answer is that the whole story is etiological, namely, it explains why the place was named as such. It does not have a historical reality for that period of time.[6] The title "King Jabin of Canaan, who reigned in Hazor," found in Judges 4:2, indicating that the city was alive and well even after Joshua, is also problematic. Yadin, citing Albright, dismissively states that this is "an editorial gloss by a later editor."[7]

All of these studies show that archaeology does not have the correct answer to our problem.

Various Solutions

Once critics realized that the biblical texts are inconsistent and archaeological evidence is inconclusive, they began to use anthropological methods in order to construct possible scenarios of the conquest, which would also take into account the little information we have from the Bible and archaeology. The following three are the most reasonable models:

1. **Military invasion**: According to this view, advocated in different variations by scholars such as Albright, Wright, Malamat, and Yadin, the Israelites militarily conquered the land, beginning in the thirteenth century B.C.E. It was a forced entry, first into the hill country and then the lowlands. However, most of these critics believe that the conquest in fact took much longer than what is recounted in the Bible. As Yadin views it, "At the end of the Late Bronze Age, semi-nomadic Israelites destroyed a number of major Canaanite cities; then, gradually and slowly, they built their own sedentary settlements on the ruins, and occupied the remainder of the country."[8]

2. **Peaceful infiltration:** This proposal was first made by the German biblical scholar Albrecht Alt in 1925 and was then adopted by several other scholars. According to this view, the conquest initially was not a military endeavor. Instead, various semi-nomadic groups gradually moved into the hill country of Canaan in order to find pastures for their herd. After a while, these people established alliances and were joined by others who were either in the land already or had come from as far away as Egypt. *YHVH* became the god of the new confederacy. The military actions followed and were completed around the time of King David in the tenth century B.C.E.

3. **Peasants' revolt:** Advocated by George E. Mendelhall and then by Norman K. Gottwald, this view rejects both the military scenario and the infiltration model. Instead, this model proposes that an internal uprising took place within the land of Canaan when poor peasants, overburdened by taxes and discrimination, revolted against powerful overlords who ruled a city-state system that functioned under the Egyptian hegemony.

All the theories mentioned above, with their different variations, attempt to present a plausible explanation of the conquest. Each one has its strengths and weaknesses. It is likely that the truth lies somewhere in between. It looks like the biblical texts have telescoped a number of events within a short period of time and attributed the entire enterprise to one leader, namely, Joshua. It is also clear that the archaeological evidence is at odds with the historical texts in the Bible. It makes more sense to assume, therefore, that the Book of Joshua (and Judges, in part) tells us about the formative stages of the Israelite nation in Canaan, compressing all kinds of stories. As one critic argued, maybe the actual situation included all the elements of the different theories above: some invasion, a gradual infiltration of outside tribes, and an uprising and confederation building by peasants trying to break free from the urban powers.[9]

The Message of the Books

The Books of Joshua and Judges portray an idealized version of the conquest of Canaan. This probably was also a religious interpretation of the events by people who represented the "official view,"[10] namely, the consensus of the intelligentsia of the Israelite society, like priests, Temple officials, and royal scribes during monarchic times, who ultimately gave shape to the traditional explanation. What ordinary Israelites believed cannot be recovered. Even the boundaries outlined in Josh. 13–21 are not historically accurate, but as one scholar argues, they represent "the territory that each tribe was responsible for conquering, not what it had already captured."[11] Critical study of the Book of Joshua shows that it is "a kind of extended etiology, written several centuries after the events it describes in order to answer the question: How did Israel get control of the Promised Land? The answer is a simple one: Yahweh did it, with Joshua as the principal human leader."[12]

The Emergence of the Israelite Nation

According to the explanation provided in the Bible, the Israelite nation emerged when the twelve sons of Jacob became the twelve tribes of Israel (Gen. 49 and Exod. 1:1–4). (Dinah, Jacob's daughter, did not have her own tribe.) Biblical scholarship disputes this assumption on the basis of the various changes in the tribal configuration before the monarchy (e.g., the Levites lost their status as a tribe [Num. 18:23]; the tribe of Joseph was divided into two, Manasseh and Ephraim [Num. 26:28]; the tribe of Dan moved north from their original location [Judg. 18]), the difficulty in relying on the historical claims of the Bible, and the lack of archaeological support. Most scholars now admit that, overall, the beginnings of the nation of Israel are shrouded in mystery. Various legends have come together in order to create a likely story that is full of accomplishments and triumphs of the Israelite people, but these do not represent historical truth.

The most likely scenario is that Israel emerged as a result of a loose confederation of various tribes. As one scholar imagines, "Some may have been immigrants from Transjordan, possibly even from Egypt. But basically Israel seems to have emerged from the 'melting pot' of peoples already in the land of Canaan at the beginning of the Iron Age. . . . Their lifestyle and material culture were essentially 'Canaanite.' Their sense of kinship with each other and separateness from other groups resulted from living in proximity with each other and from patterns of marriage and mutual support over time."[13] But they seem to have been unified by their faith in their God, *YHVH*, who, they believed, chose them from among the nations and promised protection in exchange for their ultimate loyalty.

From a theological perspective, however, the ultimate victor in the conquest is not the people of Israel or Joshua, but God. That is ultimately the message that the Book of Joshua wishes to impart. God conquered the land, and for that the Israelites owe God eternal gratitude: "The Eternal drove out before us all the people—the Amorites—that inhabited the country" (Josh. 24:18).

The Rabbinic View

In the Rabbinic period, the Sages assumed the historicity of the Book of Joshua. For the Rabbis, Joshua the son of Nun of the northern tribe of Ephraim was not only a great military leader but also a Torah scholar, who studied day and night (Josh. 1:8), even though, at times, he forgot many of the *halachot* (BT *T'murah* 16a). As "Moses's attendant" (Josh. 1:1), he was "filled with the spirit of wisdom" (Deut. 34:9), which made him faithful, humble, deserving, and wise (*B'midbar Rabbah* 12:9). He even received the Oral Torah directly from Moses, as his immediate successor (*Pirkei Avot* 1:1).

Several Rabbinic texts suggest that the conquest of Canaan may have begun before Joshua's time. He simply completed it. For example, commenting on the biblical verse, "God said: 'Lest the people repent when they see war'" (Exod. 13:17), one scholar writes, "According to an old tradition, there was an exodus from Egypt sometime before the Exodus under the leadership of Moses took place. This first exodus under the leadership of the sons of Ephraim is, according to the Midrash, referred to in I Chronicles 7:20–21, and alluded to in Psalm 78:9. The Ephraimites failed, and their undertaking resulted in disaster for them and their followers."[14]

The conquest story as found in the Book of Joshua reflects the early stages of the emergence of the Israelite nation in Canaan, and even though the entry into the land of Canaan did not happen the way it is described in the Bible, the conquest itself still constitutes a foundational myth of the Jewish people that claimed the land of promise through a military victory gained under God's direction.

11

Was King David for Real?

Michelangelo Buonarroti (1475–1564). David. 1501–1504.
Detail, three-quarter view of bust. Marble. Post–restoration.
Galleria dell'Accademia, Florence, Italy.

The Claim

King David is one of the most celebrated personalities in the Bible. In fact, the Books of Samuel and Chronicles set aside considerable amount of space to discuss his rise, accomplishments, and decline. He appears as an accomplished musician, a brave soldier, a conqueror of various lands, including the city of Jerusalem, the unifier of all the twelve tribes of Israel, an ideal king, and a messianic figure.

The role of King David has been a subject of fierce discussion among biblical historians. Some biblical minimalists have assumed that King David was a mythical personality like King Arthur who was created centuries after for ideological reasons. On the other hand, biblical maximalists have argued that the story of David is historically accurate. There is, however, also a middle ground. As Mortimer J. Cohen noted, "Each generation has shaped an image of David to appeal to its own mind and heart and its own need. This image is based in part on history, and partly on the hopes and yearnings of the Jewish people."[1] This chapter will examine the legends surrounding this great man and follow their development into the present time.

Did King David Exist?

To date, no mention of King David has been found in any ancient Near Eastern text. The name "David," which occurs more than one thousand times in the Bible, appears in Old Babylonian texts as *da-wi-da-nu-um* (early second millennium B.C.E.) or as *dwd(h)* in the Moabite language (ninth century B.C.E.).[2] The meaning of the name, however, is not clear. Some people have suggested that "David" may have been a title, like "general," but this has not been proven. One scholar suggests that it may mean something similar to "father's brother."[3]

The closest that we have come to confirm King David's existence is in the so-called "Tell Dan stele."[4] In 1993, Gila Cook, the surveyor of the Dan Project in Israel's northern Galilee, spotted an Aramaic text in some reused building stones. In the following year, two more fragments were discovered. These texts state that an unnamed king, in the ninth century B.C.E., perhaps Hazael of Aram-Damascus, defeated "[Ahaz]iahu son of [Jehoram kin]g of the House of David [*bytdvd*]." If there was a "House of David," meaning a king of the Davidic line who reigned in Judah, it is thus likely that there was a man named David who established the dynasty.

Some people have objected to the reading of *bytdvd* as *beit david* because there is no dot between *byt* and *dvd*. However, most scholars agree that "in light of Aramaic use, that is not compelling."[5] It appears likely that this is a sound reference to the existence of King David who set up the dynasty.

The Story of David the Man

King David lived in the tenth century B.C.E., possibly between 1000 and 960 B.C.E. The stories about him are found primarily in the Books of Samuel. As described in these chapters, his life story is divided into three parts: David's rise to power, consolidation of power, and David's decline.

David's Rise to Power

David was the youngest of eight sons of Jesse the Ephrathite of the town of Bethlehem in Judah (I Sam. 17:12–14). According to the Book of Ruth, he is a descendant of Ruth and Boaz (Ruth 4:22; see also I Chron. 2:12–15). A late source mentions two sisters: Abigail and Zeruiah (I Chron. 2:16). A shepherd (I Sam. 17:15; see also II Sam. 7:8) from an ordinary family, David was discovered by the prophet Samuel as the future king of Israel after Samuel and King Saul had a parting of the way.

There are two different biblical versions of how David came to know Saul. In one, he came to Saul's attention when he killed the giant Goliath, the fearsome Philistine warrior waging war against Israel (I Sam. 17). In the other, Saul needed someone to soothe his spirits when he was depressed (I Sam. 16).

After joining the royal court, David aroused Saul's jealousy. David was very popular with the public. In support of David, they chanted, "Saul has slain his thousands; David, his ten thousands!" (I Sam. 18:7). Saul thus attempted to kill him. David, with the help of his best friend, Saul's son Jonathan, escaped and became a fugitive. Living among the undesirables, he turned into a local bandit.[6] The Bible states that at this period of his life, "everyone who was in straits and everyone who was in debt and everyone who was desperate joined him, and he became their leader" (I Sam. 22:2). He took refuge with kings who were the enemies of Saul, extorted goods and services from people in Israel (I Sam. 25), and tried to stay away from King Saul, whom he refused to kill despite having many chances to do so. "The Eternal forbid," he said, "that I should do such a thing to my lord—the Eternal's anointed—that I should raise my hand against him" (I Sam. 24:7).

Up until the reign of David, the twelve Israelite tribes were loosely united. Some were clustered in the south, around the tribe of Judah, others in the north, centered around the tribes of Joseph. David was the first to unite all twelve tribes. First, being a member of the tribe of Judah, he gained the loyalty of his own tribal leaders. After Saul's death during a battle against the Philistines at Mount Gilboa (I Sam. 31), David went to Hebron in Judah and was made king "over the House of Judah" (II Sam. 2:4), acting most likely as a vassal of the Philistines. Soon after, the northern tribes recognized his leadership and anointed David in Hebron as king over all the tribes of Judah and Israel (II Sam. 5:1–3). He was only thirty-seven years old when he became the king of a united Judah and Israel (II Sam. 5:1–3; I King 2:11).

Consolidation of Power

During David's long reign, Egypt was weak and Mesopotamia was quiet. The Hurrians and the Hittites were not a threat. The Phoenicians in the north were friendly because of the commercial and political ties with Israel. David's only task was to concentrate his efforts on his immediate neighbors. He vigorously pursued them, gaining victories against the Philistines, the Moabites, and the Arameans (II Sam. 8). Thus he extended his territory to Transjordan in the east, the Sinai in the south, and the Mediterranean Sea in the west. He also became an able administrator and appointed new counselors to a variety of functions: Joab as commander of the army, Jehoshaphat as recorder, and Seraiah as scribe (II Sam. 8:15–18). Even his own sons became priests (II Sam. 8:18).

After earning the loyalty of all Israel, David quickly moved to consolidate his power. When Ish-bosheth, the son of Saul, was killed by his own people (II Sam. 4:7), all opposition against David was eliminated. Yet, David needed to rally all the tribes in a centralized place that he could call his own. So, he captured the city of Jerusalem from the Jebusites, made it the capital of the new kingdom, and renamed it "the City of David" (II Sam. 5: 9).

David's next move was to bring the Ark of the Covenant to Jerusalem. Since the time it had been captured by the Philistines during the early days of Samuel (I Sam. 4:11), the Ark had been transported from place to place, causing trouble for the local people, and finally lingered in the house of Obed-edom for a while (II Sam. 6:11). By bringing the Ark to Jerusalem, David was able to attain spiritual leadership as well. Even though his wife, Michal, the daughter of Saul, did not approve of all the celebrations, and in particular, of the way in which David kept "leaping and whirling" (II Sam. 6:16) before the Ark, it was placed inside a tent that was especially pitched by David following great celebrations. Michal wound up being barren (II Sam. 6:23), which the text views as a punishment for her criticism of David, thus eliminating the likelihood that a descendant of the line of Saul would ever take away the throne from David. All the sons of King Saul were killed either by the enemies of Israel or by their own people. Only Mephibosheth, Jonathan's son, remained, but he was crippled (II Sam. 4:4) and thus not a threat to David. In fact, David, in loyalty to his friend Jonathan, kept his son alive and hosted him at his table (II Sam. 9:13). King David was now the sole and undisputed ruler of all the twelve tribes.

Knowing that he was special to YHVH and having already built himself a sumptuous palace, David now wanted to set up a Temple to YHVH. But Nathan the prophet, speaking for God, informed David that YHVH did not need a sanctuary in which to dwell: "As I moved about wherever the Israelites went, did I ever reproach any of the tribal leaders whom I appointed to care for My people Israel: Why have you not built Me a house of cedar?"(II Sam. 7:7). Nathan added that the building of a holy temple would be accomplished by one of David's offspring: "He shall build a house for My name" (II Sam. 7:13). David accepted *YHVH*'s decree, and with the Ark of the Covenant placed in a special "tent" in Jerusalem, his city in time became known as YHVH's residence (Ps. 9:12).

As a crowning sign of his accomplishments, David also received a royal "covenant of grant" from God (II Sam. 23:5; see also Jer. 33:21), assuring him that he would always have a successor on the throne: "Your house and your kingship shall ever be secure before you; your throne shall be established forever" (II Sam. 7:16). He was viewed as a God-fearing king who "executed true justice among all his people" (II Sam. 8:15). Thus began the "royal ideology" that has influenced the rest of the Israelite history. Though various dynasties followed one another in the Northern Kingdom of Israel, from the time of King David until the destruction of the First Temple in 586 B.C.E. one of David's descendants always ruled in Judah.

David's Decline

The remaining years of David's life were troubled. He had an affair with Bathsheba (II Sam. 11–12), a married woman whose loyal husband, Uriah the Hittite, was a soldier during a battle with the Ammonites. When Bathsheba discovered that she was pregnant with David's child, David had Uriah killed and married Bathsheba, for which he was severely rebuked by the prophet Nathan. David acknowledged his mistake and repented. The child died, but Bathsheba conceived again and gave birth to Solomon.

Later, David's son Amnon raped his half-sister, Tamar (II Sam. 13) and consequently was killed in revenge by Tamar's brother, Absalom, who then quickly escaped to Geshur, in the Galilee, remaining there three years. When he was brought back to Jerusalem, Absalom began to solicit support among the people in order to depose his father (II Sam. 15). David fled Jerusalem to save his life, but with the help of his people he was able to put down the rebellion. However, during the course of the rebellion his son Absalom was killed by Joab, David's general. Even after this storm passed, the discontent of the northern tribes erupted into another rebellion, this time led by Sheba the Benjaminite (II Sam. 20).

In order to complete all the projects he had in mind, David set up a forced labor and undertook to take a census of the people, most likely for the purposes of military proscription and taxation; both made him extremely unpopular (II Sam. 24). But when a plague, interpreted by the people as a sign of God's displeasure with David's acts, devastated the country, the king repented, and calm once again was restored.

Toward the end of his life, David's son Adonijah claimed the throne and proclaimed himself king (I Kings 1:11). However, Bathsheba, supported by the prophet Nathan, prevailed upon the ailing David and ensured the succession of her son, Solomon.

David ended his days heartbroken, trying to warm himself in the embrace of a young maiden who provided some human warmth. But, as the texts states, "the king was not intimate with her" (I Kings 1:4). Upon his death, David was buried in Jerusalem. The Bible reports, "He reigned seven years in Hebron, and he reigned thirty-three years in Jerusalem" (I Kings 2:11; II Sam. 5:5).

The Books of Samuel are candid about the troubled life of David and report both the highs and the lows in his life but always maintain that he was the chosen leader of *YHVH*.

David's Story: History or Fiction?

How reliable are these stories about David? Without any recourse to external information, namely extra-biblical texts or archaeological data, it is difficult to assess their accuracy. Though many take them as historically correct, most scholars today see a particular agenda embedded in the narratives. For some scholars, the conflicts of David and Saul, for example, stand as a metaphor for the small state of Judah (represented by David) in conflict with the Northern Kingdom of Israel (represented by Saul). For others, the stories were used in order to support King Josiah's cult reform strategy in the seventh century. It is also possible to argue that the stories about David have a kernel of history but were embellished and often exaggerated in order to stress his outstanding personality. It is likely that these events about King David, which read like royal propaganda, were written by his supporters not too long after his death. Even though the throne he assumed justly belonged to one of King Saul's descendants, David's remarkable successes are attributed to *YHVH*'s expressed will. This is made clear by the prophet Nathan who, in the name of *YHVH*, assures the king: "I will never withdraw My favor from him [i.e., David's successor] as I withdrew it from Saul, whom I removed to make room for you" (II Sam. 7:15).

Royal propaganda of this kind is well-known in the ancient Near East. These kinds of texts chronicle the sovereign's accomplishments by ascribing them to the will of the gods. A good example is the *Cyrus Cylinder* (*ANET*, 315–16). This Akkadian text claims that Cyrus, the great Persian conqueror of Babylonia, in 539 B.C.E. captured the city of Babylon primarily at the request of the Babylonian god Marduk—an argument that the Babylonians would have understood as the deserved punishment for their sins against Marduk, but one that we in our days would find as totally preposterous and self-serving.

In the Books of Samuel, David is portrayed as a shrewd military strategist, a courageous warrior, an able administrator, a poet and musician, a man capable of making mistakes but taking responsibility for them, a loving father and friend, and a man utterly devoted to *YHVH*, for which he was amply rewarded by becoming God's elect and the recipient of a covenant: "David was successful in all his undertakings, for the Eternal was with him" (I Sam. 18:14).

The David Legend

Great leaders attract great legends. Over time, the reputation of David assumed mythic proportions. He was viewed as the ideal king who reigned during the golden age of the monarchy. After the destruction of the First Temple in 586 B.C.E. and sometime during the exilic period, people began to look back to him as the embodiment of all glory, and projected him into the future as a symbol of redemption from all oppressors. His name appears in a number of titles in the Book of Psalms. Fourteen of them connect the psalm with some event in David's life. In prophetic literature, David begins to assume messianic images. In a later text inserted in First Isaiah, the poet states, "A shoot shall grow out of the stump of Jesse [i.e., father of David], a twig shall sprout from his stock. The spirit of the Eternal shall alight upon him . . . he shall judge the poor with equity, and decide with justice for the lowly of the land" (Isa. 11:1–4). Similarly, Jeremiah prophesized, "See, a time is coming—declares the Eternal—when I will raise up a true branch of David's line. He shall reign as king and shall prosper, and he shall do what is just and right in the land. In his days Judah shall be delivered and Israel shall dwell secure" (Jer. 23:5–6). Living in Babylonia, the prophet Ezekiel proclaimed in the name of God: "I will appoint a single shepherd over them to tend them—My servant David. He shall tend them, he shall be a shepherd to them. I the Eternal will be their God, and My servant David shall be a ruler among them—I the Eternal have spoken" (Ezek. 34:23–24; see also

Ezek. 37:24–28). All of these passages refer to the future, when an extraordinary leader will bring peace and harmony among the people of Israel.

When the Persian king Cyrus issued his renowned edict in 539 B.C.E. enabling the Judean exiles to return to the Land of Israel, from which they had been cast out in 586 B.C.E., the people saw in it the beginning of God's fulfillment of all the promises made to them. The returnees reestablished their community, rebuilt the Temple, and were initially led by a Davidic prince by the name of Zerubbabel, a grandson of king Jehoiachin. David was now called the "anointed one" (*mashiach*) who will in the future vanquish all enemies: "I will make a horn sprout for David; I have prepared a lamp for My anointed one [*limshichi*]. I will clothe his enemies in disgrace, while on him his crown will sparkle" (Ps. 132:17–18).

During the fourth century B.C.E., when the Books of Chronicles were composed, the author reemphasized the glorification of the Davidic dynasty. But this time, David is portrayed as a completely righteous and utterly blameless man and king. Chronicles presents a whitewashed picture of David, in which his ascension to the throne is viewed as divinely decreed (I Chron. 11:1–3).

With regard to the death of Goliath, the narrator of Chronicles confronts a textual problem. Though I Samuel 17 tells us that David killed Goliath, II Samuel 19 reports that in reality Goliath was killed by someone named Elhanan son of Jaare-oregim the Bethlehemite (II Sam. 21:19). This discrepancy reveals the fact that even during the redaction of the Books of Samuel, significant historic events were attributed to David and taken away from unknown characters. Chronicles thus comes up with a creative solution. Trying to preserve David's reputation, it claims that "Elhanan son of Jair killed Lahmi, the brother of Goliath the Gittite" (I Chron. 20:5).

In the same vein, in retelling the details of the battle against the Ammonites during which King David slept with Bathsheba, Chronicles completely omits the episode (I Chron. 20:1–4), as if to suggest that David could not have committed such a terrible sin. Regarding the ill-received census during the reign of David, Chronicles assigns the blame to Satan: "Satan arose against Israel and incited David to number Israel" (I Chron. 21:1). No rebellions are mentioned in Chronicles. No palace intrigues regarding the succession. Only: "When David reached a ripe old age, he made his son Solomon king over Israel" (I Chron. 23:1). In order to reenvision David, Chronicles dispenses with many troubling elements present in the earlier David narratives.

In Rabbinic Literature

In Rabbinic literature, the reputation of King David is unprecedented. Having inherited the perspective of the Books of Chronicles, and living under oppression by the Seleucids (i.e., Syrian-Greeks) and later by the Romans, the sages began to view King David as an even stronger messianic figure who would ultimately deliver the Jews from their enemies. For example, even though the Bible portrays him as originating from an ordinary family, for the Rabbis, David, the "elect of God," had in fact royal beginnings.[7] He was, we are told, a descendant of Miriam, the sister of Moses. His great-grandfather Boaz was the same as Ibzan, one of the early "judges" of Israel. Even his father, Jesse, according to the Rabbis, was one of the Torah scholars of his time.

According to the Rabbis, David was always destined for greatness. He pursued justice and practiced charity: "When litigants came for judgment before King David, he would say to them, 'Draw up your claims.' In the event that one was found owing his fellow a mina [money], David would say to him, 'Give it back to thy fellow.' But if he could not do so, David would hand a mina of his own to the claimant and send him off in peace."[8]

The Rabbis often envisioned a David who was almost perfect. In the Rabbinic literature, David shunned sin and observed God's commandments. Even the evil inclination had no power over him. Thus, for example, in dealing with the Bathsheba affair, the Sages state that Uriah had given Bathsheba a bill of divorce before going to battle. Therefore, David did not commit adultery. David did not take Jerusalem by force but bought it from the Jebusites by paying them six hundred shekels, fifty shekels for each tribe. Even when he had made a mistake, people could turn to David and learn how to repent from his example.

David, the Rabbis insist, was a man of Torah. He spent all of his free time engaging in prayer and study. In kabbalistic literature, David assumes an even greater role. He is not only a scholar but one of the pillars of the universe. Thus, in the *Zohar*, for example, he is viewed as the fourth support of the heavenly chariot (*Zohar* 1:248b).

As a Messianic Figure

According to the Rabbis, the Messiah will be a descendant of King David and be called *Mashiach ben David* (the Messiah, son of David). In Rabbinic lore, based on Malachi's words, "I will send the prophet Elijah to you before the coming of the awesome, fearful day of the Eternal" (Mal. 3:23), we find an imaginary sequence of events: First Elijah, who never died but was taken into heaven by a whirlwind (II Kings 2:11), will arrive, announcing the appearance of the Messiah. Then, there will be two Messiahs coming, one after the other. The first Messiah, namely, "Messiah son of Joseph" (*Mashiach ben Yosef*), will make his appearance. This messianic figure will be slain in the battle of Gog and Magog (see Ezek. 38–39). Only after his resurrection will the real Messiah son of David (*Mashiach ben David*) come.[9]

Without creating a coherent and systematic approach to their teachings about the Messiah, the ancient Rabbis of the Talmud looked for signs that will usher the "days of the Messiah." Some sages believed the "son of David" will come only when even the pettiest kingdoms on earth cease to have power over Israel or when there are no conceited men in Israel (BT *Sanhedrin* 98a). For others, if and when Israel fully celebrates two consecutive Sabbaths, the Messiah will arrive (BT *Sanhedrin* 118b)

In a remarkable Talmudic passage, the Rabbis teach that there is a potential Messiah in every generation. According to the story, Rabbi Y'hoshua ben Levi met the prophet Elijah and asked him, "When will the Messiah come?" "Go and ask him," he replied. "Where will I find him?" Rabbi Y'hoshua asked again. Elijah said, "At the entrance" (perhaps of the town or, according to some, "of Rome"). So, Joshua went to see him and asked, "When will you come, Master?" "Today," he replied. When the Messiah did not come, Joshua confronted Elijah: "He lied to me, saying he would come, but did not." Then Elijah answered him: "He said, 'today' but only 'today if you hear God's voice' [Ps. 95:7]," namely, that the arrival of the Messiah is conditional upon the observance of the commandments (BT *Sanhedrin* 98a).

In the first century C.E., the early Christians maintained that the Messiah had come in the person of Jesus. The rest of the Jews rejected this claim, arguing that the Messiah is expected to reestablish Jewish sovereignty over the Land of Israel, gather in all the exiles, and establish a perfect society. Jesus did not fulfill these requirements. In response, Christians said that the Messiah would return at the end of time. Because there was no evidence for this second claim in the Bible or any of the sacred texts, many Jews refused to accept Jesus as the Messiah.

The emergence of individuals who claimed to be the long-awaited Messiah, before and after Jesus, left Jews uneasy. Ancient historians have identified various pretenders: Judah ben Ezekias (sixth century C.E.), Simon (6 C.E.), Athronges (6 C.E.), Menachem ben Judas (ca. 66 C.E.), Simon ben Giora (ca. 68 C.E.). In 133 C.E., Bar Kochba led a rebellion against Rome, and during the early stages of his victories, he was declared Messiah by no other than the great Rabbi Akiva. However, Bar Kochba was defeated, and Jews paid a heavy price. During the seventeenth century, Shabbetai Zvi was declared Messiah in the Ottoman Empire, but he too failed and ultimately converted to Islam, disappointing thousands of Jews who thought redemption was within reach. The fates of messianic pretenders David Reubeni (sixteenth century, Arabia), Jacob Frank (eighteenth century, Ukraine), and others were not less tragic for the Jewish communities and reinforced a skepticism about the possibility of a Messiah. This is reflected in the teachings of Rabbi Yochanan ben Zakkai (first century C.E.), who taught, "If you have a plant in your hand and someone comes and says the Messiah has arrived, plant the sapling first, and then go out to greet the Messiah" (*Avot D'Rabbi Natan* B31). He seems to be saying, the coming of the Messiah is far off; so go and do your daily work now.

In Medieval Times

The belief in the coming of the Messiah was strongly maintained in medieval times. According to Saadyah Gaon (Saadyah al Fayyumi, the Gaon of Sura in Babylonia [892–942]), at the end of time, the Messiah, the son of David, will come, deliver Jerusalem from the enemy, and settle there with his own people.[10] For Joseph ibn Zaddik, the twelfth-century judge of the Jewish community in Cordova, Spain, when the Messiah comes, all the pious people of the Jewish people will be brought back to life and will never die again.[11] Even a rationalist such as Maimonides states in his Thirteen Articles of Faith, "We must believe as a fact that the Messiah will come. . . . The king of Israel will come only from the House of David and the seed of Solomon. Anyone who rejects this family denies God and the prophets" (*Chelek, Sanhedrin* 10).

In his famous book *Mishneh Torah*, Maimonides describes what will happen during the days of the Messiah: "In the future, the King Messiah will arise and renew the David dynasty, restoring it to its initial sovereignty. He will rebuild the Temple and gather in the dispersed remnant of Israel. Then, in his days, all the statues will be reinstituted as in former times. We will offer sacrifices and observe the Sabbatical and Jubilee years according to all their particulars set in the Torah" (*Mishneh Torah* 14, Kings 11:1). However, he adds, "One should not entertain the notion that in the days of the Messiah any element of the natural order will be nullified, or that there will be any innovation in the work of Creation. Rather, the world will continue according to its pattern" (12:1).

In the opinion of Joseph Albo (1380–1444), "Every adherent of the Law of Moses is obliged to believe in the coming of the Messiah." However, this belief "is not such a fundamental principle that he who denies it should be called an infidel."[12] In reality, the difference between Maimonides and Albo is not about the validity of this and other dogmas but in the way in which they are classified and graded.[13]

In Modern Times

Many Jews today, including Orthodox and many Conservative Jews, reaffirm their belief in the coming of a personal Messiah at the end of time and, in fact, daily praise God "who in love will bring a redeemer [go-eil] to their children's children for God's name's sake." Additionally, they pray that God should "speedily cause the offspring of David, Your servant, to flourish, and lift up his glory by your divine help because we wait for your salvation every day."

On June 12, 1994, when the charismatic Lubavitcher rebbe Menachem Mendel Schneerson (b. 1902) died in Brooklyn, New York, some of his followers considered him a Messiah and started to proclaim his imminent resurrection. They even prayed, "May our Master, Teacher and Rabbi, the king Messiah, live forever." However, the majority of them and the rest of the Orthodox Jews around the world rejected the assertion that Schneerson is a Messiah.[14]

Early Reform Jews in Germany were not comfortable with the notion of an individual Messiah, considering it irrational. Thus, for example, in the Frankfort Platform of 1842, they declared, "A Messiah who is to lead the Israelites back to the land of Palestine is neither expected nor desired by us; we know no fatherland except that to which we belong by birth or citizenship."[15] Instead, they spoke of "the Messianic Age." As expressed in the Pittsburgh Platform of 1885, "We recognize in the modern era of universal culture of heart and intellect the approach of the realization of Israel's great Messianic hope for the establishment of the kingdom of truth, justice, and peace among all men."[16] Since that time, the concept of messianic age rather than an actual messianic figure has, so far, remained predominant in the teachings of Reform Judaism.

In the Jewish community, there are a few thinkers who reject the idea of messianism altogether. For instance, Rabbi Sherwin Wine, the founder of Humanistic Judaism, once declared, "Listening to the Jesus people [Messianic Jews] or the Lubavicher Rebbe people, it's the same thing. There is a figure sent by God who is going to rescue us. Therefore, I find all messianic thinking dangerous. I think it's one of the dangerous ideas that came out of the Jewish past. Because messianism is utopianism, and utopianism is a very dangerous thing . . . . If you wanted utopian goals, then you're going to be disappointed and frustrated all the time. The way to live the life of courage is to have goals that are realistic and appropriate."

It is remarkable how the life of David, a charismatic leader of old, was enriched through legends over the centuries. From being a local bandit to achieving messianic images, David embodied all the aspirations of the Jewish people in hopes of better times. It appears that no other person, except David, was better suited to inspire such an accomplishment.

12

Did a Whale Swallow Jonah?

Zeldis, Malcah, b. 1931 © ARS, NY.
Jonah and the Whale. Private collection.

The Claim

There is a song for preschoolers entitled "Jonah and the Whale" that is sung
to the tune of "London Bridges."

Jonah was swallowed by a whale
By a whale
By a whale.
Jonah was swallowed by a whale
Swallowed whole.

Similarly, Father Mapple, in Herman Melville's book *Moby Dick* (chapter 9) composed a hymn that begins with the following words:

The ribs and terrors in the whale,
Arched over me a dismal gloom,
While all God's sun-lit waves rolled by,
And lift me deepening down to doom.

These two examples are part of a long-standing popular tradition in the Western world that tells the story of the biblical prophet Jonah being swallowed by a whale, wherein he lived for three days and three nights and composed a prayer of deliverance. This story is also reflected in a variety of art forms, such as paintings, sculptures, poems, and books.[1]

The tale of the prophet Jonah has captivated generation after generation. Yet it raises many questions. Is it just a folktale, or could it really have happened? What is the basis of this tradition? Where did it come from? And how did it develop?

The Biblical Story

Found among the twelve Minor Prophets of the Hebrew Bible, the Book of Jonah is just four chapters long. It tells the story of Jonah, the son of Amittai, who receives word from God that he must go to the city of Nineveh, the capital of Israel's mightiest enemy, the Assyrians, in order to announce its destruction because of their corruption and moral turpitude. Jonah, however, refuses to do God's bidding and attempts to flee in the opposite direction. At the city of Joppa, today's Jaffa, he rents a boat leaving for Tarshish. During the voyage, a storm breaks out, threatening to wreck the boat. The sailors try their best to control the vessel but to no avail. Finally, they cast lots to determine who is responsible for endangering the lives of so many aboard the ship. Jonah, who called himself a "Hebrew," is identified as the culprit. Once discovered, he asks that he be thrown into the roaring sea. The kindhearted sailors first refuse his request and pray to the Israelite God, "Oh, please, Eternal, do not let us perish on account of this man's life. Do not hold us guilty of killing an innocent person!" (Jon. 1:14). At the end, they heave him overboard, and the sea miraculously calms down. The awestricken crew then acknowledges the God of Israel and offers sacrifices in gratitude.

In the water, God produces a large fish that swallows Jonah. He lives in its belly for three days and three nights and recites a prayer; thereafter, at God's command, the fish spews Jonah out onto an unspecified dry land. Now Jonah realizes that there is no escape from God and obediently accepts

God's second charge by marching through the streets of Nineveh, proclaiming the divine warning. To his utter surprise, the Ninevites take his words at heart and repent from their evil ways, thus averting God's calamitous decree.

The people's change of heart, however, angers Jonah, who expected the destruction of the city and its inhabitants. Instead of an act of justice, he witnesses an act of divine compassion. This is more than he can bear. In response, he says he wants to die.

Jonah stations himself east of the city, resting under a booth he has built. God creates a gourd that grows overnight to provide some shade. This pleases Jonah. But when the gourd withers, Jonah suffers a great discomfort, and again he prays for death. At this point God tells Jonah, "You cared about the plant, which you did not work for and which you did not grow, which appeared overnight and perished overnight. And should not I care about Nineveh, that great city, in which there are more than a hundred and twenty thousand persons who do not yet know their right hand from their left, and many beasts as well!" (Jon. 4:10–11). The answer is obviously, yes. God does care for everyone, including the animals. The story abruptly ends here. We do not know, however, whether or not Jonah accepts God's rebuke. This is left to the imagination of the readers.

History or Not?

As the text makes clear, this story is not written by Jonah but about Jonah. It is even anti-Jonah. The entire episode is told in the third person. Written or edited between the fifth and third century B.C.E., the book also contains, according to one biblical scholar, two complementary legends: the first concerns Jonah's resistance to God's commission to summon Nineveh to repentance, and the other, Jonah's dissatisfaction with God's mercy. To these was added a mythological motif of a human being swallowed and vomited out by a great sea monster.

The story of Jonah contains a number of inaccuracies that prevent it from being viewed as a historical text, as follows:

1. The title of the king of Assyria, here an unidentified ruler, was not "the king of Nineveh" (Jon. 3:6). His official title, according to archaeological evidence, was "the king of Assyria" (e.g., Tiglat-Pileser, 1114–1076 B.C.E. [ANET, 274]; Adad-Nirari, 810–783 B.C.E. [ANET, 281]; Esarhaddon, 680–669 B.C.E. [ANET, 289]).

2. The city of Nineveh was, in reality, much smaller than the claimed "three days' journey in breadth" (Jon. 3:3). Assuming Jonah walked twenty-five miles a day, the city would have been seventy-five miles from one end to another. It is highly unlikely that it was that big. During the time of the Assyrian king Sennacherib (704–681 B.C.E.), the circuit of the city's walls measured only about eight miles. All Jonah had to do was walk three miles or so, and he would have found himself in downtown Nineveh!

3. The custom of issuing decrees by the king (Jon. 3:7–9), in consultation with high officials of the kingdom, is neither Israelite nor Assyrian. The practice does appear, however, in connection with the Persian kings.

4. The psalm inserted into chapter 2, either by the author or by a later editor, reads like a prayer of gratitude after deliverance ("You brought my life up from the pit" [Jon. 2:7]) rather than one recited during an ordeal.

5. The assumption that Jonah could be swallowed whole by a great fish, live in it for three days and three nights, and even compose a prayer there strains the credulity of most readers.

6. It is also unlikely that the Assyrians would have repented because of an Israelite prophet's appeal. As a critic says, this is "a more astounding miracle that the miracle of the fish!"[2]

Most likely, Jonah is not an historical account but a legend that tries to teach a lesson. One scholar refers to the story of Jonah as a "parody" that depends on "reversals and burlesques."[3] Even though these "historical" details may or may not have been his primary concern, the author or editor apparently did want to ground his parable in a setting that had at least a semblance of historicity. He therefore chose as an example of a wicked city the city of Nineveh, the capital of Israel's archenemy, the Assyrians, which was destroyed by the Medes in 612 B.C.E. He also identified as his main character a little-known prophet who lived in the days of Jeroboam II, king of Israel, in the eighth century B.C.E. (see II Kings 14:25). He portrayed the protagonist not as a hero, but as an antihero, a narrow-minded nationalist whose concern was the well-being of Israel alone.

Fish or Whale?

The Bible tells of Jonah being swallowed by a large fish. But what kind of a fish was it? Was it just a big fish or, specifically, a whale? The biblical text states:

The Eternal provided a huge fish [*dag gadol*] to swallow Jonah; and Jonah remained in the fish's belly [*bim'ei hadag*] three days and three nights. Jonah prayed to the Eternal his God from the belly of the fish [*mim'ei hadagah*]. (Jon. 2:1–2)

Then:

The Eternal commanded the fish [*ha-dag*], and it spewed Jonah upon dry land. (Jon. 2:11)

This text mentions not a whale but a big fish. Similarly, the Aramaic translation has *nuna rabba*, and the Vulgate, the Latin translation, uses the expression *piscem grandem*, both meaning "big fish." However, when Matthew quotes this biblical passage in the Christian Bible, he states:

Just as Jonah spent three days and three nights in the belly of the whale [the Greek word here is *ketos*; in Latin, *in ventre ceti*], so will the Son of Man spend three days and three nights in the bowels of the earth. (Matt. 12:40, NAB)

This word *ketos*, used by Matthew, is the same word found in the Septuagint, the Greek translation of the Hebrew Bible. It renders Jonah's *dag gadol* as a *ketos megalos* (big fish). Similarly, when Josephus, the first-century-C.E. Jewish historian, retells the story of Jonah, he writes, "It is related that Jonah was swallowed down by a whale [*ketos*]" (*Ant.* IX, 10:2, 208). There are thus two words: one is *dag*, and the other *ketos* (in Latin, *cetus*). *Dag* means "fish" in Hebrew. But the translation of the Greek word *ketos* remains unclear.

Christian Bible translations of Matthew 12:40 use different English words for *ketos*. Some have "whale" (e.g., King James, RSV, NAB, ASV), others have "sea monster" (e.g., NRSV, NEB, Amplified Bible) or "sea creature" (e.g., ISV), and many have simply a "big/great fish" (e.g., NLT, CEV, Darby, GNB).

The generic word for "fish" in the Greek Christian Bible is *ichtus*. *Ketos* is a name applied to the genus, not to any individual fish. *Ketos* can mean a "huge fish," "sea monster," or "whale." In Greek mythology, Ketos was known as the daughter of Gaia, the land goddess, and Pontus, the ancient sea god. Personifying the dangers of the sea, Ketos was identified as a sea monster that was married to Phorys, the sea god. In Greek art, she is often drawn as a serpentine dragon, not as a whale. Most likely, the word *ketos* went through various developments. As one commentator points out, it "exhibits a pro-gressively larger size, changing from Homer's seal to Pliny's whale."[4]

It is not clear, therefore, if Matthew, the Septuagint, and Josephus viewed Jonah's fish as a sea monster or as a whale. However, when the Bible was translated into English, the King James Version of 1611 used the term "whale" in Jonah 2:1, most likely because a whale was the biggest fish known to the editors. For them the "big fish" had to be a "whale." Besides, at that time, people did not recognize the difference between a fish and a whale. A whale is a placental mammal and not a fish. This was not understood until the eighteenth century. Herman Melville (1819–1891), in his book *Moby Dick* (chapter 32, "Cetology"), points out that Carl Linnaeus (1707–1778), the Swedish botanist, did not distinguish whales from fish until 1776. How-ever, the pattern set up by King James was dominant. Ever since, the idea of Jonah being swallowed by a "whale" has captured the imagination of many people and has remained alive up until the present time.

A Fish Swallowing a Human?

Can a whale swallow a human being? Pious interpreters of the Hebrew Bible, in an attempt to provide a "rational" explanation of the incident, have come up with a variety of suggestions, including that Jonah was really picked up by a ship named "Big Fish," that he spent the night in an inn called "The Whale" or in a bathing station, or even that he dreamed the whole incident.[5]

Many scholars disagree with this approach. Marine biologists note that whales are cetacean (from the word *ketos*) mammals of two major types. Some are baleen whales, the so-called mustached whales, which include blue, hump-back, gray, bowhead, and so on. These have gullets that are only a few inches across and a strainer in their mouth. These whales cannot swallow humans. The other type, the toothed whales, include the killer, beluga, sperm, and so on. Among them, the sperm whale (*physeter catodon*) is the only one capable of swallowing a human being whole, but no such case has been documented in spite of many such stories that are found in the literature. Lastly, these whales, not known to attack humans, are primarily found in large oceans, perhaps in the Gulf of Mexico, but not in the Mediterranean Sea, where the story is placed.

Some medieval Jewish commentators were uncomfortable with the idea of a human being living safely inside a sea creature. For example, Radak (Rabbi David Kimhi, 1160–1263, of Narbonne, southern France) stated that it was "a great miracle" and that the big fish was created especially for this purpose at the time of Creation (on Jon. 2:1–2). Similarly, Rabbi Abraham ibn Ezra (1092–1167) of Tudela, Spain, argued, "A human being does not have the strength to live inside a fish, even for an hour. This was a miracle created by God" (on Jon. 2:1 and 2:2).

Given the stories that were prevalent in the mythologies of the Mediterranean basin about the role of the primordial sea monsters, with their ability to swallow humans, Jonah's "great fish" is most likely a legendary detail used by the author/editor to heighten the dramatic impact of the story. Ultimately, he wanted to make a point, and he used every literary tool at his disposal, including some that were totally incredulous.

Related Legends

Modern Hebrew does not have a proper name for "whale," but uses the biblical word *livyatan*, a word that comes from the Bible, referring to the mythological "Leviathan," the sea monster that personified the watery chaos mentioned in many of the ancient Near Eastern texts. Etymologically, the word *livyatan* means "twisted one," and was thought of as a giant serpent. Often, it is used interchangeably with the biblical words *tanin* and *rahav*, both meaning some kind of a dragon.

In prebiblical myths, during a primordial combat, the Canaanite god Baal (in other texts, it is the goddess, Anat, Baal's wife) defeats the forces of the sea, represented by "Yam" (meaning "sea"). In the Bible this victory is attributed to God: "It was You who crushed the heads of the Leviathan" (Ps. 74:14). In the long description of the Leviathan in Job 40:25–41:26, the sea monster appears like a crocodile:

> Can you draw out Leviathan by a fishhook?
> Can you press down his tongue by a rope?
> Can you put a ring through his nose,
> Or pierce his jaw with a barb? (Job. 40:25–26).

According to the prophet Isaiah, God will eventually defeat Leviathan:

> In that day the Eternal will punish,
> With God's great, cruel, mighty sword
> Leviathan the Elusive Serpent—
> Leviathan the Twisting Serpent;
> He will slay the Dragon [*tanin*] of the sea. (Isa. 27:1)

The monster vanquished by God in Psalm 74 (cf. Isa. 51:9) represented the primordial chaos. Here in Isaiah 27, it stands for the forces of evil in the present world.

Ancient people living around the Mediterranean basin believed that sea monsters roamed around freely, attacking and even swallowing human beings. In Greek mythology, in order to terrorize the city of Troy, Poseidon sends a sea monster, a *ketos*, which swallows Herakles, the hero. But in an attempt to save Hesione, the princess chained to the rocks as a sacrifice to the monster, Herakles killed this monster by hacking at its innards while living in it for three days. Furthermore, in a Corinthian red-ground crater (ca. sixth century B.C.E.) found at the Museum of Fine Arts in Boston, Massachusetts, Herakles is seen attacking a toothed serpentine dragon, most certainly a *ketos*. Also, in the myth of Jason and Argonauts, Jason is swallowed by a sea monster.

In Jewish tradition, the sea monster of Jonah is of great interest to the biblical commentators. Noting the difference between Jonah 2:1a, where the fish is called *dag*, in the masculine, and Jon. 2:1b, where it is referred to as *dagah*, in the feminine, the medieval commentator Rashi (eleventh century, France) remarks that the fish that swallowed Jonah was a male, and Jonah was able to stand in it comfortably upright, and because he was so much at ease, he felt no need to pray. At that point God asked the "fish" (*dag*) to spew him out into the mouth of a female fish (*dagah*) that was pregnant. It was inside her that Jonah felt constrained and finally compelled to utter a prayer (on Jon. 2:1). To explain the change from *dagah* of Jonah 2:2 back to *dag* again in Jon. 2:12, Metsudat David (Rabbi David Altschuler, eighteenth-century Galician exegete) adds that after the prayer, the female fish (*dagah* of Jon. 2:2) spewed him into the mouth of a male fish (*dag* of Jon. 2:11).

In his collection of Jewish legends, Louis Ginzberg adds other details: The fish that harbored Jonah was so large that "the prophet was as comfortable inside of him as in a spacious synagogue. The eyes of the fish served Jonah as windows, and, besides, there was a diamond, which shone as brilliantly as the sun at midday, so that Jonah could see all things in the sea down to its very bottom."[6]

In the Apocryphal Book of Tobit, there is a story about a man named Tobias, the son of Tobit who "went down to wash himself. A fish [in Greek, *ichtus*] leaped up from the river and would have swallowed the young man, and the angel said to him, 'Catch the fish.' So the young man seized the fish and threw him up on the land" (Tob. 6:2–3, RSV).

The Koran, the holy book of Islam, makes reference to Jonah and his fish. It writes, "Then the big fish did swallow him" (Surah 37:142). Here the word for "big fish" is *hut*. In Arabic, this word means "fish" or "whale." In the Koran, as Abdullah Yusuf Ali points out, it "may be a fish or perhaps a crocodile. If it were in an open northern sea, it might be a whale."[7]

This survey of Rabbinic and non-rabbinic literature shows that people living by the Mediterranean Sea told stories about large sea monsters roaming the wide seas as a means to tell stories of heroism and survival.

The Message

It is unlikely that the Book of Jonah recounts an historical event. So what is the message of the story of Jonah? The author, perhaps on purpose, does not make the lesson explicit. Perhaps his contemporaries were able to understand it clearly, but that is not the case for those of us who live so far away in time. Consequently, many commentators have offered their own interpretation of the narrative.

For some, the issue at hand is the tension between God's justice versus mercy. According to the Rabbis, God has two different attributes: God's application of universal justice, usually manifested in the name *Elohim*, is called *midat hadin* (the attribute of judgment). This is contrasted with God's merciful attitude (called *midat harachamim*, "attribute of mercy") toward all creatures, expressed through the name *YHVH*. These two attributes are often in tension, but the hope is that divine mercy will ultimately prevail. In our case, even though the Ninevites were wicked, God refuses to punish them severely once they repent and turn away from their evil ways.

Others argue that the author/editor wanted to stress the impossibility of escaping God. Jonah tries to get away by trying to go far away from Israel, to the city of Tarshish, an unknown location, perhaps somewhere in the Mediterranean Sea, but God still found him.

Still others read it as a rebuke to the exclusivist views of Ezra and Nehemiah after the return from the Babylonian exile. During the postexilic times, when the leaders of the new community discovered that people had adopted foreign practices and that the rate of interfaith marriages had reached a critical percentage, they decreed that the non-Israelite women had to be divorced and sent away (Ezra 10:11; cf. Neh. 13: 25). But whether or not this decree was ever implemented is not mentioned in the Bible. Nehemiah tells us that "those of the stock of Israel separated themselves from all foreigners" (Neh. 9:2), but whether that included divorcing foreign women is not clear. Some commentators argue that the Book of Jonah comes to fight this particularism by stating that some non-Israelites, such as the wicked Ninevites, are capable of turning away from sin and therefore worthy of God's care and concern like any other human being. Similarly, some critics highlight the book's universal message, without any reference to the postexilic concerns, by stressing that God's kindness extends to all humanity.

It is also possible to read the story as a lesson that we need to give others a second chance in life, just as Jonah was told to go back to Nineveh and repeat his message of repentance (Mishnah *Taanit* 2:1). For many Christians, the three days Jonah spent in the belly of the fish became symbolic of the three days from Jesus's crucifixion to his resurrection, and was depicted as a favorite theme in medieval Christian art.

There are many themes that could be identified as the main message of the book. Beyond these themes, the motif of the mythical "great fish" must be grappled with. It seems to have been used by the author/editor as a vehicle to press a social or religious agenda. The narrative points out that Jonah had failed in his mission because he refused to accept that change was possible and that God welcomed repentance. What we take away from the story of Jonah is not that we need to follow Jonah, but rather to be inspired by the message of the book as a way to deal with our fellow human beings with care and concern for their well-being.

WHERE IS TARSHISH?

The location to which Jonah tried to flee, Tarshish, has not been identified. Isaiah 2:16 (see also Isa. 23:1) mentions "*oniyot Tarshish*," which could mean either "ships going to Tarshish" or "ships of the type of Tarshish." From Ezek. 27:12 we learn that Tarshish traded with the city of Tyre, in today's Lebanon. According to Josephus, the city is located in Cilicia, in southern Turkey, where the city of modern Tarsus is found (*Ant.* IX, 10:2). Robert H. Pfeiffer says it is near Gibraltar.[8] According to Samuel Sandmel, the name Tarshish is related to Tartessa, a Spanish site that the Phoenicians had reached.[9] These are all educated guesses. Wherever Jonah went, he tried to go as far away from Israel as possible, somewhere within the Mediterranean Sea, hoping God would not find him. He was mistaken.

13

Was There a Queen Esther?

Andrea Del Castagno (1410–1457). Queen Esther. Ca. 1448.
Fresco. 47¹/₄ × 59 in. (120 × 159 cm). Uffizi, Florence, Italy.

The Claim

The Book of Esther, which provides the rationale for the festival of Purim, is extremely popular among Jews. The text presumes the historicity of the basic events in ancient Persia that ended with the rescue of the Jewish community. This happened because of the bravery of Mordecai and the charm of his cousin Esther, the queen of King Ahasuerus. The last chapter of the book urges the reader to turn to the "Annals of the Kings of Media and Persia" for further details involving King Ahasuerus and Mordecai (Est. 10:2). This chapter will discuss this claim of historicity, and point to the various literary genres of the story that gave way to the celebration of similar festivals in Jewish history using Esther as their model.

The Holiday

The biblical Book of Esther recounts events that are said to have occurred in the Jewish Diaspora of Persia and provides the reason for celebrating the holiday of Purim (the Feast of Lots). One of the most joyous, yet minor, festivals of the Jewish calendar, Purim is celebrated on the fourteenth day of Adar in February/March. The previous day is called *Taanit Esther* (the Fast of Esther) and the day after, *Purim Shushan* (Purim of Susa).

During Purim the Scroll of Esther (*M'gillat Esther*) is read in the synagogue, people dress up in costumes representing the major characters in the book, and (in the Western world) eat hamantaschen (Yiddish for "Haman's pockets"), which are three-cornered pastries filled with seeds or fruit preserves. They also tell lighthearted stories, and merrymaking becomes the order of the day. Many congregations run "Purim carnivals." According to the Talmud (BT *M'gillah* 7b), one is encouraged to get drunk to the point of not being able to distinguish between "Cursed be Haman" and "Blessed be Mordecai," though today people are advised to drink responsibly. During this holiday, it is also customary to send food or gifts, known as *mishlo-ach manot* (in Hebrew) or *shalachmanos* (in Yiddish) to friends, relatives, and the poor (Est. 9:22).

The Book and the Plot

The Book of Esther, only ten chapters long, was probably written around the second century B.C.E., although it describes events that presumably occurred in the fifth century B.C.E. Persia. The scroll itself claims that it was written by Mordecai (Est. 9:20), but in the Talmud, the redaction of the book is ascribed to the "Men of the Great Assembly" (BT *Bava Batra* 15a).

The plot is centered around King Ahasuerus; his queen, Vashti; Mordecai, a prominent Jew from the city of Susa; Mordecai's young and beautiful cousin, Esther; and the villain, Haman, a high official in the Persian administration. The book tells of the efforts of Esther, the new queen who replaced Vashti, and her relative Mordecai to save the Jews from the hands of Haman, who wanted to exterminate them and their entire people. Once Haman's plot was revealed, the king, out of affection for his wife Esther, ordered that Haman be killed instead of Mordecai, and allowed the Jewish community to exact punishment on their enemies.

Purim is the only biblical festival not mentioned in the Pentateuch, and Esther is the only book in the *Tanach* that does not appear among the Dead Sea Scroll material discovered so far. It is not surprising that the Pentateuch does not make any reference to it among the other religious holy days, because the events of Esther are presumed to have occurred during the late exilic times; by that time a good part of the Pentateuch had already taken shape. It is puzzling, however, that it is not found among the Dead Sea Scroll material unearthed in the Qumran caves since 1947. It is possible that this is simply an accident of discovery, namely, that archaeologists have not dug at the right place or that the people who lived around Qumran (usually identified with a Jewish sect called the Essenes) had a religious objection to its preservation. There is just no answer for the time being.

The Problem of Historicity

The Book of Esther raises many questions. Is it fiction or history? What is its core message? How did the festival of Purim originate and develop? The dramatic events recorded in the book have elicited various and often conflicting reactions from commentators throughout the centuries. Ancient Persian chronicles do not refer to these events at all. Therefore, without access to independent sources, which would help verify the book's claims, biblical scholars have been compelled to advance arguments both in favor and against the historicity of Esther. Let us review some of the major ones.

Historical
Even without corroboration, a number of items in the book appear probable. For example:

1. The Persian king Ahasuerus in the Book of Esther is identified with Xerxes (486–465 B.C.E.), who was the fourth king in the Achaemenian period. The Rabbis confirm this identification: "Ahasuerus is the same as Artaxerxes" (*Esther Rabbah* 1:3).
2. The Persian Empire was indeed huge and extended, as the book states, from India to Ethiopia. The king, in fact, did have a palace in the city of Susa (*Shushan*, in Hebrew).
3. The text states that the name of the holiday, Purim, comes from the Hebrew word *pur*, meaning "lot" (Est. 9:24), referring to the lot cast

by Haman for the day of the "pogrom." Though the origin of the word "Purim" is in dispute among scholars, this word has been connected with an Akkadian noun, *puru(m)*, meaning "lot." Others argue that it comes from an Aramaized form of another Akkadian verb, *purrurru*, meaning "to destroy."

4. The author of the Book of Esther correctly describes the governmental structure, the postal system, the criminal justice, and many other features of the Persian state.

5. The author is familiar with Persian words and often uses them in his book, such as *dat* (law), *partemim* (nobles), *bitan* (pavilion), and *pat-shegen* (copy). The name of Esther is related to the Persian word *stara*, meaning "star."

6. The author of Esther refers the readers to "the Annals of the Kings of Media and Persia" (Est. 10:2; see also 2:23, 6:1) regarding the full account of the events; unfortunately, these texts did not survive.

Fictional

On the other hand, there are a number of historical inaccuracies in Esther. For instance:

1. Susa was not the capital of the Persian Empire, even though it was an important administrative center and the king's spring residence.

2. There were only 20 satrapies in the Persian Empire, and not 120 as the Bible claims (Est. 1:1).

3. There is no reference to a Jewish queen in the archives of the Persian Empire. Queens came from one of the seven noble Persian families. The name of Xerxes' wife was Amestris.

4. If Mordecai were deported by Nebuchadnezzar in 597 B.C.E., as the Book of Esther claims (Est. 2:6), by Xerxes' time, he would have been more than 110 years old!

In addition, the Book of Esther contains a number of exaggerations that appear unlikely, if not comical:

1. The king's feast lasts 180 days (Est. 1:4).

2. Queen Vashti, the king's wife, refuses to obey the king's command to appear in front of his counselors (Est. 1:12).

3. The candidates for queen undergo a beauty treatment lasting twelve

months: "six months with oil of myrrh and six months with perfumes
and women's cosmetics" (Est. 2:12).

4. The king "orders" all men to become the masters of their home (Est.
1:22).

5. Mordecai, a non-Persian, becomes a high official in ancient Persia
(Est. 3:1).

6. Letters were sent out by the government in "all" languages (Est. 1:22),
instead of the imperial Aramaic, which was the official language of
the Persian state.

7. A small minority of Jews were allowed to kill thousands of Persians
(Est. 9:6, 9:15–16).

In light of these anomalies, some scholars consider the book to be unreliable. One critic characterized the book as "fiction"[1] and, in fact, claimed
that "the author of the book invented *in toto* the festival of Purim."[2] However, most scholars do not go that far and agree that, even though the Book
of Esther does not report a verifiable historical event, it is not totally devoid
of historical value. As another commentator points out, "If the Book of Esther does have a kernel of truth, then that kernel, like a grain of sand in an
oyster shell, has been covered over by layer upon layer of lustrous material."[3]

The Nature of the Book

In the ancient Near East, there was no such distinction between "religious"
and "secular" as those terms are understood today. Every piece of literature
had a religious tone to it. Yet one of the remarkable aspects of the Book of
Esther is its relatively "secular" character. In the Book of Esther there are no
references to prayer, gratitude to God, the election of the Jewish people,
covenant, or redemption; nor is there a mention of angels or afterlife. Even
more striking is the fact that the name of God is not clearly mentioned in the
text, either the proper name *YHVH* or the more general *Elohim*. However,
when Mordecai urges Esther to see the king in order to save her people, he
tells her that should she keep silent on this critical matter, "relief and deliverance will come to the Jews *mimakom acheir* [from another place]" (Est.
4:14), perhaps an oblique reference to God.

In Rabbinic literature the word *makom* frequently means God ("the
place"). According to Josephus, the reference in the Book of Esther is to
God (*Ant.* XI, 6:7). Other modern scholars argue that God is simply in the

background, implicit though not overt. One could ask, if the author really wanted to invoke God, why didn't he clearly state it? In his commentary, Arthur Cohen ventures two guesses: "Perhaps, since the Megillah was to be read at the annual merrymaking of Purim, when considerable license was permitted, the author feared that the Divine Name might be profaned, if it occurred in the reading. Perhaps he feared that the Book might be profanely treated by Gentiles, because of its story of the triumph of the Jews over their enemies."[4] To make sure that the readers would view Esther as a "religious" text, the Greek version of Esther translated in antiquity (ca. second century B.C.E.) added a number of "religious" texts, including prayers to God by Mordecai and Esther, as well as specific references to Esther's abstaining from eating forbidden food and wine.

Many scholars note that the names of Mordecai, Esther, and Vashti in the Book of Esther sound very much like Mesopotamian deities. Mordecai, they say, refers to the Babylonian god Marduk, Esther refers to the goddess Ishtar, and Vashti refers to the Elamite god Mashti. Besides, Esther's real name, "Hadassah," is equivalent to the Aramaic *hadashatu*, meaning "bride," a frequent epithet of Isthar, the goddess. These scholars argue that the story of Esther is nothing but an ancient Middle Eastern myth that has its origin in Mesopotamia but was later adopted by an Israelite writer. Other critics see a connection between the story of Esther and Persian and Greek legends. These interpretations are obviously speculative, and almost impossible to prove, but they all reflect the problems inherent in the book.

Though not considered a historical book, Esther may, however, contain a kernel of history, which through the years attracted additional material full of exaggerations and legendary material. In this case, the question of its literary genre becomes an issue; namely, if it is not a historical text, what is it? Here, too, scholars are in disagreement and provide various ways at looking at the narrative. Bruce William Jones, for example, points to the "humorous nature of the book," which tries to reconcile Jewish readers to their status as a minority among gentiles.[5] This is done through exaggeration and by the use of deliberate absurdities in the story. As he says, "It is easier to bear the pain or subjugation if one can mock those in authority or those responsible for the pain."[6] As examples, he cites the one-dimensional portrayal of the women as only beautiful, the emphasis on pleasure in the court (e.g., drinking, partying), and the foolishness of the gentiles, including Haman, the main villain. Similarly, Adele Berlin writes, "Esther is best read as comedy."[7] Rabbinic midrashim, she notes, have intuited this and added even more preposterous embellishments to the story and its characters.

For other groups of critics, Esther represents a distinct genre in biblical literature: a short story involving the "interactions between the major characters, in pairs for most of the book and in groups of three at the end";[8] or an etiological narrative to justify the origin of the Jewish feast of Purim;[9] or an historical novel based on some historical foundation;[10] or simply a "festival legend."[11]

Reactions to the Book

Though beloved among Jews, the Book of Esther has elicited negative reactions in many non-Jewish circles, because of its overwhelmingly nationalistic outlook and vengeful ending. There is no doubt that the author is happy about the downfall of Israel's enemies, including the hanging of Haman's ten sons (Est. 9:7–10). The text stresses, however, that Jews refuse to plunder the belongings of the Persians, even though they are allowed to do so (Est. 8:11, 9:10). But Jews do apparently take their revenge. On the thirteenth day of Adar they kill a total of five hundred men in the fortress of Susa (Est. 9:6). Esther asks the king permission to repeat the deed on the fourteenth of Adar, when Jews slay three hundred thousand men in Susa (Est. 9:15). In the provinces, they kill seventy-five thousand of their foes, but as the text says repeatedly, "they did not lay hands on the spoil" (Est. 9:16). This additional request, says Lillian Segal, is "completely gratuitous and mean-spirited."[12]

Christians in particular opposed inclusion of the Book of Esther in the Christian canon, seeing it as unfit to be sacred text. One of the first to react strongly to this book was Martin Luther (1483–1546). He argued against the book on the grounds that it was too Judeo-centric and not in keeping with Christianity, writing, "I am so hostile to this book [Second Maccabees] and to Esther that I wish they did not exist at all, for they Judaize too greatly and have much pagan impropriety."[13] In the twentieth century, Robert Pffeifer stated, "Such a secular book hardly deserves a place in the canon of Sacred Scriptures."[14] Eissfeldt reacted as a devout Christian when he wrote, "A book which was so closely bound up with the national spirit, and which indeed the people itself regarded as a source of its power, could not be excluded by the religion which was bound with it. This we can understand. But Christianity, extending as it does over all peoples and races, has neither occasion nor justification for holding onto it."[15]

Some Jews were also uncomfortable with the tenor of the book and the fact that God is not overtly mentioned. In ancient times, Rabbis expressed doubts as to whether Esther should be included among the sacred writings of the Bible because it may not have been written under the inspiration of the Holy Spirit (BT *M'gillah* 7a). After a long discussion, the book was canonized at Yavneh around 70 C.E. Yet, discussion of the sacred nature of the book continued until the fourth century.

Even in modern times some of these same concerns remained. Rabbi Samuel Sandmel, a twentieth-century American scholar, wrote, "The Scroll of Esther seemed to me at one time to have no place in Scripture, both because of its barbarity and what then seemed to me its unreality. But Hitler was a Haman *redivivus,* and the generation of those who were adults in 1932 discovered that the legends about the age of Xerxes came to be a traumatic experience, multiplied in numbers and intensified almost beyond belief."[16] The traumatic experience of the Holocaust made the events in Esther seem less fantasical and strengthened the relevance of the ancient story.

In the modern period, both Jews and non-Jews have defended the message of the book and provided new perspectives. In his commentary on Esther, Robert Gordis maintains that Mordecai's instructions to the Jews that they should destroy the women and children of their enemies (Est. 8:11) has been completely misunderstood. In reality, he adds, what Mordecai did was to quote the words of Haman's decrees in his own decree authorizing the Jews to defend themselves against their foes (see Est. 3:13).[17] This appears to be a forced interpretation, and perhaps unnecessary. For, as one critic writes, "Those who are offended by the blood and by the so-called Jewish nationalism are either literalists or are acting as if they were. Even when they recognize that the story is fiction, they treat it more seriously than it was intended. Pity the theologians who were offended because they could not laugh. By contract, the Jews who maintained a sense of humor in the face of adversity were better able thereby to survive that adversity."[18]

Esther in the Rabbinic Literature

In the Rabbinic period, Purim became a beloved festival. The *Midrash Mishlei* 9:2 teaches, "Should all other festivals cease to be observed, the days of Purim will never be annulled." Similarly, the Jerusalem Talmud expresses the belief that "though all other festivals be abolished, Chanukah and Purim will never be annulled" (JT *Taanit* 2:12). Similar sentiments are expressed in

Yalkut Shimoni, an anthology collected in the thirteenth century: "All the festivals will in the future be abolished except Purim and the Day of Atonement" (on Prov. 9).

The Book of Esther received fanciful elaborations in the Rabbinic literature. Many details not found in the Bible were filled in by Rabbinic interpretations. For example, even though the Bible states that the king summoned Queen Vashti to appear "wearing a royal diadem, to display her beauty to the peoples and the officials" (Est. 1:11), the Rabbis make it more dramatic by requiring her to appear as "naked" (*Esther Rabbah* 4:1). Although the Book of Esther does not state what happened to Vashti when she refused the king's command, the Rabbis claim she was killed for her infraction: "He gave the order and they brought in her head on a platter" (*Esther Rabbah* 4:11).

The fact that Esther, a pious Jew, marries a gentile (Est. 2:17) bothered many of the Sages. Some, who could not accept the fact that Esther would become pregnant by a non-Jew, preferred to say that she had a miscarriage and never bore a child again (*Esther Rabbah* 6:3). Others justified the act of marriage by stating that Esther was a martyr for a good cause and the instrument of redemption in the future: "It must be because a great disaster is going to fall on Israel, and she will deliver them (*Esther Rabbah* 6:6). One midrash adds, "The vast fortune that Haman possessed was divided into three parts: one part was given to Mordecai and Esther, the second to the students of Torah, and the third set aside for the restoration of the Temple" (*Midrash T'hillim* 22:197). For the Rabbis, the ends justified the means in this case.

Local Purims

The Book of Esther had such a huge impact in the Jewish consciousness throughout the centuries that it became paradigmatic of Jewish survival under oppression. Any time a Jewish community was threatened by a powerful enemy and was eventually rescued by circumstances beyond themselves, either through the agency of another well-meaning individual or by other social changes, they wrote down their own Scroll of Purim, following the teaching of the Talmud (BT *B'rachot* 54a) that one must recite a thanksgiving benediction on returning to the place where one was saved from danger. Numerous stories of this kind were written down by Jewish communities around the world. These escapes from danger were called "Local Purims" or "Minor Purims." Following are three typical examples:[19]

Purim of Tiberias:
In 1743 Sulaiman Pasha, governor of Damascus, came to lay siege to Tiberias, which was ruled by sheik Dair al-Amar. The Jews suffered much during the eighty-three days of the war. However, when the siege was raised (on the 4th of Elul) as well as the day on which the news of Sulaiman Pasha's death arrived (on the 7th of Elul), the Jews of Tiberias declared local Purims.

Purim of Tammuz at Algiers:
In 1774 Mohammed ibn Uman, the leader of Algiers, courageously defended his city against the Spanish army. The Jewish legend has it that flames came out of the graves of the Rabbis Isaac ben Sheshet and Solomon ben Simon Duran, and contributed to the Spanish defeat. Hence, in order to celebrate the miracle of having again escaped from the Spaniards, the Jews of Algiers instituted a Purim on the 11th of Tammuz.

Purim of Rhodes:
In 1840 the Greeks of the island of Rhodes, disturbed by Jews who were competing with them in the sponge trade, caused the disappearance of a non-Jewish child. The child was later found alive on the island of Syra. However, by that time the Jews of Rhodes had been imprisoned and tortured. Responding to complaints by Jews, the Ottoman Sultan Abd al-Majid deposed the governor, and gave the Jews a firman [royal decree] declaring that the accusation of ritual murder was false. By a curious coincidence, the imprisonment of the Jews and the granting of the firman took place on the same day of Purim (14th of Adar). Since then, the holiday has been celebrated as a double festival at Rhodes with special prayers and hymns.

The Message

The Book of Esther taught the Jewish community how to survive in a gentile world. It provided Jews with hope that things would somehow become better for them. Highlighting the courage and transformation of Esther and the wisdom of Mordecai, it reinforced the belief that they could in fact overcome the Hamans of their time. Even the lack of reference to God has received positive reinforcement. As Rabbi Shlomo Riskin writes, "The absence of God's name in Megillat Esther not only shows us how to discern invisible patterns in the unfolding of history; it also reminds us that we must be actively involved if our people are to be saved."[20]

A local event buried in lost antiquity, Purim, which was progressively enriched by legends of countless generations, still provides a strong motivation for all Jews to help one another, to display acts of courage, and to hope for the day when their enemies will disappear altogether.

14

Was Chanukah Really a Miracle?

Chanukkah lamp (menorah) from a synagogue.
Brass, in the center the Amsterdam lion.
From the Netherlands. 18th CE.
Judaica Coll. Max Berger, Vienna, Austria.

The Claim

The Rabbis explain that Chanukah is celebrated for eight days because after the Temple was rededicated by the Hasmoneans in the second century B.C.E., a "miracle" took place. A jar of oil found inside of the sanctuary, with only enough oil for one day, inexplicably lasted eight days. This chapter will advance arguments to show that this traditional interpretation is the result of a theological construct created by the Rabbis of the Talmud centuries later who wanted to emphasize God's role in the story of the liberation.

The "Miracle" of Chanukah

In the popular understanding of the word, a "miracle" refers to an amazing and wonderful occurrence. The birth of a baby often elicits the comment that it was a "miracle." Whenever we are at a loss to explain an event, people usually call it a "miracle." However, this word has also a more technical meaning. In this sense, a miracle is an exception to the natural laws, an intrusion into the regular workings of the universe by unknown forces, and often explained by God's intervention into the process of preserving nature. So, for example, if a stone were thrown into the air, the law of gravity should turn it downwards. But instead, if it goes against the natural law and continues to go upwards, that is a miracle.

The well-known story about Chanukah's "miracle" centers on an event that many believed occurred during the reign of Antiochus IV, the Greek-Syrian king who ruled over Judea in the second century B.C.E. After he desecrated the Temple of Jerusalem, Jews rebelled and defeated the enemy. During the cleansing of the Temple, so the story goes, the faithful Jews looked for oil to light the fire in the Sanctuary but could find a jar that could last only one day; a "miracle" occurred and the fire burned eight days. That is why, many people believe, Chanukah lasts eight days.

The focus on the Chanukah miracle has become part of our traditional myths and everyday language. Around the time of the holiday, articles written in the popular media mostly stress its miraculous aspect as the primary rationale for the eight days of Chanukah. Children play with dreidels (Yiddish for "spinning tops") that contain one of four different letters on each side, namely *nun, gimel, hei,* and *shin.* Traditionally these letters are an acronym for the expression *Neis gadol hayah sham,* meaning "A great miracle happened there." (In Israel, they substitute the word *po,* meaning "here," for the word *sham,* meaning "there."). On October 12, 2004, the Israeli newspaper *Haaretz* published a story by Akiva Eldar, dealing with modern Israel, entitled "A One-Time Chanukah Miracle." One of the two blessings we say over the Chanukah candles still contain the words praising God, "who has worked miracles [*nisim* in Hebrew] for our ancestors in those days, at this season."

Many people accept miracles as an explanation for historic events or even present occurrences that cannot be understood through natural causes. However, miracles bespeak a capricious God who intervenes in the regular workings of the universe, and that would make the world an unreliable place. Modern science teaches us to depend on natural laws for our understanding of how the world operates. If something happens that we cannot explain, we can only blame ourselves for our limited understanding of nature and hope that as we obtain more knowledge we will be able to resolve the causes of these problematic issues. A science-oriented individual would argue that

---

ANOTHER INTERPRETATION OF THE DREIDEL

Some people maintain that each letter of the dreidel stands for the ancient kingdoms that tried to destroy Jews but failed: *nun* for Nebuchadnezzar, king of Babylon; *gimel* for Gog, standing for Greece; *hei* for Haman, in Persia; and *sin* for Seir, meaning Rome. Others suggest that *nun* stands for *nefesh* (soul), *gimel* for *guf* (body), *hei* for *hakol* (all), and *sin* for *seichel* (mind), all together representing a human being. Most likely the original wording comes from the German and/or Yiddish: *nun* (for *nicht/nisht* (nothing): you win and lose nothing; *gimel* for *ganz* (all): take the whole kitty; *hei* for *halb* (half): you win half; and *shin* for *shtel ein* (put in): you place one object into the kitty.

God works through nature and that, in fact, nature represents the will of God.

The Bible assumes the existence of miracles. The ancient Israelites believed that the Reed Sea parted during the Exodus and that the sun stopped at the command of Joshua (Josh. 10:12–14). But the Israelites lived in pre-scientific times. The Talmudic Rabbis believed in miracles but cautioned, "We do not rely on miracles" (BT *P'sachim* 64b). Moderns, however, try to explain things by scientific methods and not by pointing to miracles.

The question about Chanukah is whether our sacred literature provides us with other interpretations of the events that help explain the reason for the eight-day celebration, rather than relying on the Talmudic interpretation of the miracle. The answer is yes. Among them, the First and Second Books of Maccabees, two books that were left out of the Hebrew Bible but are part of the Apocrypha, play a major role in shedding light on the events of Chanukah.

The First Book of Maccabees covers a period of forty years from the start of the reign of Antiochus IV, in 175 B.C.E., to the accession of the Jewish king, John Hyrcanus in 134 B.C.E. The author is unknown, but he wrote as if he were a witness to the events. The original Hebrew text has disappeared, but its Greek translation was preserved in the Septuagint.

The Second Book of Maccabees is an abridgment of a larger book written by an otherwise unknown Hellenist Jewish author, Jason of Cyrene. This book deals primarily with the deeds of Judah, called the Maccabee, who was one of the five sons of Mattathias of the Hasmonean family and led the revolt against the Syrian-Greeks. Unlike the First Book of Maccabees, this one was originally written in Greek.

In addition to the Books of the Maccabees, there are also the writings of Josephus, the Jewish historian of the first century C.E. Flavius Josephus (ca. 37–100 C.E.) was a priest, a soldier, and an historian. He was born in Jerusalem and wrote extensively about Jewish history, and primarily about the war with Rome as he witnessed it. His writings provide eyewitness accounts of pivotal moments of Jewish history. A few Rabbinic texts also shed important light on this puzzling question.

The Historical Background

The historical circumstances of the Maccabean revolt can be summarized as follows. After Alexander the Great died in 323 B.C.E., his generals divided his huge Greek Empire into three parts: Ptolemy received Egypt, Antigonus was given Greece, and Seleucus I Nicanor (312–281 B.C.E.) obtained Syria and the eastern provinces. In 301 B.C.E., Judea and Phoenicia were finally transferred to Seleucus. In those days, Jews were ruled internally by High Priests who often depended on the Greek rulers for their authority. Their positions were frequently bought by paying large sums of money to whomever was in power in Damascus, the capital of the Syrian-Greek Empire.

During this period and the following decades, two different groups of Jews in Israel clashed with each other. On the one hand, there were the more traditional Jewish Chasidim, the "pious ones" (unrelated to the Chasidism who emerged in eighteenth-century Europe), and on the other, Hellenist Jews who ingratiated themselves with the Syrian-Greek ruling powers. The latter were motivated by the desire to gain and preserve the status of *polis* for Jerusalem, which would give them some tax benefits and allow them to keep a Hellenistic lifestyle that included the right to build "a gymnasium according to the gentile custom" (I Macc. 1:14). In those days, every Greek city had a public gymnasium where young people exercised, usually in the nude. Many Jews took part in these practices. However, some assimilated Hellenistic Jews went even further, by removing the mark of their circumcision—a procedure called "epispasm" (foreskin restoration)—in order to look like other Greeks. A number of Hellenist Jews, among them the well-known members of the Tobias family, acted as tax collectors. They played a major role in transferring power from one High Priest to another.

In 175 B.C.E., when Antiochus Epiphanes IV became king, he displayed great ambitions for his empire by attempting to conquer Egypt and other surrounding countries. He even gave himself the surname "Epiphanes" (meaning "the visible god") and started to interfere in the politics of Judah. This did not sit well with many Jewish leaders (many of whom facetiously called the king "Epimanes" (meaning "the madman"). The king appointed Jason (for Joshua) (175–171 B.C.E.) as High Priest instead of his brother Onias III. However, under the influence of the Tobias family, Antiochus replaced Jason with Menelaus (for Onias) (171–167 B.C.E.), in exchange for a large sum of money (II Macc. 4:24), even though Menelaus was not a member of the High Priestly family.

In 169–168 B.C.E., Antiochus IV set out to conquer Egypt. While fighting there, Jason, the deposed High Priest, left the Ammonites, with whom he had taken refuge, and attacked Menelaus in order to regain the High Priesthood. A civil war broke out between Jason and Menelaus, and Jason successfully entered the city of Jerusalem. King Antiochus was furious. On his way back from Egypt, Antiochus attacked Jerusalem, imposed restrictions on Judea, and eventually desecrated the Temple. The First Book of Maccabees describes these tragic events as follows: "He [Antiochus IV] directed them to follow customs strange to the land, to forbid burnt offerings and sacrifices and drink offerings in the Sanctuary, to profane Sabbaths and feasts, to defile the Sanctuary and the priests, to build altars and sacred precincts and shrines for idols, to sacrifice swine and unclean animals, and to leave their sons uncircumcised" (I Macc. 1:44–48, RSV). And then, on the fifteenth day of the month of Kislev, in 167 B.C.E., the Syrian-Greeks erected "a desolating sacrilege upon the altar of burnt offering" (I Macc. 1:54, RSV). That was too much for many pious Jews. A priest by the name of Mattathias of the Hasmonean family from the town of Modein, not far from Jerusalem, along with his five sons John, Simon, Judas, Eleazar, and Jonathan, urged people to rebel forcefully. But the Chasidim refused to fight on the Sabbath, and as a result many were massacred on this holy day. Mattathias and his sons believed otherwise. They said that the Sabbath was given to Israel to live and not die. So, they urged their compatriots to carry weapons even on the Sabbath. Eventually, many of the Jews joined the Hasmoneans in their fight for freedom.

The Hasmonean revolt continued after the death of Mattathias, with considerable success. Judah (called the Maccabee), Mattathias's son, defeated the Syrians in 166 B.C.E. over Heron at Beth Horon, and in 165 B.C.E. over Gorgias at Emmaus, and then over General Lysias at Bethzur. As a result of the military victories, parts of Judea were liberated and the Temple cleaned. After three years of defilement, the Temple was purified and rededicated to the worship of the one invisible God "with songs and harps and lutes and cymbals" (I Macc. 4:54). This dedication, literally *chanukah* in Hebrew, took place on the twenty-fifth day of Kislev, 165 B.C.E. According to Josephus, the historian, on this day the victorious Jews, "lighted the lamps that were on the candlestick, and offered incense upon the altar [of incense], and laid the loaves upon the altar [of showbread], and offered burnt-offerings upon the new altar [of burn-offerings]" (*Ant.* XII, 7:6). The festival of Chanukah celebrates this major achievement.

In Jewish life today it is customary to light one additional candle every night until we reach the number eight. During this festival, a special menorah, also known as a *chanukiyah*, a candelabrum with eight branches and an extra small branch called a *shamash* (meaning "a helper"), is used. The rationale for adding one candle every night is that "we promote (in matters of) sanctity but do not reduce" (BT *Shabbat* 21b).

Why Eight Days?

Like other festivals, Chanukah developed over a long period of time. The First Book of Maccabees, which was written during the last decade of the second century B.C.E., tells the story of the liberation and then adds, "Judah and his brothers and all the assembly of Israel determined that every year at that season the days of the dedication of the altar should be observed with gladness and joy for eight days, beginning with the twenty-fifth day of the month of Kislev" (I Macc. 4:59, RSV). Here Chanukah appears simply as a festival of rededication of the Temple of Jerusalem, with no reference to lights or a miracle.

In the Second Book of Maccabees, composed later on, perhaps during the second half of the first century B.C.E., Chanukah is described differently. Here the holiday appears not only as a festival of dedication but also as a belated Festival of Booths, namely, Sukkot: "It happened that on the same day on which the Sanctuary had been profaned by the foreigners, the purification of the Sanctuary took place, that is, on the twenty-fifth day of the same month, which is Kislev. And they celebrated it for eight days with rejoicing, in the manner of the Feast of Booths, remembering how not long before, during the Feast of Booths, they had been wandering in the mountains and caves like wild animals. . . . They decreed by public ordinance and vote that the whole nation of Jews should observe these days every year" (II Macc. 10:5–6, 10:8, RSV). Because of the war, the Jews did not have an opportunity to celebrate Sukkot (which lasts eight days) that year, but when the rededication took place, they realized that it would be appropriate to mark the pilgrimage festival of Sukkot as free individuals, even if it were a bit later. Here, too, there are no references to lights or to a miracle.

The author of the Book of Second Maccabees reinforces the notion of a belated Sukkot, by notifying the Jews of Egypt: "Since on the twenty-fifth day of Kislev we shall celebrate the purification of the Temple, we thought it necessary to notify you, in order that you also may celebrate the Feast of Booths and the Feast of the Fire [see II Macc. 1:19–36] given when Nehemiah, who built the Temple and the altar, offered sacrifices" (II Macc. 1:18, RSV). The first reference to lights is found in the writings of Josephus, two centuries later. This is the way he describes the festival: "Now Judah celebrated the festival of the restoration of the sacrifices of the Temple for eight days . . . and from that time to this, we celebrate the festival and call it 'Lights.' I suppose the reason was that liberty beyond our hopes appeared to us and since then was this name given to that festival" (Ant. 7:7). It is interesting to note that during the days of Josephus the holiday was known as Chag HaOrim, the "Holiday of Lights," and not Chanukah. He seems to know nothing about the "miracle of oil."

The Mishnah, the law code assembled by Y'hudah HaNasi in the early part of the third century C.E., does not mention lights. The "miracle of oil" appears in the Talmud, about seven hundred years after the time of the Maccabees. Thus, we read:

What is [the reason for the celebration] of Chanukah? Our Rabbis taught: On the twenty-fifth of Kislev (begin) the days of Chanukah, which are eight in number, during which a lamentation for the dead and fasting are forbidden. For when the Greeks entered the Temple, they defiled all the oils in it, and when the Hasmoneans prevailed against them and defeated them, they searched and found only one cruse of oil that lay with the seal of the High Priest. It was sufficient only for one day's lighting. But a miracle [neis in Hebrew] occurred, and they lit (the lamp) with it for eight days. The following year, they set up these days as a festival with the recital of Hallel and thanksgiving. (BT Shabbat 21b)

In the Talmud, the Hebrew word *neis* (miracle) is used to describe the event. In fact, we are told that a cruse of oil that could last one day "miraculously" lasted eight. Some scholars have argued that the meaning of the word *neis* here does not mean "miracle," but instead means "an extraordinary event." This appears to be a rationalization and not a good explanation. The Rabbis often believed in miracles, even though some people in the modern world do not.

The Talmudic explanation of the holiday appears to be an elaboration of a note found in *M'gillat Taanit*, an early tannaitic text in Aramaic that deals with days in the Jewish calendar on which fasting is forbidden: "On the twenty-fifth (day of Kislev), is the day of Chanukah. During eight days mourning is forbidden." However, the Scholium, Rabbinic glosses written in Hebrew (ca. seventh century C.E.) and appended to *M'gillat Taanit*, repeats the story of the "miracle of oil," but only in one of its versions. The other version contains a totally different explanation. Here, as well as in *P'sikta Rabbati*, a medieval midrash regarding the festivals, we are told that when the Hasmoneans entered the Temple, they found there eights iron spears. They stuck candles on these spears and kindled them (*P'sikta Rabbati* 2:1). This explanation may not be historical, and perhaps is meant to be more poetic and moral in nature, such as weapons turning into lights, but at least it does not deal with an unproven "miracle."

The Talmudic story of the so-called "miracle of oil" became popular throughout the centuries. According to the dominant scholarly view, the ancient Rabbis shifted the focus of the legend away from the Hasmoneans, placing it on God, who wrought a "miracle" on behalf of the Jewish people. The reason may have been because of the Rabbis' opposition to the Hasmonean dynasty's grab for power. Thus, the traditional prayer read during Chanukah, *Al HaNisim*, "For the Miracles," referred to in the Talmud (BT *Shabbat* 24a; *Maseket Sof'rim* 20:8) but fully found for the first time in the prayer book of Amram Gaon (ninth century C.E., Sura), contains the following words: "We thank you for the miracles, the redemptions, the mighty deeds, and the victorious battles that You did for our ancestors in those days at this season. In the days of Mattathias, son of Yochanan, the Hasmonean, the High Priest and his sons, the wicked Greek government rose up against Your people Israel. . . . But You delivered the strong in the hand of the weak. . . . Your children entered the Holy of Holies of Your house, cleansed Your Temple, purified Your Sanctuary, kindled lights in Your holy courtyards, and established these days of Chanukah to give thanks and praise to

Your great name." It is interesting to note that the credit for the victory is here assigned solely to God. It is also noteworthy that the text does not clearly mention the "miracle of oil."

Chanukah: A Minor Holiday?

In Jewish tradition, Chanukah, like Purim, is considered a minor holy day. There are few demands made on Jews during these days. Work is permitted and fasting prohibited. The most important requirement during Chanukah is to light the candles every night with the appropriate blessings. These candles are considered holy and cannot be used for practical purposes; for example, they cannot be used to read by their light or to light the Sabbath candles. It is a mitzvah to "advertise the miracle," and therefore the Chanukah menorah must be displayed prominently. This was the custom among the Spanish Jews in Spain, but Ashkenazi Jews, because of virulent anti-Semitism in Eastern Europe, were sometimes allowed to place it indoors.

In the Western world, however, and especially in the northern hemisphere, Chanukah has become a major holiday because of its proximity to Christmas in the secular calendar. Jews living in Islamic countries do not treat Chanukah with the same level of importance. Even in South America, Chanukah is not considered a major holiday, because it happens during the summer, when the sun is bright and shining, and does not need to compete with "White Christmas."

In some circles, Chanukah has turned into a sort of Jewish Christmas. In fact, the *Needham Times*, a suburban newspaper that appears in one of the western suburbs of Boston, Massachusetts, published an article in December 1988 entitled "Hanukkah: The Jewish version of Christmas." It is not uncommon today to see Santa Claus spinning a dreidel, an angel lifting up a menorah, a Christmas tree that contains a Star of David, or a tree called a "Chanukah bush." Many card companies promote mixed messages during these holidays that appeal to marginal Jews, some interfaith married couples, or totally assimilated Jews. The Jewish religious establishment does not like it, because Chanukah is very different from Christmas, in terms of its background, history, and religious message. Whereas Christmas celebrates the birth of Jesus, Chanukah commemorates a military victory over an oppressor. Christmas is a major Christian holy day, but Chanukah is not. Many in the Jewish community also disapprove of mixing the symbols of the two festivals because of what the Rabbis (based on Lev. 18:3) often call *hukkat hagoyim,* "copying the custom of the gentiles."

The proximity to Christmas has radically altered the nature of Chanukah. Today in the Western world, it is placed among the major festivals of the Jewish year, with some customs taken over from the Christian world, such as gift giving, home decorations, family gatherings, and dinners. In traditional Judaism, the time to give gifts is during Purim. But the trend is almost irreversible, and Chanukah will continue to play a major role among us in the Jewish calendar.

The Message

The traditional sources on Chanukah contain more than one explanation as to why it is celebrated for eight days. Some are legendary, some more historical. What becomes clear is that the popular view regarding the "miracle of oil" as the only valid interpretation of Chanukah's length of eight days cannot be maintained.

In spite of Rabbinic objection, the festival of Chanukah will continue to be a major holiday, and it has all the ingredients for it. The fact that Chanukah is not mentioned in the Hebrew Bible may have contributed to the fact that it played a minor role in the Jewish year. But that alone does not diminish its importance or the powerful message it conveys. As Anne Roiphe writes, "I see Chanukah as a time when, as we light the candles, we pause in awe before the Jewish people whose survival through adversity brings light into the darkness of the human soul."[1]

Chanukah proclaims the need to have pride in one's Jewish identity, the necessity to protect and preserve Jewish values and religious traditions, the celebration of Jewish survival amid all circumstances and conditions, along with the values of courage, rededication, thanksgiving, and, above all, the right to be different. The Maccabees did not fight for civil liberties alone; this is what Antiochus IV was already offering the Judeans in exchange for their willingness to accept the Hellenistic way of life. The Hasmoneans fought primarily for the right to live according to their own tradition. This right must be cherished and respected in order to preserve the values of freedom and inclusivity that we hold dear.

15

Did the Israelites Live in Booths?

Oppenheim, Moritz Daniel (1800–1882). Sukkot (Tabernacles), 1867.
Oil on canvas. Gift of the Oscar and Regina Gruss Charitable
and Educational Foundation, Inc., 1992–1999.
Photo by Richard Heri. The Jewish Museum, New York, NY, U.S.A.

The Claim

According to the biblical account, after leaving Egypt, the Israelites lived in "booths" during the wilderness period (Lev. 23:43). This chapter will dispute this assertion by pointing out that "booths" are temporary abodes, which are exposed to the elements and, as such, not suitable to wilderness living as permanent abodes. It will argue that the biblical claim is a projection back from an agricultural setting of the life in Canaan into the wilderness period centuries before, by priestly writers who wanted to justify the use of "booths" during the celebration of Sukkot, the main fall harvest festival of the year. It will also analyze the development of the festival through the centuries.

The Pilgrimage Festivals

Ancient people, much like today, regularly set aside a number of special dates in their calendar to mark important occasions, such as a military victory, a major national catastrophe, the phases of the moon or sun, or the conclusion of the harvest. Agricultural societies often depend on the regularity of the seasons and particularly on the availability of rain and water. In the past, some were more fortunate than others. Egypt could rely on the Nile for its water needs, and Mesopotamia had the Tigris and the Euphrates as its major water resources. Ancient Canaan was not so lucky. The Jordan River was not sufficient to meet all the hydration requirements of the local farmers, and dry spells often caused major problems for the regional subsistent-level economy.

There are a number of textual references to famines in ancient Israel caused by droughts. For example, Abraham had to leave for Egypt because of a "famine" (*raav*) (Gen. 12:10). Similarly, Isaac went over to the land of Abimelech, king of the Philistines in Gerar, on account of a famine (Gen. 26:1). During the days of Joseph in Egypt, "all the lands came to Egypt to buy provisions from Joseph, for the famine [*haraav*] had taken hold in every land" (Gen. 41:57; see also 47:13). Among those who came down were the children of Jacob, who were instructed by their father, "Look—I have heard that there are provisions for sale in Egypt; go down that way and buy provisions from there, that we may live and not die" (Gen. 42:2). There were similar famines during the reigns of David (II Sam. 21:1) and Ahab (I Kings 17:1, 18:5), during the days of Elisha (II Kings 4:38, 8:1), and others. Often, lack of bread was viewed as a punishment from God (e.g., Amos 4:7; Ezek. 5:16). On the contrary, a rich harvest was a divine blessing (e.g., Lev. 26:3–5) and worthy of celebration, to give gratitude to God, who, the Israelites thought, caused the rain to fall.

Of the many holy days in the Hebrew calendar, the Three Pilgrimage Festivals are the most significant: Passover (Pesach), Weeks (Shavuot), and Booths (Sukkot), the last one mistakenly translated as "Tabernacles." Each one is called a *chag* in Hebrew, originally meaning "pilgrim feast." This word is related to the Arabic *hajj*, referring to the obligation of every Muslim to go on a pilgrimage to Mecca at least once in a lifetime.

According to biblical injunctions, every Israelite male was expected to come to the local temple during the Three Pilgrimage Festivals: "Three times a year all your males shall appear before the Sovereign, the Eternal" (Exod.

23:17). The Book of Deuteronomy makes it even more explicit: "Three times a year—on the Feast of Unleavened Bread, on the Feast of Weeks, and on the Feast of Booths—all your males shall appear before the Eternal your God in the place that [God] will choose. They shall not appear before the Eternal empty-handed, but each with his own gift, according to the blessing that the Eternal your God has bestowed upon you" (Deut. 16:16–17). Even though the text speaks only of males being required by law to "appear before the Eternal" (by the time of Deuteronomy, this meant Jerusalem), other sources state that even women and children took part in the pilgrimage to Zion (Deut. 16:11, 16:14; see also 12:12, 12:18).

The Three Pilgrimage Festivals celebrate different agricultural and historical events in the history of the Israelites: Passover, originally a spring festival, comprised two distinct holy days, "the Festival of Passover" (Chag HaPesach) and "the Festival of Unleavened Bread" (Chag HaMatzot); both were eventually connected with the Exodus from Egypt. Shavuot, the wheat harvest during the summertime, in time became associated with God's Revelation at Mount Sinai and the reception of the Torah. Finally, Sukkot, a fall festival marking the gathering and storing of grain and new wine, commemorates the fact that during the Exodus from Egypt (i.e., during their wandering in the Sinai), the Israelites lived in the wilderness, presumably in booths or temporary dwellings.

It is important to note, however, that like many other holy days, all these pilgrimage festivals underwent significant changes throughout the centuries. Minor festivals eventually assumed major roles in the calendar (e.g., Chanukah), whereas other highly important holy days lost their luster and popularity. The festival of Sukkot is such a holy day.

In the Hebrew calendar, Sukkot (formerly called Chag HaAsif, the Feast of the Ingathering, cf. Ex. 23:16) is celebrated on the fifteenth of Tishrei, only five days after Yom Kippur (in September/October). According to the Bible, it lasts seven days (Deut. 16:13). The first day and the last day (or the first two and last two in the Diaspora[1]) are considered full holy days, with all the ritual requirements and restrictions (e.g., no work, no eulogies, no fasting). The seventh day is called Hoshana Rabbah. The eighth day, which is added to the festival as a separate holy day called Sh'mini Atzeret, includes a special prayer for rain. The celebration ends on the ninth day with Simchat Torah (Rejoicing over the Torah).[2] In addition to the sukkah, a temporary booth set up for this occasion, Jews use the *lulav* ("a palm branch" and other leaves) and the *etrog* (citron) in their worship services (see below for details). The intermediate days, called Chol HaMo-eid, last five or six days (depending on the length of the festival) and are considered "half holy days," with the requirement to continue to "dwell" in the sukkah; however, one can resume daily activities with greater ease during this period.

Sukkot in the Bible

From the biblical texts we gather that at the end of the year, perhaps after the fall fruit harvest, the Canaanites, including the early Israelites, celebrated a festival with great rejoicing. Thus, for example, we read that during the days of the Israelite Judges, Gaal son of Ebed, an opponent of Abimelech son of Gideon (also called Jerubaal, one of the "Judges"), together with his men, passed through the city of Shechem, and gained the confidence of her citizens. Subsequently, "they went out into the fields, gathered and trod out the vintage of their vineyards, and a made a festival. They entered the temple of their god, and as they ate and drank, they reviled Abimelech" (Judg. 9:26–27). The Israelites, being part of the greater Canaanite culture that included a celebration of the fall harvest, transformed it into a holy day reflecting their own ideology. As revealed in the discovery of the Gezer Calendar, an Israelite document of the tenth century B.C.E., from a very early time the ingathering of fruit was marked as a special occasion.

In the earliest cultic calendar of the Bible, Sukkot is mentioned as one of the Three Pilgrimage Festivals and referred to simply as Chag HaAsif (the Feast of Ingathering): "the Feast of Ingathering at the end of the year, when you gather in the results of your work from the field" (Exod. 23:16). It is interesting to note that here no specific date is assigned, nor an explanation of what kind of a harvest it was; there is not even a rationale for the celebration. Its meaning was taken for granted by everyone. The expression "ingathering" refers to the autumnal storing of the grain and first fruits, such as grapes and olives. The reference to "the end of the year" is obscure. Some take it as "the end of the harvest year," whereas others think it means "the end of the calendar year." In Exodus 34:22, it is said that the festival occurred "at the turn of the year," implying the transition to a new agricultural season.

The fall harvest was considered to be very important—perhaps the most important of all the harvests. The holy day provided an opportunity for people to travel to local temples and express gratitude for the abundance provided by God during the past year. This pilgrimage was done yearly, as we derive from the case of Elkanah, the husband of Hannah and Peninnah, who "used to go up from his town every year to worship and to offer sacrifice to the God of Hosts at Shiloh" (I Sam. 1:3). It was at this city, located north of Bethel, on Mount Ephraim, that an annual festival called *chag YHVH* (feast of the Eternal) was held (see Judg.'21:19). Not only were special sacrifices of gratitude offered on this occasion, but there was also great merriment in the community. Women would come out of their vineyards and join in the dancing in open fields (Judg. 21:20).

The end of the calendar year was the season for other major celebrations. King Solomon, for example, dedicated the new Temple in Jerusalem during the festival of Sukkot: "All the men of Israel gathered before King Solomon at the Feast [*bechag*], in the month of Ethanim—that is, the seventh month" (I Kings 8:2). What is remarkable in this statement is the importance given to Sukkot. It is simply called "the Festival" (see also II Chron. 7:8; Ezek. 45:25), namely, the most important festival of the year, and presumably, everyone knew what that meant.

After the death of King Solomon, when the kingdom split into two, Jeroboam I became the king of Israel in the north and settled in Shechem. Wanting to make sure that the northerners would sever their relationship with the southern kingdom of Judah, he implemented two major reforms: he set up two golden calves for purposes of worship, one in Bethel, his southern border with Israel, and the other one in Dan, far up in the north. He said to the Israelites, "This is your god, O Israel, who brought you up from the land of Egypt!" (I Kings 12:28; cf. Exod. 32:4). He also appointed non-Levitical priests to minister in the new sanctuaries. The other change had to do with the holy days. We are told that he "established a festival on the fifteenth day of the eighth month, in imitation of the festival of Judah" (I Kings 12:32). It seems that the holy day of the fifteenth day of the "eighth" month corresponded to Sukkot, but whether King Jeroboam changed it from the traditional seventh to the eighth month because he wanted to make sure his citizens would not go down to Jerusalem during the traditionally scheduled date in the south or because he was adapting the festivals to the agricultural conditions of the north is not clear. One scholar has suggested that "the dating of the festival in the seventh month, reckoning from the vernal equinox as in Mesopotamia, may reflect exilic usage, the festival in pre-exilic times being according to the harvest, perhaps later as in that of Jeroboam."[3]

Deuteronomy provides a longer explanation of the festival: "After the ingathering from your threshing floor and your vat, you shall hold the Feast of Booths [*Chag HaSukkot*] for seven days" (Deut. 16:13). These instructions also include the information that this pilgrimage festival ought to be celebrated "in the place that the Eternal will choose" (Deut. 16:15), a code name for Jerusalem.

This passage is noteworthy for several reasons: for the first time, the holy day is called "Sukkot." Furthermore, for the first time it is stated that the festival should last seven days, without, however, providing a specific date in the calendar. The law emphasizes that Sukkot must be celebrated in Jerusalem, implying not at other local temples, perhaps because they were considered "illegitimate" after the cultic concentration in Jerusalem that began with King Hezekiah and then King Josiah in the seventh century B.C.E. Deuteronomy also teaches that the celebration should involve "rejoicing," *v'samachta* (Deut. 16:11). Other biblical texts state that "rejoicing" involves good food and wine (Deut. 12:7, 14:26). This is echoed in later Rabbinic texts that say that "rejoicing" involves, eating, drinking, fancy garments, and study of Torah (BT *P'sachim* 109a, 68b). Deuteronomic law repeats the law in Exodus requiring that no one should appear empty-handed when they make a pilgrimage to the Temple of Jerusalem, "but each with his own gift, according to the blessing that the Eternal your God has bestowed upon you" (Deut. 16:17). Finally, Deuteronomy requires that the Torah be read aloud every seven years during the Feast of Booths in the presence of all Israel (Deut. 31:10–11), most likely because Sukkot attracted the largest attendance of pilgrims to Jerusalem.

Sukkot in Priestly Texts

The fullest explanation of Sukkot is found in priestly texts (P) that deal with festival calendars and other ritual matters in the Temple. In the cultic calendar of Leviticus we read, "On the fifteenth day of this seventh month there shall be the Feast of Booths [*Chag HaSukkot*] to the Eternal, [to last] seven days" (Lev. 23:34). This festival is to take place "when you have gathered in the yield of your land" (Lev. 33:39). On the first day of the festival, Israelites are commanded to "take the product of *hadar* [meaning unknown] trees, branches of palm trees, boughs of leafy trees, and willows of the brook, and you shall rejoice before the Eternal your God seven days" (Lev. 23:40). Furthermore, the law enjoins all Israelites to live in booths (*sukkot*) for seven days, "in order that future generations may know that I made the Israelite people live in booths when I brought them out of the land of Egypt" (Lev. 23:43). An extra holy day is tacked onto Sukkot, to be celebrated on the eighth day as a "sacred occasion," *atzeret* (Lev. 23:36). During Sukkot and *atzeret*, given the importance of the festivals, large amounts of sacrifices were offered on the altar (Num. 29:12–35). Several points require comment here:

1. By this time, Chag HaSukkot has been firmly established as the name of the festival. The old name, Chag HaAsif (the Feast of Ingathering), is no longer used.

2. A new ritual object, made of a mixture of branches and greens, is used during the festival. However, we are not told what to do with these branches, which later on would come to be called a *lulav*. In postexilic times, the instruction was "to go out to the mountains and bring leafy branches of olive trees, pine trees [*alei eitz shemen*, meaning uncertain], myrtles, palms and [other] leafy trees [*eitz avot*, meaning uncertain] to make booths" (Neh. 8:15). Here these branches are used to build booths, but are not waved, as will become the custom in later years.

3. As in Deuteronomy, Israelites are asked to "rejoice" (*us'machtem*) during the festival before God, namely, within the Temple compound.

4. For the first time, the festival is given a historical rationale: booths are connected with the experience of the Israelites' ancestors dwelling in the wilderness during the Exodus. According to the Bible, the first place where the Israelites rested after leaving Egypt was called "Sukkot" (Exod. 12:37). In our priestly text, this location is associated with the dwelling places of the exiles during the wilderness period. This connection is puzzling on two levels: Biblical sources clearly state that the Israelites in the Sinai lived in "tents" (*ohel*) and not in booths made of tree branches (see Num. 11:10, 16:26). Secondly, even if some Bedouins live in booths made of palm dates at the end of summer and during early autumn, as Ze'ev Meshel suggests[4] these are temporary dwellings during the calendar year, and not permanent abodes as the Bible seems to suggest (cf. Lev. 23:43). Furthermore, the use of booths fits better in an agricultural setting, during or after the harvest, in the Land of Israel and afterwards. In fact, Isaiah clearly states that grape harvesters kept "a booth" (*sukkah*) in their vineyards (Isa. 1:8). According to the agricultural practice of the time, in order "to protect the olive orchards in the month of harvest [September], their owners used to guard them by night, standing in shelters constructed of branches and vines."[5] Jeffrey Tigay, a contemporary Jewish scholar, suggests that

Leviticus might not have meant "booths" in its literal sense but, based on some midrashic and modern commentaries, that it could also refer to God's protective cloud that shielded the Israelites in the wilderness just as a booth protects one from the elements.[6]

When the festival received an additional historical interpretation is unclear. The dominant scholarly opinion is that this secondary explanation became more and more popular after the destruction of the First Temple in Jerusalem, in 586 B.C.E., and during the Israelites' stay in Babylonia. By that time the people were uprooted from their land and needed an additional purpose to keep the holy day alive. The historical explanation was then projected back and applied to the peregrinations in Sinai.

Sukkot in the Second Commonwealth and Beyond

During the postexilic period, when the Israelites rebuilt the Second Temple, the festival of Sukkot continued to play an important role in the religious calendar of the people. The Book of Ezra states that "the Festival of Booths" was celebrated in the seventh month in Jerusalem "with its daily burnt offerings in the proper quantities, on each day as is prescribed for it" (Ezra 3:4). In the Book of Nehemiah, a puzzling statement appears about Sukkot: on the second day of the festival, when the leaders of the people gathered around Ezra, they found written in the Torah a law requiring the Israelites to dwell in booths during the festival of the seventh month; so, they went out, gathered some branches and leaves, made themselves booths in private and public places, for "the Israelites had not done so from the days of Joshua son of Nun to that day" (Neh. 8:17). This text could imply that booths were not used since the days of the conquest of Canaan or that the Israelites had not built booths "like these" for a very long time.

The pilgrims continued to come to Jerusalem from all over the area to celebrate Sukkot. In a cryptic biblical note we are told that those who were not inclined to make a pilgrimage would not receive any rain, and even Egypt would suffer some sort of punishment in spite of the fact that people there could depend on the Nile for their water needs (Zech. 14:16–19). The historian Josephus reports that during Sukkot, the city of Lydda would empty out, "for the whole multitude were gone up to Jerusalem" (*Wars* II, 19:1).

Once in Jerusalem, the pilgrims offered their sacrifices at the Temple and brought in their second tithe and the first fruits, each carrying a *lulav* in hand. They also participated in colorful ceremonies, most of which dealt with water, in gratitude for the past and in prayer for the future. For example, on the morning of the first day, they witnessed a libation of water (*nisuch hamayim*) on the altar (*Mishnah Sukkah* 4:9). At night they attended the burning of fire torches during what was called *simchat beit hasho-eivah*, literally, "the festivity of the water drawing" (meaning uncertain) (*Mishnah Sukkah* 5:1–4). The Mishnah states that this ceremony included flute playing, dancing, singing, prayers, and songs and adds, "He who has never seen the joy at the *beit sho-eivah* ceremony has never seen joy in his life" (*Mishnah Sukkah* 5:1). According to Rabbi Baroka, there was also "the day of beating the palm branches" (*yom chibut harayot*) during which they used to beat the palm trees on the ground at the side of the Temple's altar (*Mishnah Sukkah* 4:6). On the seventh day, called Hoshana Rabbah, priests marched around the altar seven times, beating the earth with their willow branches and reciting prayers, *Hoshia na* (Save us). It is interesting to note that many of these ceremonies have to do with the need for water, and the rituals contain residues of old sympathetic magic by which the deity is "urged" or "forced" to produce certain results and, specifically in this case, using willows, an old symbol of fertility, to produce water for the next year. Even during the Rabbinic period, the prayer for rain occupied an important part of the liturgy. As the Mishnah states, "On Sukkot, [divine] judgment is passed in respect of rain" (*Mishnah Rosh HaShanah* 1:2).

The eighth day, the day after Sukkot, called *atzeret* in the Bible (Num. 29:35; see also Neh. 8:18; II Chron. 7:9), was considered a holy day in its own right, with its own appropriate sacrifices, but without the use of the palm branch and booth.

Toward the end of the biblical period, Sukkot maintained its dominance in the Jewish religious calendar. Even when the festival could not be observed because of foreign persecution, such as during the early Maccabean period, Jews celebrated a belated Sukkot once the Hasmoneans rededicated (*chanukah*) the Temple to the worship of one God (II Macc. 10:6).

During the first century c.e., the origin of Sukkot was assigned all the way back to Abraham: "He was the first to celebrate the Feast of Sukkot on the earth, and to dwell in booths" (Jubilees 16:21). In the writings of Philo of Alexandria, in addition to the priestly rationale for living in booths during the wilderness period during the Exodus, there is another, more naturalistic, explanation of booths: "The labor of farmers no longer requires that they live in the open air when all the fruits are being gathered in" (*Special*

Laws 2:204). Similarly, Josephus writes that Moses bid every family to build tents, "so that we may preserve ourselves from the cold of that time of the year" (*Ant.* III, 10:4).

For the Rabbis, whose task it was to preserve Judaism after the destruction of the Temple in 70 C.E., Sukkot continued to be a major festival, even though there was no Temple to which Jews could bring sacrifices or where they could celebrate it with the old rituals of water and fire. For them, the building of the sukkah, the waving of the *lulav* together with the *etrog* (interpreted now as the "fruit of the *hadar* tree" [Lev. 23:40]) during the *Hallel* service, and the recitation of appropriate prayers for rain became paramount.

The Rabbis debated all the details about the building of the sukkah, for example, whether it should be considered a permanent abode or, as eventually became normative in Jewish life, a temporary shelter (BT *Sukkah* 23a). They argued about its size and location, the obligation to "dwell" in it for seven days, the qualities of the *lulav* and *etrog*. They also added an extra day to the holy day for those who live outside of Israel, called "the second day for the Exile" (*yom tov sheini shel galuyot*), and recorded their memories of the Temple celebration (see *Mishnah Sukkah*). It was considered a mitzvah to rejoice during Sukkot, which was referred to as *Z'man Simchateinu* (the Season of Our Rejoicing).

During medieval times, following the Babylonian custom of reading the entire Torah in one year, it became the practice of the synagogues around the world to take out the scroll of the Torah on the day after Sh'mini Atzeret, read the last portion, and immediately begin reading from Genesis. This was an occasion for celebration and became known as *Simchat Torah* (the Joy of Torah). The spirit of happiness was maintained, but as Hayyim Schauss aptly states, "Jews celebrated not because of the grapes and the other crops, but because of the Torah."[7]

Each of the four symbols of Sukkot (called *arbaah minim*) was clearly identified based on a Rabbinic interpretation of Leviticus 23:40: the *lulav*, a palm branch; the *hadas,* a myrtle; the *aravah,* a willow; the *etrog,* a citron. The *etrog* was a new addition and has kept its own separate identity. Three myrtle branches and two willows fit in the reed holder of the *lulav*. On every day of Sukkot (except Shabbat), during the recitation of the *Hallel* (festival psalms), the *lulav* and *etrog* are held together and waved in four directions and up and down, not as in earlier times to force the divinity to produce rain, but to indicate God's sovereignty over the entire universe.

These symbols have also received extensive interpretations in the literature. In the case of the *lulav,* just as the four species cannot exist without water, so the entire world cannot exist without rain. For others, the four components represent the three patriarchs and Joseph, or the four matriarchs, namely, Sarah, Rebekah, Rachel, and Leah. Some argue that the citron stands for the heart, the palm branch for the backbone, the myrtle for the eye, and the willow for the mouth. Yet, all must be submitted to the service of God.

In the opinion of some commentators, the citron has taste and aroma, referring to Jews who know Torah and practice it; the palm has taste but no aroma, referring to Jews who know Torah but do not practice it; the myrtle has aroma but no taste, referring to Jews who do good works but do not know Torah; and, finally, the willow has neither aroma nor taste, referring to Jews who do not know Torah, nor do they practice it. Yet, the failings of one are compensated by the virtues of the others. God requires us to bring them all together in one bond of concerned individuals.

A popular interpretation of the sukkah is that since the sukkah is small and cozy, it reminds us that we need to find room for all people irrespective of their status in life. Furthermore, being weak and flimsy, the sukkah teaches us that human beings need to recognize their limitations. According to another opinion, as a temporary structure, the sukkah is a symbol of our ephemeral life.

Kabbalistic literature places emphasis on the guests (called *ushpizin*) that are invited to be part of a meal within the sukkah. Not only are ordinary individuals asked to join in a community meal, but by invoking their names, many of the patriarchs and ancient Jewish leaders, both male and female, such as Joseph, Moses, Aaron, and David, but also, Sarah, Rachel, Miriam, Hannah, and others, are also symbolically invited in to be part of the celebration.

In Modern Times

In our time, the festival of Sukkot has lost much of its biblical importance. Coming right after the intensive High Holy Days and due to our increased urbanization that disconnects us from the soil, the importance of Sukkot has been marginalized. It is still in the Jewish calendar as one of the Three Pilgrimage Festivals, but the rituals do not have the same relevance as they did in the past. Reform Jews, following the biblical calendar in Israel, celebrate it only seven days, and combine Sh'mini Atzeret with Simchat Torah. Except for some traditional Jews, only a small portion of American Jews build sukkot, and only a few carry a *lulav* and *etrog*. Many synagogues now set up a sukkah but use it only one or two days. On the other hand, there are some young people, few in number though, who are committed to revitalizing the festival of Sukkot and, using prefabricated kits, are now building "booths" in their backyards, organizing "sukkah hopping" parties, and turning the booth into a place of hospitality for family and friends. It remains to be seen, however, if this renewed interest in Sukkot can be sustained in our industrial society.

Though the celebration of Sukkot is on the decline, Simchat Torah seems to have taken a bigger role in Jewish life today. During the *hakafot*, the circling within the synagogue with Torah scrolls carried on arms, congregants dance in the aisles and, in some neighborhoods, even into the streets. Reform Jews have added the custom of consecrating the students entering religious school in the younger grades, thus attracting hundreds of enthusiastic parents who wish to see their children carrying little Torah flags and reciting the *Sh'ma* before the full congregation.

In order to revitalize the festival, there has been an attempt to connect Sukkot with the environment, stressing our dependence on the soil for whose fruits we must express our gratitude to the Source of Life. Thus, the message of Sukkot is being used to foster programs on affordable housing, homelessness, poverty, or solar power. Many congregations in the United States are opening up soup kitchens or congregational shelters or sponsoring food and clothing drives. Some have environmental groups operating out of religious establishments in this spirit of Sukkot, such as Teva ("Nature") or Adam va-Adamah ("Adam and Earth"). By extension, many are urging vegetarian diets and healthy eating. It is suggested that "the sukkah is a practical lesson in non-attachment to the material world—an eight day meditation-in-practice that helps us remember that no material goody can really give us security, that real security comes only from remaking the world in a just way."[8]

A very old festival, most likely taken over from the local Canaanites, and based on some very primitive myths and magical thinking, Sukkot has undergone tremendous changes. From being the most important agricultural *chag* in the calendar, it became historicized in the exilic period, but progressively fell from grace after the destruction of the Second Temple, only to regain new interpretations in our time, away from its historical moorings, in the hope of infusing new life into it.

16

Do Jews Believe in Heaven and Hell?

Scenic view of the Valley of Hinom in Jerusalem. (Courtesy of American Colony.)
Photo by Eric Matson, 1910. From Israel Government Press Office.

The Claim

Many people, among them some Jews, claim that Judaism does not have a concept of afterlife or, to be more exact, that it does not believe in heaven and hell or in hell and paradise. This chapter will examine the veracity of this assumption, arguing that even though the concept has undergone many changes through the centuries, Judaism has always maintained a belief in the afterlife.

The Mystery of Death

Death is one of the greatest mysteries of life and creates different levels of anxiety among individuals. Intellectually, we all know that we are going to die one day. As Ecclesiastes succinctly states, there is "a time for being born and a time for dying" (Eccles. 3:2). But emotionally, we are seldom ready to accept it. Often, we do not even want to use the proper verb to describe the act of departing from this world, namely "to die." Instead we say, "he is gone," "she is with God," "he is in heaven," "she is resting in peace," "he is no longer with us," "she passed on," "he was laid to rest," not to mention "he croaked" or "he kicked the bucket."

There is no escaping from death. It is the destiny of everyone and everything that breathes. As the Psalmist reminds us, "What man can live and not see death?" (Ps. 89:49). In the Talmud (BT *B'rachot* 17a), Rabbi Yochanan quips, *Sof adam lamut*, "The end of a human being is to die." Sometimes death comes peacefully, at other times as a result of pain and suffering. We reluctantly accept the reality of death when it happens after a long and fulfilling life but are devastated when it affects a young person or occurs violently.

There are some people who actually welcome death, especially after a long life or because of a painful condition. There is a famous Talmudic story about Rabbi Akiva, a second-century sage, who was tortured by the Romans. When he was being taken out for execution, it was the hour to recite the *Sh'ma* (Deut. 6:4). His students marveled at his resiliency. But Akiva said, "All my life I have been troubled about the implication of the commandment to love God with 'all your soul' [Deut. 6:5]. Now I have a chance to fulfill it." He died while prolonging the last word of the *Sh'ma*. Thereupon God proclaimed, "Happy are you Akiva, that your soul departed with the word *echad* [one]" (BT *B'rachot* 61b).

Most people fear death. Not ready to give up, they feel they still have the energy to accomplish more or enjoy more here on earth. Some are concerned about those they leave behind or terrified about what will happen to them after they are gone. One of the main reasons for this apprehension is that we do not know what awaits us beyond the grave. The unknown is always a troublesome source of anxiety. The prayer book gives voice to this feeling when it states, "Though we cannot understand, we accept life as the gift of God. Yet, death, life's twin, we face with fear. But why be afraid? Death is a haven to the weary, a relief for the sorely afflicted."[1]

Death is not a state we can experience and share with others. It is final and cannot be recounted. Those who have had a so-called near-death experience seem to repeat stories that are usually framed by the culture in which the individual lives.

Because no one has come back to tell us about life after death, the only thing we can do is project our expectations and hopes for the world beyond the grave. A survey conducted by *Newsweek* (March 1987) found that although the pulpit may be full of agnostics, the pews are filled with believers in life after death. Religion gives shape to most of these images. And adherents of different faith traditions follow those beliefs formulated by their ancient or modern sages. Our imaginations and creative thinking about the afterlife reveal more about our own values. Our expectations for the life beyond are colored mostly by how we live our lives here on earth.

Throughout the centuries, humanity has tried to defeat death in an attempt to live forever, only to realize that this is a vain pursuit. In the ancient Near East, Gilgamesh, the legendary ruler of the city of Uruk, learns the secret of immortality from Utnapishtim, the hero of the Flood story, but fails to obtain it when a serpent steals the magical plant he was about to ingest (*ANET*, 96). Similarly, Adapa, the Sumerian king of Eridu, misses a chance to gain immortality when the gods trick him (*ANET*, 102). In the Bible, God banishes Adam (and presumably Eve) from the Garden of Eden, fearing that they might eat from the "Tree of Life" and consequently live forever (Gen. 3:22–24).

The Hebrew Bible contains a few examples of people who apparently never died or were later on revived. For example, "Enoch walked with God and then was no more, for God had taken him" (Gen. 5:24). The expression "[Enoch] was no more, for God took him" is problematic. Does it mean he never died or that he died prematurely? We are not sure. Similarly, Elijah, the prophet, did not die a human death, because he "went up to heaven in a whirlwind" (II Kings 2:11). Both Elijah (I Kings 17:17–24) and his disciple Elisha (II Kings 4:17–37) revived people. There is also the case of a man who was buried, but when his bones came in contact with Elisha's bones, "he came up to life and stood up" (II Kings 13:21). These legendary cases, however, do not deal with the resurrection of the body leading to eternal life but, being exceptional, only with revivification through God's miraculous powers.

Various Opinions

The three main religions that claim the patriarch Abraham as their ancestor, namely, Judaism, Christianity, and Islam, teach that after death there is an afterlife. Generally speaking, both Judaism and Islam maintain that after death, the wicked go to hell and the righteous to heaven. In addition, many Christians believe in an intermediate place called "purgatory," which is a temporary dwelling or condition for those who died in grace but are imperfectly purified. The stay in purgatory can last a short time or much longer, depending on the gravity of one's sin.

Throughout the centuries, Jewish teachers have developed various images of life beyond the grave, and there is no unanimity of thought on this subject among Jews today. Unlike other religions, which have formulated strict dogmas about the afterlife, Judaism has historically welcomed alternative options regarding the world beyond. In our time, based on early Rabbinic teachings, Orthodox and a number of liberal Jews still affirm that in *olam haba* (the world-to-come), occurring sequentially right after the coming of the Messiah, the *t'chiyat hameitim* (the resurrection of the body), and the final judgment, all individuals will end up either in paradise or in hell. This idea of resurrection as well as hell and paradise has heavily influenced both Christianity and Islam, who affirm it in their Holy Scriptures and religious writings.

There is a multitude of mainstream Jewish beliefs on these topics. Though the belief in resurrection together with hell and paradise is the dominant view in Rabbinic Judaism, some modern Jews put their faith in the immortality of the soul, which has been a cardinal position in Reform Judaism for decades. Others defend the idea of reincarnation, especially those who subscribe to kabbalistic teachings. Still others argue that we can transcend death in a variety of ways, such as through our children, our people, our humanity, our influence on others, or our good deeds. There are also a few who state that after death there is total disintegration, with nothing remaining behind.[2]

Life After Death in the Bible

During much of biblical time, the Israelites believed that when individuals die, they go down to a place called Sheol. In fact, "to go down to Sheol" simply means to die (e.g., Gen. 37:35, 42:38). The meaning of the Hebrew word *sheol* is not clear. The Bible also refers to it as *shachat* (the ditch [Job 33:24]), *afar* (the dust [Gen. 3:19]), *avadon* (perdition [Job 26:6]), *kever* (the grave [Ezek. 32:22]), and *bor* (the pit [Ps. 88:5]) and describes it as a large hole beneath the earth, or under the waters, or at the base of the mountains. It is important to note, however, that these expressions are used metaphorically and at times refer to those individuals who are suffering and/or on the brink of death.

Sheol is understood to be a place of darkness, a place of silence. It is not necessarily set aside for punishment, because everyone who dies goes down there. In fact, in some unusual occasions, such as when the Witch of Endor brought up the long-deceased Samuel (I Sam. 28:13–15), the dead could even be brought up temporarily from the grave. The mere fact that necromancy, that is, communication with the dead to foretell the future, was prohibited in the Bible (Lev. 19:31; Deut. 18:10–11) clearly indicates that some ancient Israelites were engaged in this practice (see also Isa. 8:19; II Chron. 33:6).

During their stay in Sheol, according to the biblical text, the bodies are left there but are not obliterated. In fact, they seem to live a shadowy kind of existence. "I am a helpless man," states the Psalmist (most likely metaphorically), "abandoned among the dead" (Ps. 88:5). The prophet Isaiah tells us that after the death of the king of Babylon, "Sheol below was astir, to greet your coming" (Isa. 14:9–11). In Sheol, bodies, often called "shades" (Ps. 88:11), at times "chirp" (Isa. 29:4), remain "without strength" (Ps. 88:5), and are "freed from the sickness of the flesh" (Job 3:17). God can hear their voices (Jon. 2:3).

The Israelites viewed Sheol in the same way as most people in the ancient Near East, who called it "the Land of No Return" (*ertzet la tari*, in Akkadian)[3]: "Whoever goes down to Sheol does not come up" (Job 7:9). The dead cannot reach out to God, and those who go down cannot expect to receive divine grace (Isa. 38:18; Pss. 6:6, 115:17). When the child of King David and Bathsheba became sick, David prayed and fasted, but when the child died, he rose up and ate. His courtiers were surprised at his behavior, but he said to them, "Now that he is dead, why should I fast? Can I bring him back again? I shall go to him, but he will never come back to me" (II Sam. 12:23). However, just as God has power over the entire universe, God can also draw out of Sheol those who are worthy (Pss. 30:4, 49:16, 116:8, 139:8).

Resurrection of the Body

According to a rabbinic scholar, "The primary eschatological doctrine of Judaism is the resurrection, the revivification of the dead."[4] However, when and how this idea entered Jewish consciousness is uncertain. Louis Jacobs argues that "the doctrine of the Hereafter came into full prominence during the Maccabean period when many good men were dying for their faith and the older view of reward and punishment in this life became untenable."[5] According to Milton Steinberg, the source is either Zoroastrianism, with its teachings of resurrection and last judgment, or Hellenism, which emphasized the belief in immortality.[6]

Obviously, ancient Israelites knew of the Canaanite belief in the death and reemergence of Baal, the fertility god at the turn of the seasons, but whether they learned about resurrection leading to eternal life from others or whether the idea emerged from within is difficult to determine. The idea of a resurrection that leads to eternal life solidified only in the later stages of the biblical times. Though the idea may have had roots in the past, it made its clear appearance for the first time in the postexilic period. In Ezekiel's famous prophetic passage of the "Valley of the Dry Bones," God promises that the Jewish community as a whole would reawaken, in a symbolic way, for better times. God says to Ezekiel, "O mortal, these bones are the whole House of Israel. . . . I am going to open your graves, O My people, and bring you to the land of Israel" (37:11–12). Here, resurrection is imagined happening not for individuals but for the whole nation, as a metaphor, after the final judgment. A more specific reference is found in Daniel, where individual resurrection would occur before the final judgment, but only for a limited few: "Many of those that sleep in the dust of the earth will awake, some to eternal life, others to reproaches, to everlasting abhorrence" (Dan. 12:2; see also late additions to Isa. 25:8, 26:19).

The belief in resurrection was highly debated in the early Rabbinic periods. Josephus, the first-century Jewish historian, writes that the Sadducees rejected the idea, whereas the Pharisees strongly supported it (*Ant.* XVIII, 1:3.4; *Wars* II, 8:14; see also Acts 23:8). Jesus ben Sira, a Sadducee and professional scribe who lived in the first quarter of the second century B.C.E., denied resurrection by saying, "Do not forget, there is no coming back" (Ben Sira 38:21). Eventually, however, the belief in resurrection was turned into a cardinal principle of Rabbinic Judaism by Rabbis who were the disciples of the early Pharisees. They tried to demonstrate that this idea was grounded in the teachings of the Torah (BT *Sanhedrin* 91b) and, in fact, stated that those who deny this assumption do not have a share in the world-to-come (*Mishnah Sanhedrin* 10:1).

According to Rabbinic doctrine, "all righteous gentiles will be resurrected" (*Tosefta Sanhedrin* 13:2) and "all Israel will have a share in the world-to-come" (*Mishnah Sanhedrin* 10:1). However, there are exceptions, reflecting the ancient Rabbis' opposition to certain kinds of people or behaviors. For Rabbi Chanina, the adulterer, anyone who puts his fellow to public shame, or one who calls another by an opprobrious nickname will not be resurrected (BT *Bava M'tzia* 58a). For Rabbi Elazar, those who live outside the Holy Land, the ignorant, and whoever is slack with his Torah studies will not return (BT *K'tubot* 111a–b). Rabbi Akiva is even stricter in his opinion and denies resurrection to anyone who reads alien books or engages in magic (*Mishnah Sanhedrin* 10:1). Some ancient kings were considered so wicked that they do not deserve resurrection at all: Jeroboam, Ahab, and Manasseh (*Mishnah Sanhedrin* 1:2). The same applies to the generation of the Flood (*Mishnah Sanhedrin* 10:3). In all of these cases, the Rabbis' assessment seems to be that some people are not worthy of eternal life because of their wickedness.

The belief in the resurrection of the body held sway for a long time among Jews. This idea was rejected by some Jewish philosophers during the Enlightenment period, including Moses Mendelssohn (1729–86) and Abraham Geiger (1810–74), as well as many Reform Jews in Germany. Yet the Orthodox Jewish prayer book continues to this day to praise God "for reviving the dead" (*m'chayeih meitim*). In contrast, in light of Reform Judaism's affirmation of the immortality of the soul after death, the *Union Prayer Book* of 1940 had, "Praised be Thou, who has implanted within us eternal life." In *Gates of Prayer* of 1975, the same prayer read, "Blessed is the Lord, the Source of Life [*m'chayeih hakol*]."

However, in more recent times, there has been a shift toward acceptance of the belief in the resurrection of the body. Even among those Reform Jews who are willing to affirm it, it is often understood in its most general sense, perhaps as a metaphor. As Richard Levy wrote, "Each morning's arising [is] a little resurrection."[7] The new prayer book of the Reform Movement, *Mishkan T'filah* (CCAR, 2007), retains both statements, namely, *m'chayeih hakol* and, in parentheses, *m'chayei hameitim*, allowing the worshiper to choose between the two ideologies.

Paradise

In Judaism two different but related terms are used to designate the place of final bliss for individuals after death: *Gan Eden* and *Pardes*. In English, paradise is often referred to as "heaven." The word *Gan Eden* (literally, "the Garden of Eden") refers to the special garden set aside by God for Adam and Eve at the beginning of Creation and from which they are expelled because of their disobedience (Gen. 2–3; see also chapter 4 of this book).

The second term, *Pardes*, the root of our modern English word "paradise," is of Persian origin, and it simply means "garden" (see Neh. 2:8; Song of Songs 4:13; Eccles. 2:5). In the third century B.C.E., the Septuagint brought the two concepts (namely, *Gan Eden* and *Pardes*) together when it translated the reference to the garden in Genesis 2 as *paradeisos*. In the later biblical times, the idea of "paradise" was connected with the end of times. In the Apocrypha, for example, it became the final "place of rest" (II Esd. 7:36) and contrasted with hell (II Esd. 4:7). In the Rabbinic period, paradise was viewed as the abode of the righteous after death. In fact, around the first or second century C.E., in addition to the earthly garden ("the lower *Gan Eden*"), with its abundant vegetation and fertility (see I Enoch 32; Jubilees 4:26), one finds many references to the heavenly garden ("the higher *Gan Eden*") for the ultimate repose of the righteous (see BT *Chagigah* 14b–15a; IV Esd. 4:7–8; Testament of Abraham 20:14; II Cor. 12:2–4; Apocalypse of Moses 40:2). In Jewish mystical texts, paradise, both earthly and heavenly, is viewed as being part of the divine emanations, because the central object in it, namely the Tree of Life, is identified with the tree of the *s'firot*.

There are only a few references in the early Rabbinic literature describing the features of paradise. For some of the Rabbis of this period, the present world is a foretaste of paradise in the world-to-come, which is a place of reward for the righteous, with its celebration of Shabbat, sunshine, and sex (BT *B'rachot* 57b). For others, it is a place where the righteous sit at golden tables (BT *Taanit* 25a) or on golden stools (BT *K'tubot* 77b), participating in lavish banquets (BT *Bava Batra* 75a). Rav, a third-century sage, gives us a longer description, when he states, "In the world-to-come there is neither eating nor drinking; no procreation of children or business transactions, no envy or hatred or rivalry; but the righteous sit enthroned, their crowns on their heads, and enjoy the luster of the Divine Presence" (BT *B'rachot* 17a).

One of the most colorful and imaginative descriptions of paradise is found at the end of *Machbarot Immanuel*, by the thirteenth-century Jewish writer Immanuel ben Solomon of Rome, also known as Manoello Guideo, who was both a poet and a scholar. Immanuel wrote many books on Bible but is most famous for his satiric verses. He was a contemporary of Dante Alighieri of Florence and then Rome (1265–1321), the well-known author of the *Divine Comedy*, and most likely wrote under his influence. In his long poem entitled *Tophet and Eden*,[8] Immanuel tells us that when he was an old man of sixty, Daniel, "a man of delight," led him through the halls of hell and paradise. He describes paradise in two different ways:

And as on the higher steps we did alight, the God of the World came into sight, and there the heavens new and a new earth we saw; therein was nothing foul, no loathsome flaw, only as earth purified, where holiness is in store, and steps are prepared for the holy-souled that lower, second, and third degrees enfold. There is the perfect light of which the wise have told, that it is a sevenfold light as that of the seven days of old. For what beauty and excellence therein is found! No weariness is there, none who fall to the ground; in those souls purity is rife.

And:

Tables and candlesticks, thrones and crowns were there to be seen; they were for the souls that were pure and clean; and there was a throne of ivory, great in size, overlaid with gold in wealth, giving life unto those who reached it, and unto their flesh giving health; and the stones of a crown shone forth upon it on high; while garments of blue and purple and scarlet were spread, and about it did lay like polished copper gleaming, unto all lands their beauty beaming.

According to Rabbinic Judaism, it is hoped that all righteous Jews will end up in paradise as a reward for their good deeds on earth.

Hell

There are various terms by which "hell" is identified in ancient sources. In the Hebrew Bible, the primary word is *Geihinom* (*Gehenna* in Greek and Latin), referring to "the Valley of Hinnom" (in Hebrew *Gei Ven-hinom*), the present Wadi al-Rababi, a ravine south of Jerusalem (Josh. 15:8). This was the scene of an idolatrous Canaanite cult that was involved with passing children through fire in sacrifice to the god Molech. Part of this valley was also called Tophet (Jer. 7:31; II Kings 23:10), which stood for the place of torture and punishment after death. The word "Hades" (from the Greek for "the unseen") is also found in Greek mythology referring to the underworld and the god of the dead.

During the monarchic times, some Israelites, following Canaanite customs, put their children to death in this Valley of Hinnom, most likely in expectation of appeasing Molech, the local god. We are told, for example, that King Ahaz of Judah "made offerings in the Valley of Ben-hinnom and burned his sons in fire" (II Chron. 28:3; II Kings 16:3). Similarly, King Manasseh of Judah "consigned his sons to the fire in the Valley of Ben-hinnom" (II Chron. 33:6; II Kings 21:6). Many prophets forcefully denounced this idolatrous practice. Accusing the people of Judah, Jeremiah states in the name of God, "They have built the shrines of Tophet in the Valley of Ben-hinnom to burn their sons and daughters in fire—which I never commanded, which never came to My mind" (Jer. 7:31; see also Jer. 32:35). During the seventh century B.C.E., when the cult was centralized in Jerusalem, one of the shrines that was destroyed was the one found in *Gei-hinom*: "He [King Josiah] also defiled Tophet, which is in the Valley of Ben-hinnom, so that no one might consign his son or daughter to the fire of Molech" (II Kings 23:10).

By the first century C.E., *Geihinom* was already viewed as a place of fiery torment for the wicked after death or after the Last Judgment. In the Apocrypha, *Geihinom* is "a pit of torment" (II Esd. 7:36). In the New Testament, too, *Geihinom* is reserved for the punishment of the wicked (Matt. 5:22, 13:42). According to the Rabbis, after death two gates are open: "*Geihinom* for the wicked and paradise for the righteous" (BT *Eiruvin* 19a). *Geihinom* is so vast that it was even compared to a pot whose lid was formed by the rest of the world (BT *P'sachim* 94a). It was the "pit of destruction" for the wicked (*Pirkei Avot* 5:19) and the abode of the shameless (*Pirkei Avot* 5:20). Those who neglect the study of Torah "inherit *Geihinom*" (*Pirkei Avot* 1:5).

According to the school of Shammai, there will be three groups of people on the Day of Judgment: the thoroughly righteous, the thoroughly wicked, and those in the middle. The first are doomed to *Geihinom*. The second are entitled to everlasting life in paradise. "The intermediate will go down to *Geihinom* and squeal [because of their punishment], and rise again" (BT *Rosh HaShanah* 16b–17a). Rabbi Akiva, on the other hand, restricts the time spent in hell for some people: "the judgments of the unrighteous in *Geihinom* shall endure twelve months" (*Mishnah Eduyot* 2:10). Similarly the midrash tells us "the judgment upon the wicked in hell lasts twelve months" (*Midrash Mishlei* 17:1).

In medieval times, Immanuel ben Solomon in *Tophet and Eden* depicts *Geihinom* in frightening terms. First he writes:

> Now, as we journeyed thence, men once in violence fleet, dismembered as to their thumbs and the toes of their feet, hanging on gallows of trees, we did meet. Their flesh was being eaten by some fowl wild and fierce, and their eyes the young eagle and raven of the valley did pierce. Hail and fire did upon them continuously rain; their fruit from above, their roots below, were caught in destruction's train.

He then offers a second description:

> We journeyed thence, and lo, there were pits full of serpents, poisonous and flying, hundreds and thousands of lions and leopards were dying, and round about angels of death with their swords were plying, and torrents of mighty waters in floods were lying, making the hearts of onlookers gasp with sighing.

The terrifying scenes of "hell" were meant to discourage people from acting wickedly and, instead, to choose a path of righteousness that would bring blessings to themselves and to their families.

Preparing for the World Beyond

We all hope that when our final moment arrives, it comes late in life and free of pain. In reality, death is part of life. "I often feel," writes Rabbi Joshua Loth Liebman, "that death is not the enemy of life, but its friend, for it is the knowledge that our years are limited which makes them so precious."[9] Similarly, in another context, he adds, "Judaism teaches us to understand death as part of the Divine pattern of the universe. Actually we could not have our sensitivity without fragility. Mortality is the tax that we pay for the privilege of love, thought, creative word."[10]

Just before he died in January 2007, the humorist Art Buchwald wrote an article in which he lamented all the opportunities that went by him: "I am now punishing myself for having passed up so many good things earlier in the trip."[11] There is an echo of this sentiment found in the Rabbinic literature. In the Jerusalem Talmud (JT *Kiddushin* 48:2–4), it is stated in the name of Rav that when we stand before the Holy One at the final judgment, we will have to give account for every permissible pleasure in this world that we could have enjoyed and did not. Note that the "pleasure" must be "permissible," namely, legitimate and not damaging to anyone. Not to take full advantage of the gift of life is a sin. We must, therefore, learn how to live our life fully, richly, creatively, and nobly (see Eccles. 5:17–19). For many traditional Jews, the means to this end are the performance of the divine commandments. In the ethical literature of the late medieval times, Moshe Chayim Luzzatto (1707–46) of Padua, Italy, states that "man was placed in this world first, so that by these means [i.e., the mitzvot] which were provided for him here, he would be able to reach the place which had been prepared for him, the World to Come, there to be sated with the goodness which he acquired through them."[12]

The old myth of hell and paradise, elaborated so much throughout the centuries, still energizes our imagination today and prompts those who believe in it with the proper incentive to lead a good life here on earth.

Epilogue

Is the Bible True?

The Bible: A Best Seller

The Bible is the world's all-time best seller. Translated into all imaginable languages around the globe, it has the widest appeal of all books. According to the 2006 Scripture Language Report of the United Bible Society, there are 2,426 versions of the Holy Scriptures floating around. However, only a relatively small percentage of people study the Bible seriously. Samuel Sandmel, a biblical scholar, once wrote, "More people praise the Bible than read it. More read it than understand it, and more understand it than conscientiously follow it."[1]

There are a number of reasons for this. The Bible is a library of books that was written centuries ago; hence, it reflects a very different viewpoint of the world and society. More often than not, we try to inject into the old texts ideas that are taken for granted in our days (an endeavor known as "eisegesis") and assume that they were accepted in years past as well. Often, this approach misconstrues their message.

Throughout time, people have used and misused the Bible to promote their own agenda. For example, in the United States, both abolitionists and pro-slavery advocates made reference to the biblical material to defend their position.[2] It may be difficult for us to accept that the people in biblical times, living in an agrarian society and prescientific world, would conceive of the universe in a way that is often radically different from us. Yet, we must.

Many people think they can pick up a Bible, read it, and easily make sense of it. The reality is much different. Like any other text written in the past, the Bible needs to be studied, not just casually read, in order to understand its message. It is for this purpose that one uses commentaries that establish a context, resolve internal contradictions, clarify certain words, point to its relevance today, and allow us to react to its lesson. That is also why the ancient Rabbis surrounded the traditional texts with a variety of commentaries that span the centuries, each one taking a different take on a particular passage. Often, they interpreted the Scriptures in light of their own time and place and therefore made the texts speak to the needs of their contemporaries. Though subscribing to the presupposition that "Moses received the Torah at Mount Sinai" (*Pirkei Avot* 1:1), who then transmitted it, both in written and oral form, from one generation to another, the Rabbis still built layers upon layers of meaning, on the assumption that their new interpretation was already imbedded in the old text. As Yochanan ben Bag Bag taught, "Turn it [Torah], turn it again, for everything is in it" (*Pirkei Avot* 5:24). In other words, we are taught to study the Torah over and over, because it is a complete guide to life in general. But this requires dedication to study. Today we may or may not accept the Rabbis' assumption that the entire Torah comes verbally from Mount Sinai. However, the complexities of the text require us to admit that the Bible cannot simply be read but must be studied diligently. Not too many people, however, are willing or able to do just that.

The Challenge of Biblical Criticism

The results of modern biblical criticism denying the traditional point of view regarding the authorship and date of many of the biblical books (see chapter 1) have bewildered many ordinary readers who have not been exposed to these issues in a disciplined manner. The Bible claims that a number of books were specifically written by certain individuals, such as the Pentateuch by Moses, Psalms by David, and Proverbs by Solomon. On the other hand, biblical scholars maintain that scriptural texts, often attributed to specific authors, were in reality reedited many times through the centuries and attributed to people in the past. The believer is, therefore, in a quandary: if the Bible is the word of God, and therefore inerrant, how does one deal with the challenges of modern biblical criticism? Once doubt sets in, faith is in jeopardy.

People often ask: Were Adam and Eve the first human beings? Did the parting of the Reed Sea take place the way the Bible describes it? Or, did the sun really stop during the days of Joshua? If your answer is yes, then your belief in the inerrancy of the Bible is affirmed. But if the answer is maybe or no, then your religious convictions based perhaps on your childhood education, in which these teachings were taken for granted, get a big jolt. Furthermore, if you maintain that Bible critics are correct in some areas but not in others, where do you stop? How do you choose to accept this conclusion but not the others?

On what basis can you make this judgment? Michael Coogan is right in stating, "Study may lead to disbelief."[3]

I can attest to this crisis of faith because I went through it in my younger days. Coming out of an Orthodox Jewish environment that insisted on the acceptance of the Bible as the literal word of God, my exposure to biblical criticism was spiritually unnerving. Every time I learned that certain events in biblical times did not or could not have happened the way they are described, I felt as if the ground under me was falling away, as if my spiritual anchors were disappearing one at a time. Gradually, however, I regained my balance through continuous studies over a period of many years and a reevaluation of my previously naïve understanding. Consequently, I developed a new appreciation and, hopefully, a better understanding of the biblical message.

In the last few decades a number of popular articles have appeared that discuss the question of whether or not the Bible is true.[4] In April 2001, a Conservative rabbi in California, Rabbi David Wolpe, an author of many popular studies in Judaism, created a furor by questioning the historicity of the Exodus story.[5] The question revolves around the reliability of the biblical text. Some, based on biblical claims that the text is the *ipsissima verba* of God, simply reject the teachings of modern biblical critics. For them, the Bible cannot be wrong because it is what God actually said and, therefore, it is authoritative and binding. Others will admit that the text is an inspired work but still comes from a divine source. And there are others who, though admitting that it is an inspired document, argue that it is a human document written by fallible individuals.

Regrettably, the population at large does not always accept the historical-critical method used by most biblical scholars today. Rarely do the results of modern exegetical studies trickle down to the congregational level and become readily accepted. One of the reasons, writes Michael Coogan, is that the critical method represents a challenge to the authority of ecclesiastical leaders: "If the Bible is not true in any simple sense of that term, not free from error and not consistent, then so too must be subsequent formulations, whether conciliar, pontifical or episcopal."[6] This has created a major gap between biblical scholarship and the pews. Consequently, most worshipers are left without updated information on this subject. Stephen J. Patterson argues that exegetes "must be willing to share the results of their exegetical and historical work with the widest possible public, regardless of the unpleasant consequences that such intellectual openness may sometimes seem to produce." To do anything less, he adds, is "intellectual malpractice."[7]

Levels of Interpretation

Historically speaking, the study of biblical texts has been done by using various methodologies and through the lenses of different perspectives. In the first century C.E. in Alexandria, Egypt, the Jewish philosopher Philo argued that the Bible could be read on two different levels. In addition to its surface and simple meaning, the texts have a deeper and more profound significance. Philo maintained that the best way to understand the Bible is allegorically. For example, when Genesis mentions Noah's children (Gen. 5:32), these names, he noted, really represent symbols: "Shem" is good, "Ham" stands for evil, and "Japheth" for the indifferent (see "On Genesis," 1:88).

The ancient Rabbis argued that the biblical texts have four different levels of interpretation called *PARDES* (an acrostic of a Hebrew word meaning "orchard"): *p'shat* is the philological, basic meaning; *remez* is the allegorical level; *d'rash* is the homiletic or interpretative; and *sod* is the esoteric and mystical.

For Maimonides, the great medieval Jewish philosopher, the best way to read the Bible was metaphorical. For example, when the Bible mentions "God's finger" (Exod. 31:18), "God's feet" (Exod. 24:10), and "God's hand" (Exod. 9:3), these should not be taken literally. Instead, they refer to God's greatness. "All these expressions," he writes in his *Mishneh Torah*, "are adapted to the mental capacity of the majority of humanity that has a clear perception of physical bodies only. The Torah speaks in the language of human beings. All these phrases are metaphorical" (Knowledge: Basic Principles 1:9; see also *Guide of the Perplexed* 1:1–30).

It is also clear that no one reads or studies the Bible in a vacuum. Jews usually read the Scriptures through the eyes of the Rabbis, and Christians read it through the lenses of the interpreters of the church. For example, Christians consider the temptation of Adam and Eve in the Garden of Eden as the cause for "the fall of man" and the reason for the "original sin," requiring Jesus's intervention for human salvation. As noted in Chapter 4, many Jewish commentators interpret the same story as the beginning of humanity's emergence as discerning individuals. Without fall or original sin, there is no need for a belief in Jesus as the intercessor. Jews are encouraged to carry out mitzvot to fulfill their human destiny.

Furthermore, the Hebrew Bible is written in Old Hebrew (and partly in classical Aramaic), which is often different from Modern Hebrew in its nuance and meaning. At times, we simply do now know what certain Hebrew words mean and have no way of finding out because they are *hapax legomena*, that is, they occur only once in the entire corpus. Especially in books such as Job or Hosea, the number of uncertainties is so vast that we even have a hard time making sense of the message. Biblical translations, which are really interpretations, deal with these problems either by guessing or simply by stating, "Meaning unclear." These are among the many reasons why numberless biblical commentaries have been published to deal with textual issues from linguistic, historical, and theological perspectives.

God's Interest in History

One of the great difficulties in understanding the Bible in our time resides in the fact that ancient Israelites had a very different concept of history than ours, which relies on human evaluation of events without divine intervention. In the opinion of the biblical authors, God is intimately involved in the history of the people of Israel, and biblical history reflects this belief. God made a special covenant with them at Sinai, took them out of Egypt, accompanied them through their peregrinations in the wilderness, gave them the Land of Israel, and even went into exile with them. But the God of Israel, a universal God, is also involved in the fate of other nations. The prophet Amos berated the people in the Northern Kingdom, saying, "To Me, O

Israelites, you are just like the Ethiopians—declares the Eternal. True, I brought Israel up from the land of Egypt, but also the Philistines from Caphtor and the Arameans from Kir" (Amos 9:7). Second Isaiah declared the Persian king Cyrus a "messiah" (Isa. 45:1), promising him success in his endeavors: "I call you by name, I hail you by title, though you have not known Me" (Isa. 45:4).

At times, the God of Israel uses other nations to punish the Israelites. Thus, according to the prophet Isaiah, God will call upon "a nation afar off" (possibly alluding to the Assyrians) in order to oppress Judah (see Isa. 5:26, 10:5–6). In Jeremiah, the rod of God's anger is the "enemy from the north" (maybe the Babylonians), and it is commissioned by God in order to punish the Southern Kingdom (see Jer. 1:15, 4:6, 5:15).

In the Bible, God is at times viewed as a warrior, and military victories are often attributed to God. In Exodus 15, the poet refers to God as *ish milchamah* (the Warrior), who has cast into the sea Pharaoh's chariots and his army (Exod. 15:3–4). After the Israelites crossed the Jordan, the Book of Joshua tells us, many of the local people fought against them, but, "I [God] delivered them into your hands" (Josh. 24:11). Similarly, when David is ready to fight Goliath, he exclaims, "For the battle is the Eternal's" (I Sam. 17:47).

The image of the Israelites' God getting personally involved in the life of the people is consistent with the conception of gods in the ancient Near East. There, too, we find that divinities have a deep interest in the actions of their own people, often protecting them against enemies. In fact, it is the gods who fight against other people's gods during a battle. Furthermore, in royal chronicles, all victories or defeats are ascribed to the gods who made these possible. For example, in a Sumerian letter addressed by one of the last rulers of the third dynasty of Ur, the author states, "Enlil [the god] did give the kingship to a worthless man, to Ishbi-Irra, who is not of Sumerian seed" (*ANET*, 481). In an old Babylonian text on King Sargon, we are told, "Enlil [the god] did not let anybody oppose Sargon, the king of the country" (*ANET*, 267). In Assyria, reporting about the siege of Jerusalem, King Sennacherib (705–681 B.C.E.) says that he successfully marched against the Hatti land, and Luli, the king of Sidon, because "the awe-inspiring splendor of the weapon of Ashur, my lord, overwhelmed his strong cities" (*ANET*, 287). Similarly, when Esarhaddon (681–669 B.C.E.), king of Assyria, was fighting to obtain his throne from his enemies, he specifically credits the gods for his success: "The gods made me stay in a hiding place in the face of these evil machinations, spreading their sweet protecting shadow over me and (thus) preserving me for the kingship" (*ANET*, 289).

As in the Bible, in Mesopotamian myths too, the gods at times use other nations to punish their own people. For example, in the Sumerian text called the "Curse of Agade," Naram-Sin, the fourth king of the dynasty of Akkad, destroyed the Ekur, which was the god Enlil's great sanctuary in Nippur. However, because Naram-Sin failed to obtain the permission from the god Enlil to rebuild it, Enlil brought down the wild Gutians from the mountains in order to avenge his temple (*ANET*, 649). In the "Cyrus Inscription" (sixth century B.C.E.), we are told that because of social injustice in the land as well as cultic wrongs, Marduk, the god of Babylon, sought out Cyrus, a Persian, and ordered him to march against Babylon (*ANET*, 315). According to the Mesha Stone (ninth century B.C.E., Moabite), the reason why Omri, the king of Israel, defeated Moab was because "Chemosh was angry at his land" (*ANET*, 320).

Thus, when ancient Near Eastern historians wrote their history, they often included the deeds of their gods in conjunction with human achievements. God and humans worked together. Biblical historians did the same regarding the God of Israel, except that they credited only one invisible God for all the victories and defeats. Admittedly, we do not know how Israelites viewed the past. We can only guess based upon the evidence we have at hand. The theology underlying their composition appears to be treated as an essential part of their history. Thus, for them, even the "events" in Genesis 1–11, which deal with Creation, the Flood, and others, were considered history, not myth or fiction. They readily assumed that the God of Israel was part of the historical process.

The biblical canon, which contains the historical records of the ancient Israelites, was assembled by those in power (such as priests or royal scribes) in Judah, from among a collection of writings that were subsequently discarded, ignored, or simply lost. The Bible itself mentions a number of books in circulation among the educated elite that did not survive. Among them are the "Book of the Wars of the Eternal" (Num. 21:14), the "Book of Yashar" (Josh. 10:13), and various chronicles, such as "Chronicles of the Kings of Israel" (II Kings 14:28), "Chronicles of the Kings of Judah" (II Kings 15:6), and sundry other collections, such as "the history of Samuel the seer, the history of Nathan the prophet, and the history of Gad the seer" (I Chron. 29:29) and "the chronicle of the prophet Nathan and [in] the prophecies of Ahijah the Shilonite and [in] the visions of Jedo the seer" (II Chron. 9:29).

We do not know why these books did not survive. It is possible that they were written on perishable material; maybe they were not worthy of

196 · Did Moses Really Have Horns?

preservation; maybe there were problems in copying; it is even possible that they were deliberately eliminated by the compilers (see BT *Bava Batra* 14a). And what about those that survived? According to Nahum Sarna, "The books of the Bible survived because men firmly and fervently believed them to be the inspired word of God, sacred literature."[8]

The Bible, of course, includes what the editors felt was historical data worthy of preservation. They tell us plenty about the Exodus from Egypt, the entry into the Canaan, the monarchy, the exile, and the return. They also introduce us to some charismatic leaders who changed the course of history. Because of them we learn about the Patriarchs, Moses, various prophets, and many kings and priests. The material is laid out for us in historical progression, from the Creation of the universe to almost the Maccabean period in the second century.

In spite of all the historical information included in the narratives, it is remarkable that certain critical events are omitted and others are simply passed over in one or two sentences. For example, from the chronicles of the Assyrian king Shalmaneser III (who reigned 858–824 B.C.E.) we learn that in 853 B.C.E., during the reign of Ahab, king of Israel, there was a major war called the "Battle of Qarqar" near Hamath, north of Damascus. On the one side was the mighty Assyrian war machine, and on the other a coalition of Canaanite armies, to which Ahab contributed "two thousand chariots and ten thousand foot soldiers" (*ANET,* 279)—the largest contingent of all the allies. Even though the Assyrians claimed victory, the battle was inconclusive because right afterward, Shalmaneser discontinued his advance toward Syria. Not a single word of this is mentioned in the Bible. Similarly, after giving all the details about the discovery of a major "scroll of the Torah" (II Kings 22:8) during the reign of Josiah, king of Judah (seventh century B.C.E.), the Bible adds a short note saying, "In his days, Pharoah Neco, king of Egypt, marched against the king of Assyria to the River Euphrates; King Josiah marched against him, but when he confronted him at Megiddo, [Pharaoh Neco] slew him" (II Kings 23:29). That's it! We are not told why Josiah went to battle Neco. He simply went. In reality this was a major defeat for Judah that changed the balance of power not only in the ancient Near East, but also within the small kingdom of Judah. Not only did Judah become a vassal of Egypt, but also until the destruction of Jerusalem in 586 B.C.E., it kept changing loyalties from Egypt to Babylonia, with Judean kings aligning themselves with either one or the other power. Some biblical historians speculate that Josiah, as an ally of Babylonia, tried to stop the Egyptian advance but failed.

In some historical cases the information is so scant that we are totally left in the dark as to the reason for the event or the way it occurred. Thus, for example, we are told that one of the judges, Tola son of Puah "arose to deliver Israel" (Judg. 10:1), but the text fails to tell us from whom. Discussing the fate of one of the kings of the Northern Kingdom of Israel, the Bible simply states, "So Tibni died" (I Kings 16:22). No other detail is provided.

The impression is thus created that the biblical historians were not interested in reporting these details, however important in their context, because the facts were insignificant in their eyes or did not suit the narrators' theological agenda.

Another problem that makes the analysis of numerous biblical texts unreliable is the use of numbers in many of the historical texts. They look more like literary devices. It is known, for example, that certain numbers have special significance in the biblical world, such as three, seven, forty, and others. For example, we read that Abraham lived 175 years (Gen. 25:7), which equals $5 \times 5 \times 7$; Isaac was 180 when he died (Gen. 35:28), $6 \times 6 \times 5$; and Jacob reached 147 years when he passed on (Gen. 47:28), $7 \times 7 \times 3$. Regarding this, Nahum Sarna notes, "In this series, the squared numbers increased by one each time while the coefficient decreases by two."[9] Therefore, beyond simply counting numbers, we have the impression that the author really is trying to make a point, though it is not always easy to discern. Similarly, one wonders how Sarah gave birth to Isaac when she was 90 years old (Gen. 17:17), when, even by her own admission, she was beyond childbearing age (Gen. 18:12). Maybe the narrator wanted to highlight here the miraculous intervention of God. Moses living 120 years (Deut. 34:7) appears to correspond to the maximum life span allotted to human beings (Gen. 6:3). It becomes clear that these numbers are theologically motivated but cannot be considered historical.

In many books of the Bible a certain religious framework appears to be superimposed. For example, in the Book of Judges, all historical events during the pre-monarchical times, such as the ones that took place during the time of Othniel (Judg. 3:5–11), are subjected to a cyclical pattern: first a sin is committed; this is followed by divine punishment, and ultimately the people are rescued. Similarly, all kings in Judah as well as in Israel are judged according to Deuteronomic standards as to whether they followed God's teachings or not; for example, "He [Jotham, a king of Judah] did what was pleasing to the Eternal, just as his father Uzziah had done" (II Kings 15:34), but, "He [Pekahiah, the king of Israel] did what was displeasing to the Eternal; he did not depart from the sins which Jeroboam son of Nebat had caused Israel to commit" (II Kings 15:24).

The most remarkable aspect of biblical historiography is that the editors do not appear to be interested in history per se unless the events they relate have religious significance. Thus, they often refer the reader to other historical sources they knew were available at their time; for example, "The other events of Pekahiah's reign, and all his actions, are recorded in the Annals of the Kings of Israel" (II Kings 15:26), or, "The other events of Ahaz's reign, and his actions, are recorded in the Annals of the Kings of Judah" (II Kings 16:19). We are forced to conclude, therefore, that the main concern of the Bible is theology rather than factual accuracy.

The Question of Truth

The previous chapters have critically examined many of the foundational myths and legends in the Hebrew Bible. We analyzed a number of religious festivals and a few major biblical personalities. In all of them, through a historical and linguistic analysis, we discovered that these building blocks of Jewish faith were often subjected to constant editorial changes. Myths and legends were revised, reformulated, and enlarged; popular leaders attracted new legends, and mistranslations led people astray regarding events and people of the past. All of this raises the emotional question for the serious reader of the Scriptures: is the Bible true?

What do we mean when we ask if the Bible is true? If the word "true" refers to agreement with facts as they happened, we can confidently state that most of the events, personalities, and occasions described in the Bible, especially those in the earlier part of the biblical history, are not verifiable. The main reason is because the Bible is not meant to be a chronicle of historical events but a collection of religious teachings deemed to be valid for all time. As we noted above, when the biblical historians wished to function as chroniclers, they usually sent their readers to other annals of history (e.g., II Kings 14:28, 15:6), which regrettably did not survive. There is confirmation available of some of the events in the late monarchical period in a few of the ancient Near Eastern texts, but these too are few in number. In addition, they often have their own particular political or religious agenda that can make them unreliable as a basis for establishing historicity. Archaeology can be helpful in discovering the material remains of the local culture, but it can hardly elucidate the beliefs and concepts of the ancient Israelites.

However, there is another way of looking at the "truth" of a statement. The historical claim, one could argue, may not be factually true, but can still be religiously or morally correct. For example, when we affirm that "God is my Shepherd" (Ps. 23:1), we don't really think of God as a human shepherd taking care of the flock, but understand it as a metaphor, pointing to God's presumed protective role. Similarly, when the maiden in the Song of Songs identifies herself saying, "I am a rose of Sharon, a lily of the valleys" (Song of Songs 2:1), no one expects that this sentence would be factually true; obviously, the young woman is talking about her beauty. Thus, though a phrase may be factually inaccurate, it can convey a sentiment that is metaphorically true. When it comes to sacred Scriptures, the question to ask is not, "Is it historically correct?" but, "Is the teaching religiously sound as an explanation of the mysteries of life?"

Truths and Values

A critical survey of the biblical material shows that the main concern of the biblical narrators was not to report an event, but to use the event in order to impart a religious lesson. In the case of the Bible, the editors used the events of the past to tell us what was significant about the name of that location or to teach about God, about moral values that we must internalize, or about individuals who tell us how to behave as human beings created in the divine image. In that respect, the Bible is, in the words of Rabbi Plaut, "a book about humanity's understanding and experience of God" that "had its origin in the hearts and minds of the Jewish people."[10] The narrators considered their interpretations of the events and the lessons they derived from them as being religiously "valuable" and morally edifying, even if their facts were not always literarily true.

Conclusion

The Hebrew Bible is primarily a religious document. The critical analysis of the Bible does not in any way diminish its religious and moral significance. Though the Bible reflects the thinking of the ancient Israelites, it contains valuable lessons for us to ponder and emulate. Throughout the ages, commentators have attempted to understand its message and adapt it to the needs of their own time. Serious students of the Bible continue in the same path. Modern biblical criticism enables us to ask probing questions, looking not for historical accuracy, but for human growth, spiritual uplift, and moral development, an endeavor that is richly rewarded.

Abbreviations

ANET	*Ancient Near Eastern Texts Relating to the Old Testament* (ed. James B. Pritchard)
Ant.	*Antiquities* (by Josephus)
ASV	American Standard Version
B.C.E.	Before the Common Era
BT	Babylonian Talmud
C.E.	Common Era
CEV	The Contemporary English Version
Chron.	Chronicles
Cor.	Corinthians
Dan.	Daniel
DBY	Darby Bible
Deut.	Deuteronomy
Eccles.	Ecclesiastes
Esd.	Esdras

Est.	Esther
Exod.	Exodus
Gen.	Genesis
GNB	Good News Bible
Hab.	Habakkuk
Isa.	Isaiah
ISV	International Standard Version
JB	Jerusalem Bible
JT	Jerusalem Talmud
Jer.	Jeremiah
Jon.	Jonah
Josh.	Joshua
JPS	Jewish Publication Society (translation of the Bible)
Judg.	Judges
KJV	King James Version
Lev.	Leviticus
Macc.	Maccabees
Mal.	Malachi
Matt.	Matthew
Mic.	Micah
NAB	New American Bible
NEB	New English Bible
Neh.	Nehemiah
NJPS	New Jewish Publication Society (translation of the Bible)
NLT	New Living Translation
NRSV	New Revised Standard Version
Num.	Numbers
Pet.	Peter
Prov.	Proverbs
Ps., Pss.	Psalm, Psalms
Rom.	Romans
RSV	Revised Standard Version
Sam.	Samuel
Sir.	Sirach
Wisd. of Sol.	Wisdom of Solomon

Glossary

cult/cultic: From the Latin, *cultus* (meaning "religious veneration"); usually referring to temple rituals or priestly matters.

Gemara: Rabbinic discussion (mostly in Aramaic) of the Mishnah. The Mishnah and Gemara make up the Talmud. The Jerusalem Talmud was completed around 450 C.E., and the Babylonian Talmud around 500 C.E.

halachah; halachic (adj.): From the Hebrew verb *halach*, "walk"; refers to Jewish law.

midrash (pl. **midrashim**); **midrashic** (adj.): A collection of Rabbinic stories, folklore, legends, and homilies about many of the biblical texts. There are two types: *midrash halachah* deals with legal matters; *midrash aggadah* covers legends, parables, and lore.

Mishnah: The compilation of the Oral Law in sixty-three tractates (divided into six orders) by Rabbi Y'hudah HaNasi at the beginning of the third century C.E. It is written mostly in Hebrew, with a number of references in Aramaic and a few words in Greek.

Sifrei: A midrash to Numbers and Deuteronomy.

s'firah (pl. *s'firot*): According to Kabbalah, the revealed attributes of the divinity, or agencies by means of which God is manifested in the creation and preservation of the universe.

stele (or, **stela**): A carved or inscribed stone slab, mostly used for commemorative purposes.

Tanna (pl. *Tannaim*); **tannaitic** (adj.): A teacher mentioned in the Mishnah or who lived during the Mishnaic period (first to third century C.E.).

Tosefta: A collection of Rabbinic teachings not included in the Mishnah, usually attributed to Chiya bar Abba, end of the third century C.E.

Notes

INTRODUCTION

1. Neil Gillman, *The Death of Death* (Woodstock, VT: Jewish Lights, 1997), 27.

2. Otto Eissfeldt, *The Old Testament*, trans. P. R. Ackroyd (New York: Harper and Row, 1965), 33. See also Nahum M. Sarna, *Understanding Genesis* (New York: Schocken, 1970), 6.

3. W. Gunther Plaut, ed., *The Torah: A Modern Commentary*, rev. ed. (New York: URJ Press, 2005), xxxix.

4. *Merriam-Webster's Collegiate Dictionary*, 11th ed., s.v. "legend."

5. Eissfeldt, *The Old Testament*, 34.

6. Plaut, *The Torah*, xxxix.

7. William W. Hallo and William Kelly Simpson, *The Ancient Near East: A History* (New York: Harcourt Brace Jovanovich, 1971), 166.

8. Claus Westermann, *Genesis*, trans. David E. Green (Grand Rapids, MI: William B. Eerdmans, 1987), 45.

9. E. A. Speiser, *Genesis* (Garden City, NY: Doubleday, 1964), 46.

10. William M. Schniedewind, *How the Bible Became a Book* (New York: Cambridge University Press, 2004), 25.

11. Adele Berlin and Marc Zvi Brettler, eds., *The Jewish Study Bible* (Oxford: Oxford University Press, 2004), 521.

CHAPTER 1

1. Commentary on the Mishnah, *Sanhedrin* 10, the Thirteen Principles of Faith. See translation in *A Maimonides Reader*, ed. Isadore Twersky (New York: Behrman, 1972), 420.

2. See www.wayoflife.org/fbns/fbns249.html.

3. Yehuda Radday (*Omni*, Aug. 1982), quoted in Russell Grigg, "Did Moses Really Write Genesis?" *Creation* 20, no. 4 (Sept. 1998): 43–46.

4. For the text, see *Ancient Near Eastern Texts Relating to the Old Testament*, ed. James B. Pritchard (Princeton, NJ: Princeton University Press, 1969), 376–78.

5. There is an extensive literature on this subject. See, for example, *The Anchor Bible Dictionary* (New York: Doubleday, 1992), 6:605–22; Richard Elliott Friedman, *Who Wrote the Bible?* (New York: Summit, 1987).

CHAPTER 2

1. For various God concepts in Judaism, see Rifat Sonsino and Daniel B. Syme, *Finding God: Selected Responses* (New York: UAHC Press, 2002).

2. A. Leo Oppenheim, *Ancient Mesopotamia* (Chicago: University of Chicago, 1964), 184.

3. A grammatical form marking the one who is addressed.

4. Louis Jacobs, *A Jewish Theology* (New York: Behrman, 1973), 139.

5. An ostracon is usually a broken earthenware vessel on which people recorded messages.

6. Ruth Hestrin, "Understanding Asherah," *Biblical Archaeological Review*, September/October 1991, 50–58.

7. Ze'ev Meshel, "Did Yahweh Have a Consort?" *Biblical Archaeological Review*, March/April 1979, 24–35.

8. J. Glen Taylor, "Was Yahweh Worshipped as the Sun?" *Biblical Archaeological Review*, May/June 1994, 52–61, 90–91.

9. The ending -*ai* is usually in pausal form and represents a grammatical problem. It can either be a personal pronoun ("my master") or an emphatic ending, meaning "lord by excellence." See H. F. W. Gesenius et al., *Gesenius' Hebrew Grammar*, 2nd ed. (Oxford: Oxford University Press, 1922), 135 and note 2.

10. Nahum M. Sarna, *Exodus*, The JPS Torah Commentary (Philadelphia: Jewish Publication Society, 1991), 18.

11. Quoted in Martin S. Jaffee, *Early Judaism* (Upper Saddle River, NJ: Prentice Hall, 1997), 230.

12. Judith Plaskow, *Standing Again at Sinai* (San Francisco: Harper and Row, 1990), 169.

13. Solomon B. Freehof, *Recent Reform Responsa* (Cincinnati: Hebrew Union College, 1963), 53.

14. Marcia L. Falk, *The Book of Blessings* (San Francisco: Harper SanFrancisco, 1996).

CHAPTER 3

1. Gerhard Von Rad, *Genesis*, trans. John Marks, The Old Testament Library (Philadelphia: Westminster Press, 1961), 145.

2. Joseph H. Hertz, ed., *The Pentateuch and Haftorahs* (London: Soncino, 1971), 5.

3. Ibid., 6.

4. Quoted in Plaut, *The Torah*, 46.

5. Elyse Goldstein, *Re-visions* (Toronto: Key Porter Books, 1998), 54–55.

6. Lawrence Boadt, *Reading the Old Testament* (New York: Paulist Press, 1984), 119.

7. For the full text, see *ANET*, 60–72, 501–3.

8. Richard J. Clifford, *Creation Accounts in the Ancient Near East and in the Bible*, Catholic Biblical Quarterly Monograph Series 26 (Washington, DC: Catholic Biblical Association of America, 1994), 98.

9. *Interpreter's Dictionary of the Bible*, ed. Buttrick George Arthur (New York: Abington Press, 1962) Vol 1: 725.

10. Poem recited during the Rosh HaShanah Shofar Service, first found in the *Seder Rav Amram Gaon*, ninth century, Sura.

11. Some texts omit the words "from Israel." See, e.g., the Parma edition of the Mishnah (Biblioteca Palatina 3173) or JT *Sanhedrin* 23a.

12. About Philo's "logos," see Rifat Sonsino and Daniel B. Syme, *Finding God: Selected Responses* (New York: UAHC Press, 2002), 48–50.

13. Nahum M. Sarna, *Genesis*, The JPS Torah Commentary (New York: Jewish Publication Society, 1989), 5.

14. Von Rad, *Genesis*, 47.

15. Sarna, *Understanding Genesis*, 2–3.

16. Westermann, *Genesis*, 12.

17. Sarna, *Understanding Genesis*, 2–3.

18. Roland B. Gittelsohn, *Wings of the Morning* (New York: UAHC Press, 1969), 144.

19. Avivah G. Zornberg, *Genesis: The Beginning of Desire* (Philadelphia: Jewish Publication Society, 1995), 36.

20. Quoted in Louis I. Newman, *Hasidic Anthology* (New York: Schocken, 1975), 61–62.

CHAPTER 4

1. See, e.g., the old JPS, Soncino, King James, NRSV.

2. Speiser, *Genesis*, 26.

3. Harry M. Orlinsky, *Notes on the New Translation of the Torah* (Philadelphia: Jewish Publication Society, 1969), 60.

4. Von Rad, *Genesis*, 76.

5. Ibid., 86.

6. See, e.g., NJPS and Donald Senior and John J. Collins, eds., *The Catholic Study Bible*, 2nd ed. (New York: Oxford University Press, 2006).

7. Adapted from *Midrash Rabba, Genesis*, trans. H. Freedman (New York: Soncino, 1983), 122–24.

8. Louis Ginzberg, *Legends of the Jews* (New York: Simon and Schuster, 1961), 40.

9. *Interpreter's Dictionary of the Bible*, 1:175.

10. The *New York Times* reported on Feb. 7, 2005, "Syria to Buy Apples from Israel-Occupied Golan Heights."

11. *Anchor Bible Dictionary* (New York: Doubleday, 1992), 2:807. On apricot for *tapuach*, see p. 806.

12. Plaut, *The Torah*, 25, n. 6; Michael D. Coogan, *The Old Testament* (New York: Oxford University Press, 2006), 18. See also Gerhard von Rad, *Genesis*, trans. John H. Marks, The Old Testament Library (Philadelphia: Westminster, 1956), 88.

13. See, e.g., Rom. 5:12–19; I Cor. 15:21–22

14. Westermann, *Genesis*, 28.

15. Quoted in Nehama Leibowitz, *Studies in Bereshit*, 4th rev. ed. (Jerusalem: WZO, n.d.), 18–19.

16. Ibid., 19.

17. Tamara Cohn Eskenazi and Andrea L. Weiss, eds., *The Torah: A Women's Commentary* (New York: URJ Press, 2008), 14.

18. Avivah Gottlieb Zornberg, *Genesis: The Beginning of Desire* (Philadelphia: Jewish Publication Society, 1995), 25.

19. Harold S. Kushner, *How Good Do We Have to Be?* (Boston: Little, Brown, 1996), 21.

20. Ibid., 21–22.

21. In the Bible, "knowledge," at times, means sexual awareness, knowing someone carnally. See, e.g., Gen. 24:16, 38:26.

22. Plaut, *The Torah*, 39.

23. Eskenazi and Weiss, *The Torah: A Women's Commentary*, 13.

CHAPTER 5

1. Speiser, *Genesis*, 56.

2. Eric H. Cline, "Raiders of the Faux Ark," *Boston Globe*, sec. D, September 30, 2007.

3. *Matnot K'huna*, a Rabbinic commentary on *B'reishit Rabbah*, mistakenly states that Cordyene is Mount Ararat (see comment on *B'reishit Rabbah* 33:4).

4. It is most likely that P, the later editor, did not like the idea of Noah, a non-priest, offering sacrifices to God. Therefore, in his own account, P reduced the number of pair of animals in the boat.

5. *Zohar* 1:67b, quoted in *Gates of Repentance* (New York: Central Conference of American Rabbis, 1996), 240–41.

6. Ginzberg, *Legends of the Jews*, 66–85.

7. Maimonides states that six precepts were given to Adam and an additional one, namely the prohibition against eating the flesh of a living animal, to Noah. See his *Mishneh Torah*, Kings 9:1; see also *B'reishit Rabbah* 16:6.

8. Sarna, *Understanding Genesis*, 38.

9. John H. Tullock and Mark McEntire, *The Old Testament Story*, 7th ed. (Upper Saddle River, NJ: Pearson Prentice Hall, 2006), 45.

10. Bernhard W. Anderson, *Understanding the Old Testament*, 5th ed. (Upper Saddle River, NJ: Pearson Prentice Hall, 2007), 150–51.

11. Tikva Frymer-Kensky, "What the Babylonian Flood Stories Can and Cannot Teach Us about the Genesis Flood," *Biblical Archaeological Review* 4, no. 4 (Nov./Dec. 1978): 41.

12. W. Gunther Plaut, "Noah and How We Live with One Another in Our Time," in *Living Torah: Selections from Seven Years of Torat Chayim*, ed. Elaine Rose Glickman (New York: URJ Press, 2005), 14.

CHAPTER 6

1. For details, see Ruth Mellinkoff, *The Horned Moses in Medieval Art and Thought* (Los Angeles: University of California, 1970).

208 · NOTES

2. Everett Fox, *The Five Books of Moses* (New York: Schocken, 1995), 459.

3. Sarna, *Exodus*, 221n.

4. See, e.g., JB, NAB, NRSV, ASV, NEB, even King James.

5. On Exod. 34:29.

6. For these theories, see John I. Durham, *Exodus* (Waco, TX: Word Books, 1987), 466.

7. A. Leo Oppenheim, *Ancient Mesopotamia* (Chicago: University of Chicago Press, 1964), 98.

8. H. H. Ben-Sasson, *A History of the Jewish People* (Cambridge: Harvard University Press, 1976), 484.

9. On Exod. 34:29.

10. William H. Propp, "Did Moses Have Horns?" *Biblical Review* 4, no. 1 (Feb. 1988): 32.

11. See Rashi's comment on Exod. 34:33.

CHAPTER 7

1. Harold Kushner, *When Bad Things Happen to Good People* (New York: Schocken Books, 1981), 56.

2. In extra-biblical texts, the earliest mention of "Israel" as a people comes from the Egyptian king Mernepta's victory stele, dated ca. 1200 B.C.E.

3. There are various theories as to why the sea was called "Red," including an account of the red corals that lie along its shores, the reddish color of the mountains of Edom and Arabia, and a certain kind of algae that floats on the surface of the water, giving a reddish color to the water when the algae die off.

4. For example, see ASV, KJV, NAB, NRSV, NEB, DBY.

5. Mentioned by Brevard S. Childs, *The Book of Exodus*, The Old Testament Library (Philadelphia: Westminster, 1974), 237.

6. On Exod. 13:18.

7. See, for example, JB, NJPS, Fox.

8. Durham, *Exodus*, 182.

9. On Rephidim, see *Anchor Bible Dictionary*, 5:677–78.

10. Florentino Garcia Martinez, *The Sea Scrolls Translated* (New York: Brill, 1994), 235.

11. For details, see John R. Huddlestun, *Anchor Bible Dictionary*, 5638ff.

12. Ibid., 640.

13. Bernard F. Batto, "Red or Reed Sea," *Biblical Archaeology Review* 10, no. 4 (July/Aug. 1984): 59. See his longer article, "The Reed Sea," *Journal of Biblical Literature*, March 1983, 27–35.

14. On Exod. 13:18.

15. Batto, "Red Sea or Reed Sea," 61.

16. Michael D. Coogan, *The Old Testament*, 95.

17. On Exod. 14:21.

18. In his *Legum Alleg.* 2:102; quoted by Childs, *The Book of Exodus*, 231.

19. *Targum Neophyti*, on Exod. 14:1314; quoted by James L. Kugel, *The Bible As It Was* (Cambridge, MA: Harvard University Press, 1998), 339–40.

20. *Moses*, 2:249; quoted by Kugel, *Bible As It Was*, 340.

21. On other Rabbinic material on this subject, see Nehama Leibowitz, *Studies in Shemot-Exodus* (Jerusalem: Haomanim, 1986) 1:256–62.

22. For the list, see Ginzberg, *Legends of the Jews*, 355.
23. Ibid., 359.
24. Ibid., 360.
25. Coogan, *The Old Testament*, 95.
26. Huddlestun, *Anchor Bible Dictionary*, 5:635.
27. Gerhard von Rad, *Old Testament Theology*, trans. D. M. G. Stalker (Edinburgh: Oliver and Boyd, 1963), 1:13.

CHAPTER 8

1. G. W. Wright, *Interpreter's Dictionary of the Bible* 4:377.
2. On Deut. 5:2.
3. See list in *Biblical Archaeology Review*, June 1988, 36–37. See also Israel Finkelstein, "Raiders of the Lost Mountain: An Israeli Archaeologist Looks at the Most Recent Attempt to Locate Mt. Sinai," *Biblical Archaeology Review* 15, no. 4 (July–Aug. 1988): 46–50.
4. For details, see Itzhaq Beit-Arieh, "The Route through Sinai," *Biblical Archaeology Review* 15, no. 3 (May–June 1988): 28–37.
5. S. R. Driver, *Deuteronomy*, The International Critical Commentary (New York: Scribner's Sons, 1903), 84.
6. Brevard S. Childs, *The Book of Exodus*, The Old Testament Library (Philadelphia: Westminster, 1975), 360.
7. Judah Halevi, *The Kuzari* (New York: Schocken Books, 1964), 62–63.
8. Abraham Joshua Heschel, *God in Search of Man* (New York: Meridian Books, 1962), 217.
9. Mordecai M. Kaplan, *The Meaning of God in Modern Jewish Religion* (New York: Reconstructionist Press, 1962), 303.
10. Eugene B. Borowitz, *Renewing the Covenant* (Philadelphia: Jewish Publication Society, 1991), 274.
11. See Rashi on Deut. 29:14.
12. Central Conference of American Rabbis, "A Statement of Principles for Reform Judaism." Available at http://ccarnet.org/documentsandpositions/platforms/.
13. Quoted in Maurice S. Friedman, *Martin Buber: The Life of Dialogue* (New York: Harper Torchbook, 1960), 246.

CHAPTER 9

1. *New York Times*, Nov. 14, 2003.
2. H. W. F. Saggs, *The Greatness That Was Babylon* (New York: Hawthorn Books, 1962), 366.
3. Quoted by H. Cazelles, "Ten Commandments," *Interpreter's Dictionary of the Bible*, Supplementary Volume, ed. Keith Crim, 1976, 876.
4. Moshe Weinfeld, "The Uniqueness of the Decalogue," in *The Ten Commandments in History and Tradition*, ed. Ben-Zion Segal (Jerusalem: Magnes Press, 1990), 3.
5. See the responsum by Solomon B. Freehof, *Recent Reform Responsa*, 50–55.
6. Some object to this point of view and refer to Prov. 6:32–35, where the offense seems to be against the husband. But this is a wisdom text, not a legal document. See Moshe

Greenberg, "Some Postulates of Biblical Criminal Law," in *The Jewish Expression*, ed. Judah Goldin (New York: Bantam, 1970), 18–37.

7. Hertz, *Pentateuch and Haftorahs*, 299.

CHAPTER 10

1. Abraham Malamat, "Origins and Formative Period," in *A History of the Jewish People*, ed. H. H. Ben-Sasson (Cambridge, MA: Harvard University Press, 1969), 59.

2. Yigael Yadin, "Is the Biblical Account of the Israelite Conquest of Canaan Historically Reliable?" *Biblical Archaeology Review* 8, no. 2 (March–April 1982): 19.

3. David Ussishkin, "Lachish: Key to the Israelite Conquest of Canaan?" *Biblical Archaeology Review* 13, no. 1 (Jan.–Feb. 1987): 18–39.

4. Abraham Malamat, "How Inferior Israelite Forces Conquered Fortified Canaanite Cities?" *Biblical Archaeology Review* 8, no. 2 (March–April 1982): 33.

5. Bryant G. Wood, "Did the Israelites Conquer Jericho? A New Look at the Archaeological Evidence," *Biblical Archaeology Review* 16, no. 2 (March–April 1990): 44–57.

6. Yadin, "Is the Biblical Account of the Israelite Conquest," 23.

7. Ibid.

8. Ibid.

9. Lawrence Boadt, *Reading the Old Testament* (New York: Paulist Press, 1984), 205.

10. Joseph A. Callaway, revised by J. Maxwell Miller, "The Settlement in Canaan," in *Ancient Israel*, ed. Hershel Shanks (Washington, DC: Biblical Archaeology Society, 1999), 58.

11. Tullock and McEntire, *Old Testament Story*, 107.

12. Coogan, *The Old Testament*, 206.

13. Callaway, "Settlement in Canaan," 82.

14. *Mekhilta de-Rabbi Ishmael*, trans. Jacob Z. Lauterbach (Philadelphia: Jewish Publication Society, 1961), 1:172, note 6.

CHAPTER 11

1. Mortimer J. Cohen, "David the King," in *Great Jewish Personalities in Ancient and Medieval Times*, ed. S. Noveck (Washington: B'nai B'rith Department of Adult Jewish Education, 1965), 44.

2. *Anchor Bible Dictionary* 2:41.

3. Hans W. Hertzberg, *I and II Samuel*, The Old Testament Library (Philadelphia: Westminster, 1964), 139.

4. For the text, see W. Hallo, ed., *The Context of Scripture* (Leiden: Brill, 2000), 2:161–62.

5. Ibid. See also David N. Freedman and Jeffrey C. Geoghegan, "'House of David' Is There!" *Biblical Archaeology Review* 21:2 (March–April 1995): 78–79.

6. Israel Finkelstein and Neil A. Silberman, *David and Solomon* (New York: Free Press, 2006), 31ff.

7. For all Rabbinic legends about David that are mentioned in the text, see Ginzberg, *Legends of the Jews*, 533–52.

8. Judah Goldin, *The Fathers According to Rabbi Nathan* (New York: Schocken Books, 1955), 132.

9. About these two Messiahs, see the *Targum* to Songs of Songs 4:5 and BT *Sukkah* 52a.

10. Isaac Husic, *A History of Medieval Jewish Philosophy* (Philadelphia: Jewish Publication Society, 1940), 45.

11. Ibid., 149.

12. Joseph Albo, *Sefer Ha-'Ikkarim*, trans. Isaac Husic, vol. 4, bk. 2 (Philadelphia: Jewish Publication Society, 1946), 413–14.

13. Ibid., 416.

14. See David Berger, *The Rebbe, the Messiah, and the Scandal of Orthodox Indifference* (London: Littman Library of Jewish Civilization, 2001).

15. In W. Gunther Plaut, *The Rise of Reform Judaism* (New York: World Union for Progressive Judaism, 1963), 52.

16. "Declaration of Principles" ["Pittsburgh Platform," 1885]. Available at http://ccarnet.org/documentsandpositions/platforms/.

17. Sherwin Wine, interview by Hershel Shanks, "Judaism Without God," *Moment* (February 1999), 50.

CHAPTER 12

1. See, for example, James Limburg, "Jonah and the Whale through the Eyes of Artists," *Bible Review* 6, no. 4 (Aug. 1990): 18–25.

2. Julius A. Bewer, *The Literature of the Old Testament* (New York: Columbia University Press, 1957), 403ff.

3. Michael Orth, "Genre in Jonah," in *The Bible in the Light of Cuneiform Literature*, Ancient Near Eastern Texts and Studies, vol. 8, ed. William M. Hallo et al. (Lewiston, NY: Edwin Mellen Press, 1990), 261.

4. Jack Sasson, *Jonah*, The Anchor Bible 24B (New York: Doubleday, 1990), 149. Pliny lived in the first century C.E.

5. Elias Bickerman, *Four Strange Books of the Bible* (New York: Schocken Books, 1967), 4.

6. Ginzberg, *Legends of the Jews*, 605.

7. Abdullah Yusuf Ali, *The Meaning of the Holy Qur'an* (Beltsville, MD: Amana Publications, 2001), 1154, n. 4122.

8. Robert H. Pfeiffer, *Introduction to the Old Testament* (New York: Harper, 1948), 587.

9. Samuel Sandmel, *The Hebrew Scriptures* (New York: Alfred A. Knopf, 1963), 494.

CHAPTER 13

1. Pfeiffer, *Introduction to the Old Testament*, 737.

2. Ibid., 747.

3. Carey A. Moore, "Eight Questions Most Frequently Asked about the Book of Esther," *Bible Review*, Spring 1987, 31.

4. Arthur Cohen, *The Five Megillot* (Hindhead, Surrey: Soncino, 1946), 164.

5. Bruce William Jones, "Two Misconceptions about the Book of Esther," *Catholic Biblical Quarterly* 39, no. 2 (April 1977): 171.

6. Ibid., 172.

7. Adele Berlin, "Esther," in Berlin and Brettler, *Jewish Study Bible*, 1,623.

8. Tullock and McEntire, *Old Testament Story*, 376

9. Ibid., 377.

10. Eissfeldt, *Old Testament*, 507.

11. Georg Fohrer, *Introduction to the Old Testament*, trans. David E. Green (Nashville: Abingdon Press, 1968), 255.

12. Lillian Segal, "The Feminine Divine in the Book of Esther," *The Bible in the Light of the Cuneiform Literature*, Ancient Near Eastern Texts and Studies, vol. 8, ed. William M. Hallo et al. (Lewiston, NY: Edwin Mellen Press, 1990), 398.

13. Quoted in Eissfeldt, *Old Testament*, 512.

14. Pfeiffer, *Introduction to the Old Testament*, 747.

15. Eissfeldt, *Old Testament*, 511.

16. Sandmel, *Hebrew Scriptures*, 504.

17. Robert Gordis, *Megillat Esther* (New York: Rabbinical Assembly, 1974), 56.

18. Jones, "Two Misconceptions about the Book of Esther," 180–81.

19. All taken from the *Jewish Encyclopedia*, 1906, s.v. "Purims, Special."

20. Rabbi Sholomo Riskin, "The Final Step Is Ours to Take," *Jerusalem Post*, International Edition, week ending March 6, 1993, 15.

CHAPTER 14

1. Anne Roiphe, "Taking Down the Christmas Tree," *Tikkun* 4, no. 6 (1989): 60.

CHAPTER 15

1. The ancient Rabbis added an extra day for those who live in the Diaspora. Orthodox and Conservative Jews keep that custom. Reform Jews and Jews in Israel follow the biblical injunction and celebrate it for seven days.

2. In Israel, Sh'mini Atzeret and Simchat Torah are celebrated together right after the seventh day of Sukkot. In the Diaspora, Simchat Torah is the second day of Atzeret. Reform Jews in the United States usually combine Simchat Torah and Sh'mini Atzeret on the seventh day of the festival.

3. John Gray, *I and II Kings* (Philadelphia: Westminster, 1970), 318.

4. "Wilderness Wanderings," *Biblical Archeology Review* 34, no. 4 (2008): 32–39.

5. *Interpreter's Dictionary of the Bible*, 1:455.

6. Jeffrey Tigay, *Deuteronomy*, The JPS Torah Commentary (Philadelphia: Jewish Publication Society, 1996), 469.

7. Hayyim Schauss, *Guide to Jewish Holy Days* (New York: Schocken Books, 1961), 187.

8. *Tikkun Magazine* 6 (1991): 5.

CHAPTER 16

1. *Gates of Prayer*, ed. Chaim Stern (New York: CCAR, 1975), 624.

2. For details, see Rifat Sonsino and Daniel B. Syme, *What Happens After I Die?* (New York: UAHC Press, 1990); or Neil Gillman, *The Death of Death: Resurrection and Immortality in Jewish Thought* (Woodstock, VT: Jewish Lights Publishing, 1997).

3. See, for example, "Descent of Ishtar to the Nether World," line 1, in *ANET*, 107.

4. George Foot Moore, *Judaism* (Cambridge, MA: Harvard University Press, 1962), 2:379.

5. Jacobs, *A Jewish Theology*, 306.

6. Milton Steinberg, *Basic Judaism*, (NY: Harcourt, Brace and World, 1947), 163.

7. Richard Levy, "Upon Arising: An Affirmation of Techiyat Hameitim," *Journal of Reform Judaism*, Fall 1982, 12–20.

8. *Tophet and Eden*, trans. Hermann Gollancz (London: University of London Press, 1921).

9. Quoted in Sidney Greenberg, *A Treasury of Comfort* (Hollywood, CA: Wilshire Book Company, 1967), 54.

10. Ibid., 59.

11. Art Buchwald, "Goodbye, my friends," *Boston Globe*, Jan. 19, 2007, 13.

12. Moshe Chayim Luzzatto, *The Path of the Just*, trans. Shraga Silverstein (Jerusalem: Feldheim, 1990), 17.

EPILOGUE

1. Sandmel, *Hebrew Scriptures*, 3.

2. Rifat Sonsino, "Bible and Politics," *Judaism* 32, no. 1 (1983): 77–83.

3. Michael D. Coogan, "The Great Gulf between Scholars and the Pew," *Bible Review*, June 1994, 48.

4. See, for example, "How True is the Bible?" *Time*, Dec. 30, 1974, 34–41.

5. Tom Tugend, "Furor over L.A. rabbi's reading of Exodus, *Jewish Telegraphic Agency* (jta.org), Apr. 26, 2001.

6. Coogan, "Great Gulf between Scholars and the Pew," 46.

7. Stephen J. Patterson, "My View: Bridging the Gulf between Bible Scholarship and Religious Faith," *Bible Review*, Dec. 1990, 44.

8. Nahum Sarna, *Understanding Genesis*, xix.

9. *Genesis*, 324.

10. Plaut, *The Torah*, xxxvii.

Bibliography

Albo, Joseph. *Sefer Ha-'Ikkarim.* Translated by Isaac Husic. Philadelphia: Jewish Publication Society, 1946.

Ali, Abdullah Yusuf. *The Meaning of the Holy Qur'an.* Beltsville, MD: Amana Publications, 2001.

The Anchor Bible Dictionary. New York: Doubleday, 1992.

Batto, Bernard F. "Red Sea or Reed Sea?" *Biblical Archaeology Review* 10, no. 4 (July–Aug. 1984): 56–63.

———. "The Reed Sea: Requiescat in Pace." *Journal of Biblical Literature* 102, no. 1 (March 1983): 27–35.

Beit-Arieh, Itzhaq. "The Route through Sinai." *Biblical Archaeology Review* 15, no. 3 (May–June 1988): 28–37.

Ben-Sasson, H. H., ed. *A History of the Jewish People.* Cambridge, MA: Harvard University Press, 1976.

Berlin, Adele, and Marc Zvi Brettler, eds. *The Jewish Study Bible.* New York: Oxford University Press, 2004.

Bewer, Julius A. *The Literature of the Old Testament.* New York: Columbia University Press, 1957.

Bickerman, Elias. *Four Strange Books of the Bible.* New York: Schocken Books, 1967.

Boadt, Lawrence. *Reading the Old Testament.* New York: Paulist Press, 1984.

Borowitz, Eugene B. *Renewing the Covenant*. Philadelphia: Jewish Publication Society, 1991.

Buber, Martin. *On the Bible*. New York: Schocken Books, 1968.

Callaway, Joseph A., revised by J. Maxwell Miller. "The Settlement in Canaan." In *Ancient Israel*, edited by Hershel Shanks, 55–89. Washington, DC: Biblical Archaeology Society, 1999.

Cazelles, H. "Ten Commandments." *Interpreter's Dictionary of the Bible*, Supplement, 1976, 876.

Childs, Brevard S. *The Book of Exodus*. The Old Testament Library. Philadelphia: Westminster, 1975.

Clifford, Richard J. *Creation Accounts in the Ancient Near East and in the Bible*. The Catholic Biblical Quarterly Monograph Series 26. Washington, DC: Catholic Biblical Association of America, 1994.

Cline, Eric C. "Raiders of the Faux Ark." *Boston Globe*, Sept. 30, 2007, sec. D.

Cohen, A. *The Five Megillot*. Hindhead, Surrey: Soncino, 1946.

Cohen, Mortimer, J. "David the King." In *Great Jewish Personalities in Ancient and Medieval Times*, edited by S. Noveck, 44–60. Washington: B'nai B'rith Department of Adult Jewish Education, 1965.

Coogan, Michael D. *The Old Testament*. Oxford: Oxford University Press, 2006.

———. "The Great Gulf between Scholars and the Pew." *Bible Review*, June 1994, 44–48, 55.

Driver, S. R. *Deuteronomy*. The International Critical Commentary. New York: Scribner's Sons, 1903.

Durham, John, *Exodus*. Word Biblical Commentary. Waco, TX: Word Books, 1987.

Eissfeldt, Otto. *The Old Testament*. Translated by P. R. Ackroyd. New York: Harper and Row, 1965.

Eskenazi, Tamara Cohn, and Andrea L. Weiss, eds. *The Torah: A Women's Commentary*. New York: URJ Press, 2008.

Falk, Marcia L. *The Book of Blessings*. San Francisco: HarperSanFrancisco, 1996.

Feiler, Bruce. "In Search of the Maccabees." *Reform Judaism*, Winter 2005, 44–45, 66–68.

Finkelstein, Israel. "Raiders of the Lost Mountain: An Israeli Archaeologist Looks at the Most Recent Attempt to Locate Mt. Sinai." *Biblical Archaeology Review* 15, no. 4 (July–Aug. 1988): 46–50.

Finkelstein, Israel, and Neil A. Silberman. *David and Solomon*. New York: Free Press, 2006.

Fohrer, Georg, *Introduction to the Old Testament*. Translated by David E. Green. Nashville: Abingdon Press, 1968.

Freedman, David N., and Jeffrey C. Geoghegan. "'House of David' Is There!" *Biblical Archaeology Review* 21, no. 2 (March–April 1995): 78–79.

Freehof, Solomon B. *Recent Reform Responsa*. Cincinnati: Hebrew Union College, 1963.

Friedman, Maurice S. *Martin Buber: The Life of Dialogue*. New York: Harper Torchbook, 1960.

Friedman, Richard Elliott. *Who Wrote the Bible?* New York: Summit, 1987.

Fromm, Erich. *The Art of Loving*. New York: Harper, 1956.

Frymer-Kensky, Tikva. "What the Babylonian Flood Stories Can and Cannot Teach Us about the Genesis Flood." *Biblical Archaeology Review* 4, no. 4 (Nov.–Dec. 1978): 32–41.

Gates of Repentance. Edited by Chaim Stern. New York: Central Conference of American Rabbis, 1996.

Gesenius, H. F. W., et al. *Gesenius' Hebrew Grammar*, 2nd ed. Oxford: Oxford University Press, 1922.

Ginzberg, Louis. *Legends of the Jews.* New York: Simon and Schuster, 1961.

Gittelsohn, Roland B. *Wings of the Morning.* New York: UAHC Press, 1969.

Goldin, Judah. *The Fathers According to Rabbi Nathan.* New York: Schocken Books, 1974.

Goodman, Philip. *The Shavuot Anthology.* Philadelphia: Jewish Publication Society, 1974.

Gordis, Robert. *Megillat Esther.* New York: Rabbinical Assembly, 1974.

Gray, John. *I and II Kings.* Philadelphia: Westminster, 1970.

Greenberg, Moshe. "Some Postulates of Biblical Criminal Law." In *The Jewish Expression,* edited by Judah Goldin, 18–37. New York: Bantam, 1970.

Halevi, Judah. *The Kuzari.* New York: Schocken Books, 1964.

Hallo, William W., and William Kelly Simpson. *The Ancient Near East: A History.* New York: Harcourt Brace Jovanovich, 1971.

Hertz, J. H. *The Pentateuch and Haftorahs.* London: Soncino, 1971.

Hertzberg, Hans, W. *I and II Samuel.* The Old Testament Library. Philadelphia: Westminster, 1964.

Heschel, Abraham J. *God in Search of Man.* New York: Meridian Books, 1962.

Hestrin, Ruth. "Understanding Asherah." *Biblical Archaeology Review* 17, no. 5 (Sept.–Oct. 1991): 50–59.

Husic, Isaac. *A History of Medieval Jewish Philosophy.* Philadelphia: Jewish Publication Society, 1940.

Interpreter's Dictionary of the Bible. Edited by George Arthur Buttrick. New York: Abington Press, 1962.

Jacobs, Walter, ed. *American Reform Responsa.* New York: Central Conference of American Rabbis, 1983, 139–41.

Jaffee, Martin S. *Early Judaism.* Upper Saddle River, NJ: Prentice Hall, 1997.

Jones, Bruce William. "Two Misconceptions about the Book of Esther." *Catholic Biblical Quarterly* 39, no. 2 (1977): 171–81.

Josephus, Complete Works. Translated by William Whiston. Grand Rapids, MI: Kregel, 1963.

Kaplan, Mordecai M. *The Meaning of God in Modern Jewish Religion.* New York: Reconstructionist Press, 1962.

Kugel, James L. *The Bible As It Was.* Cambridge, MA: Harvard University Press, 1998.

Kushner, Harold S. *How Good Do We Have to Be?* Boston: Little, Brown, 1996.

———. *When Bad Things Happen to Good People.* New York: Schocken Books, 1981.

Leibowitz, Nehama. *Studies in Shemot.* Jerusalem: Haomanim, 1986.

Levy, Richard. "Upon Arising: An Affirmation of Techiyat Hameitim." *Journal of Reform Judaism,* Fall 1982, 12–20.

Limburg, James. "Jonah and the Whale through the Eyes of Artists." *Bible Revew* 6, no. 4 (Aug. 1990): 18–25.

Maimonides, M. *The Guide of the Perplexed.* Translated by Shlomo Pines. Chicago: University of Chicago Press, 1963.

Malamat, Abraham. "Origins and Formative Period." In *A History of the Jewish People,* ed. H. H. Ben-Sasson, 3–87. Cambridge, MA: Harvard University Press, 1969.

———. "How Inferior Israelite Forces Conquered Fortified Canaanite Cities." *Biblical Archaeology Review* 8, no. 2 (March–April 1982): 24–35.

Martinez, Florentino Garcia. *The Sea Scrolls Translated.* New York: Brill, 1994.

Mekhilta de-Rabbi Ishmael. Translation and notes by Jacob Z. Lauterbach. Philadelphia: Jewish Publication Society, 1961.

Meshel, Ze'ev. "Did Yahweh Have a Consort?" *Biblical Archaeology Review* 5, no. 2 (March–April, 1979) 24–35.

————. "Wilderness Wanderings," *Biblical Archaeology Review* 34, (July-August, 2008) 32–39.

Mishkan T'filah: A Reform Siddur. New York: Central Conference of American Rabbis, 2007.

Moore, Carey A. "Eight Questions Most Frequently Asked about the Book of Esther." *Bible Review,* Spring 1987, 16–31.

Newman, Louis I. *Hasidic Anthology.* New York: Schocken Books, 1975.

Oppenheim, Leo A. *Ancient Mesopotamia.* Chicago: University of Chicago Press, 1964.

Orth, Michael. "Genre in Jonah." In *The Bible in The Light of Cuneiform Literature.* Ancient Near Eastern Texts and Studies, vol. 8, edited by William M. Hallo et al. Lewiston, NY: Edwin Mellen Press, 1990, 257–81.

Patterson, Stephen J. "My View: Bridging the Gulf between Bible Scholarship and Religious Faith." *Bible Review,* Dec. 1990, 16, 44.

Pfeiffer, Robert H. *Introduction to The Old Testament.* New York: Harper, 1948.

Plaskow, Judith. *Standing Again at Sinai.* San Francisco: Harper and Row, 1990.

Plaut, W. Gunther. *The Growth of Reform Judaism.* New York: World Union for Progressive Judaism, 1965.

————. *The Rise of Reform Judaism.* New York: World Union for Progressive Judaism, 1963.

————. ed. *The Torah: A Modern Commentary.* Rev. ed. New York: Union for Reform Judaism, 2005.

————. "Noah and How We Live with One Another in Our Time." In *Living Torah: Selections from Seven Years of Torat Chayim.* Edited by Elaine Rose Glickman. New York: URJ Press, 2005, 13–14.

Pritchard, James B., ed. *Ancient Near Eastern Texts Related to the Old Testament.* 3rd ed. Princeton, NJ: Princeton University Press, 1969.

Propp, William H. "Did Moses Have Horns?" *Bible Review* 4, no. 1 (Feb. 1988): 30–37.

Rad, Gerhard von. *Genesis.* Translated by John Marks. The Old Testament Library. Philadelphia: Westminster Press, 1961.

————. *Old Testament Theology.* Translated by D. M. G. Stalker. Vol. 1. Edinburgh: Oliver and Boyd, 1963.

Riskin, Shlomo. "The Final Step Is Ours to Take." *Jerusalem Post,* International Edition, week ending March 6, 1993, 15.

Roiphe, Anne. "Taking Down the Christmas Tree." *Tikkun* 4, no. 6: 58–60.

Safire, William. "Chappy Chanukah." *New York Times Magazine,* Dec. 1989.

Saggs, H. W. F. *The Greatness That Was Babylon.* New York: Hawthorn Books, 1962.

Sandmel, Samuel. *The Hebrew Scriptures.* New York: Alfred A. Knopf, 1963.

Sarna, Nahum M. *Exodus.* The JPS Torah Commentary. Philadelphia: Jewish Publicaiton Society, 1991.

————. *Exploring Exodus.* New York: Schocken Books, 1989.

————. *Genesis.* The JPS Torah Commentary. New York: Jewish Publication Society, 1989.

————. *Understanding Genesis.* New York: Schocken Books, 1970.

Sasson, Jack. *Jonah.* The Anchor Bible, vol. 24B. New York: Doubleday, 1990.

Schauss, Hayyim. *Guide to Jewish Holy Days.* New York: Schocken Books, 1961.

Schniedewind, William M. *How the Bible Became a Book.* Cambridge: Cambridge University Press, 2004.

Scholem, Gershom. *On the Kabbalah and Its Symbolism.* New York: Schocken Books, 1965.

Segal, Lillian. "The Feminine Divine in the Book of Esther." *The Bible in the Light of the Cuneiform Literature.* Ancient Near Eastern Texts and Studies, vol. 8, edited by William M. Hallo et al. Lewiston, NY: Edwin Mellen Press, 1990, 381–411.

Senior, Donald, and John J. Collins, eds. *The Catholic Study Bible*, 2nd ed. New York: Oxford University Press, 2006.

Sonsino, Rifat. "Bible and Politics." *Judaism* 32, no. 1 (1983): 77–83.

Sonsino, Rifat, and Daniel B. Syme. *Finding God: Selected Responses*. New York: UAHC Press, 2002.

Speiser, E. A. *Genesis*. The Anchor Bible. Garden City, NY: Doubleday, 1964.

———. *Oriental and Biblical Studies*. Philadelphia: University of Pennsylvania, 1967.

Taylor, Glen J. "Was Yahweh Worshipped as the Sun?" *Biblical Archaeology Review* 20 (May–June 1994): 52–61, 90–91.

Tigay, Jeffrey H. *Deuteronomy*. The JPS Torah Commentary. Philadelphia: Jewish Publication Society, 1996.

Tullock, John H., and Mark McEntire. *The Old Testament Story*. Upper Saddle River, NJ: Pearson Prentice Hall, 2006.

Twersky, Isadore, ed. *A Maimonides Reader*. New York: Behrman House, 1972.

Ussishkin, David. "Lachish: Key to the Israelite Conquest of Canaan?" *Biblical Archaeology Review* 13, no. 1 (Jan.–Feb. 1987): 18–39.

Weinfeld, Moshe. "The Uniqueness of the Decalogue." In *The Ten Commandments in History and Tradition*. Edited by Ben-Zion Segal. Jerusalem: Magnes Press, 1990, 1–44.

Westermann, Claus. *Genesis*. Grand Rapids, MI: Eerdmans, 1987.

Wood, Bryant G. "Did the Israelites Conquer Jericho? A New Look at the Archaeological Evidence." *Biblical Archaeology Review* 16, no. 2 (March–April 1990): 44–57.

Yadin, Yigael. "Is the Biblical Account of the Israelite Conquest of Canaan Historically Reliable?" *Biblical Archaeology Review* 8, no. 2 (March–April 1982): 16–23.

Zornberg, Avivah Gottlieb. *Genesis: The Beginning of Desire*. Philadelphia: Jewish Publication Society, 1995.